11/04

2/04

Understanding
The Lord of the Rings

Understanding
The Lord of the Rings

THE BEST OF
TOLKIEN CRITICISM

EDITED BY

Rose A. Zimbardo and Neil D. Isaacs

HOUGHTON MIFFLIN COMPANY

BOSTON NEW YORK 2004

For information about permission to reproduce selections from
this book, write to Permissions, Houghton Mifflin Company,
215 Park Avenue South, New York, New York 10003.

Visit our Web site: www.houghtonmifflinbooks.com.

Library of Congress Cataloging-in-Publication Data
Understanding The lord of the rings : the best of Tolkien
criticism / edited by Rose A. Zimbardo and Neil D. Isaacs.
p.   cm.
Includes bibliographical references (p.) and index.
ISBN 0-618-42251-X
1. Tolkien, J. R. R. (John Ronald Reuel), 1892–1973.
Lord of the rings. 2. Fantasy fiction, English—History
and criticism. 3. Middle Earth (Imaginary place)
I. Zimbardo, Rose A. II. Isaacs, Neil David, 1931–
PR6039.032L63775 2004
823'.912—dc22 2004047274

Printed in the United States of America

MP 10 9 8 7 6 5 4 3 2 1

In loving memory of MARTIN STEVENS

> *he loved poesie*
> *Trouthe and honour, freedom and curtesie*

And for JACOB REECE ISAACS,

> *halfling of Dan and Tammy,*
> *who will soon guide him*
> *to Middle-earth and beyond*

> *with love from Grandpa*

CONTENTS

Understanding
The Lord of the Rings

NEIL D. ISAACS

On the Pleasures of (Reading and Writing) Tolkien Criticism

IT IS ALMOST forty-three years since Rose Zimbardo pointed me toward Middle-earth. I was a relatively late arrival, the phenomenal success of *The Lord of the Rings* having already been well established — to the dismay of some establishment defenders of the traditional canon.

Throughout the sixties, three aspects of that phenomenon seemed to dominate perceptions of the value of the book. One was the persistent resistance by the arbiters of literary taste to afford critical recognition to a work that had proven its abundant appeal to a wide *popular* and, worse, *youthful* audience. Another was the fact that the book's commercial success was not the product of hype: the early popularity of *The Lord of the Rings* was produced by a word-of-mouth groundswell that preceded the reactive attention of the mass media. It was a matter of reporting the phenomenon rather than precipitating it, though the reportage added fuel to the fire.

The third was that some of the features and attractions of the book and its created world inevitably elicited an infectious outbreak of "faddism and fannism, cultism and clubbism," as I called it in "On the Possibilities of Writing Tolkien Criticism." In that introduction to our first collection of critical essays I was lamenting that these factors, particularly "the feverish activity of the fanzines," were counterproductive to the development of a climate for serious critical attention to Tolkien's masterpiece.

More than a decade after the novel's appearance, as an example if not a proof of the shocked attention still being paid to a literary phenomenon by an uncomprehending coterie of critics (including Edmund Wilson, Germaine Greer, and Philip Toynbee), the *New York Herald Tribune's* *Book Week* published on its front page (February 26, 1967), beginning in large type and accompanied by a cartoon, what amounted to a confession of ignorance by a prominent critic, Paul West. Part of my response in "On the Possibilities of Writing Tolkien Criticism" neatly summarizes, I think, the nature of the problem:

On what bases does West attack *The Lord of the Rings*?

1. He is baffled by it, baffled into numbness. I cannot argue with this; he demonstrates both bafflement and numbness throughout.

2. With a nostalgia for the last century's discarded theories, he laments that Tolkien created his world and its creatures alone, without some folksy community origin. But if Tolkien is sole owner and proprietor of Middle-earth, I would prefer to give him all my admiration than to betray any envy for his creative imagination.

3. *The Lord of the Rings* is a game, only a game, and has no bearing on humanity. Now this is a *serious* objection, to which I would offer a pair of categorical adversatives: first, without the sense of play as an essential element in literature, we would have to do without much of Chaucer, Shakespeare, Joyce, Proust, Nabokov — for in a sense all art is a game, the game of putting form to matter; second, the game of *The Lord of the Rings* is miraculously designed to be played and won by anyone who takes part, but the reader who doesn't see the significance of its urgent bearing on humanity will always be a loser.

4. The society from which people must escape into Tolkien's world is very bad indeed. I offer no comment on this argument, but I wonder if West hasn't simply used Tolkien's popularity as a way to make this last general point; it has no direct (or logical) bearing on the relative excellence of the book.

It may be unfair to hold West up as epitomizing the negative attitudes toward Tolkien. After all, few attentive readers had actually been driven to the simplistic notions that the book features "a virtue that triumphs untested," an "evil that dies uninvestigated," and one protagonist, Frodo, who is "the goodie hobbit." But even West acknowledged that the cultism and clubbism were irrelevant to — indeed barriers to — considerations of literature, that is, serious criticism. In such a climate, Rose Zimbardo and I designed *Tolkien and the Critics* as a small contribution toward a major project, saving what we believed was a great novel from the "faddists and button makers" whose enthusiasm contributed to clouding some critical judgment.

An obligatory if presumptuous request to Professor Tolkien to consider supplying a brief foreword for the collection brought a gentle but firm response:

> I am very grateful for your attention and interest. But I am wholly occupied, or should be, with new work of my own, and I am obliged to say "no" to all requests for articles in reviews, opinions, forewords, or anything of the kind. I think it is essential to a writer who is still writing to avoid the distraction of external criticism, however sensitive or well-informed.

That the contributions to our book were to varying degrees "sensitive and well-informed" may be attested to by the warm welcome it received from reviewers. The fourteen essays, about equally divided between original pieces and reprints of the best available material, formed what one review (perhaps the least flattering of all) called "largely an unstructured dialectic on the meaning and value of the whole trilogy." What was most gratifying to us about its success (as measured within the limited aspirations of academic, university press publication) was its threefold accomplishment: its samples of general appreciations by prestigious writers, its examples of illuminations of specific aspects of the novel by critics with focused interests, and its anticipations of an abundance of critical attention yet to come. In a way, the collection was an announcement of assurance that, in due course, *The Lord of the Rings* would have to be given its rightful place among the major fictional works of our time.

Within the following decade an astonishing amount of critical work on Tolkien appeared. The variety of critical approaches that Middle-earth had spawned was as great as that of the imagined species in Tolkien's world, a kind of secondary "sub-creation." There were doctoral dissertations and papers at professional meetings, guides for innocent readers, collections of learned essays, memoirs, bibliographies, explorations of source material, and contextualizings from one perspective or another. The enormous appeal of *The Lord of the Rings* had spread to include not only its increasing mass audience but also a cottage industry of scholarly study. Medievalists and philologists had a field day mining the rich veins of their disciplines' ore with tools both venerable and au courant. Allegorists of many persuasions, especially of the Christian and historical orientations, had their innings. And the psychological, the archetypal, and the structuralist schools were staking their claims.

Into this thick growth Zimbardo and Isaacs ventured once more, proposing a second collection. Dissuaded from calling it "Tolkien and the Critics II" or some variation of "The Second Generation," we settled for *Tolkien: New Critical Perspectives*. If we had been motivated the first time around by the wish to justify Tolkien's admission to the canon, we now faced the more formidable task of separating well-intentioned appreciations of *The Lord of the Rings* and the proliferating attention to extraneous, external, tangential, devotional, and personal matters from what we regarded as appropriate approaches to the book that would foster substantial literary criticism.

In most ways, the second collection was as good as the first. Equally divided, again, between reprinted and original material, it may have lacked the clout of contributions by C. S. Lewis and W. H. Auden. But it made up for that, in part, by including a chapter from Paul Kocher's *Master of Middle-earth,* at that point the best book-length study of Tolkien's work, and an original essay by Verlyn Flieger, her first published work on her way to a distinguished career as a scholar of Tolkien in particular and of fantasy and Faërie in general. Our second collection received much less attention from reviewers, but one astute critic, in an otherwise favorable notice, took me to task for an "ill-tempered" introduction, "On the Need for Writing Tolkien Criticism."

He was right; the book was marred by my approach, which focused not on the strength of the collected contributions but on carping critiques of material we had deemed unworthy of inclusion. Looking back, I find this indefensible, but I believe I know the reason for my critical distemper (though I would leave the differential diagnosis of mood disorder or personality disorder to others). It was that the publication of *The Silmarillion,* some four years before our second collection, had altered both the public perception of, and the critical climate for, Tolkien's work.

The problem was a double-edged sword. On one hand, critics with negative attitudes toward *The Lord of the Rings* used *The Silmarillion* to bolster their positions, disregarding the wholly different natures of the two works and illogically applying their distaste for the latter to the former. On the other hand, devotees used *The Silmarillion* to range far beyond *The Lord of the Rings* in their enthusiasm for Tolkien's created world, thereby deflecting attention from, and appreciation for, a major work of fiction, in precisely the ways we had feared. Of the provision of new scripts for video games to come I will not speak here.

There may well have been as much sadness as anger in my mood vis-à-vis Tolkien scholarship and readership at the time, as a couple of short passages from my review of *The Silmarillion* featured in the *Washington Star* on Sunday, September 11, 1977, will attest:

> *The Silmarillion* is a sacred text. It is an editor's attempt to set forth in an orderly way a great body of traditions, lore, and mythology that stands behind the great narrative of *The Lord of the Rings*. It is cosmogonical, cosmological, and apocalyptic. It is also a seemingly endless series of names (personal and place) and events chronicled without the distinction of detail that would temper the repetitiveness. Above all it is solemn, as befits a sacred text.
>
> Readers who love *The Lord of the Rings* for its narrative power, its droll charm, its intricate playfulness, and the physical and psychological details that give life to its fully realized world will not be very happy with *The Silmarillion*. Its style will stun many, particularly those who know Tolkien as the author of "*Beowulf*: the Monsters and the Critics," still the most lucid and readable essay in all Old English scholarship. This book is persistently Biblical. The Book of Numbers comes most often to mind. And so it is that, beyond all hope, Christopher son of J.R.R. has brought the new Tolkien to light in the world of men.

That the ill temper faded over time I attribute not to any mellowing but to an appreciation for later developments. With Christopher Tolkien's gathering, editing, and publishing of successive volumes of the history, legends, lore, and mythology of Middle-earth, there came a plethora of rewards for the devotees. But the voices of carping critics faded in large part, I think, because the attention of serious literary scholarship to *The Lord of the Rings* reinforced the book's importance and won its canonical recognition even as it attracted new generations of a mass readership.

One great fear remained. Translated to the screen, I thought, the book would be reduced and its meaning lost to serious readers. However, as soon as we saw Peter Jackson's *The Fellowship of the Ring* all such fears dissipated. Indeed, the monumental triumph of Jackson's movies has given us a road back to Middle-earth, a road already well traveled by yet another generation of appreciative readers.

From the moment Rose Zimbardo first suggested to me that it was time for us to conclude our own trilogy of Tolkien essay collections, I have thought of this edition as a "greatest hits album." Such an enterprise has its own built-in pitfalls for the compilers, not to mention the writer of the liner notes. Why the obvious "Pretty Woman" for the Roy Orbison selection and not the more representative "Ooby-Dooby"? Why the Licia Albanese reading of Puccini's "Vissi d'arte" and not a remastered Claudia Muzio? In any case we are obligated to spell out our general criteria for choices — which are certain to be challenged.

Our first decisions were nearly automatic. We intended to collect the best critical work available that focused on *The Lord of the Rings*. Moreover, we had no intention of presenting a "balanced" view. There would be no representative of those voices — strident, cynical, sardonic, dismissive, supercilious, condescending — that articulated negative views of the book. All the naysayers had one thing in common. Whether they objected to prose style, poetic insertions, assumed allegorical simplicities, self-indulgent allusiveness, character stereotyping, derivative clichés, sociopolitical bias, Christian apologetics, or puerile taste, to make their case they all had to shift focus away from the *story*.

The Lord of the Rings is an adventure story par excellence, and as such it is one of the great works of twentieth-century fiction. If it has elements of myth, archetype, epic structure, and adolescent fantasy, not to mention deep moral, psychological, and geopolitical insights, so much the better for its performance as narrative. This collection assumes that argument about the value and power of *The Lord of the Rings* has been settled, certainly to the satisfaction of its vast, growing, persistent audience, but also of a considerable body of critical judgment. (For a summary of the case, with explicit refutation of the losing arguments, we refer readers to Tom Shippey's book *J.R.R. Tolkien: Author of the Century.*)

Another early decision was to eschew biographical approaches, of which there are many available. From personal memoirs to carefully documented accounts, this material is often charming or illuminating, particularly when it places Tolkien's experience in such broader contexts as the group of his fellows called Inklings, his experiences in World War I, and his immersion in medieval languages and literature. Without denying the validity of the many connections between the author's life and his work, we determined to focus on the latter. That decision has cost us the option of reprinting an excerpt from Humphrey Carpenter's estimable biography, but that book is still available in print.

We extended that principle of focus into a much broader criterion of exclusion. Many worthy pieces of individual scholarship exploring specific aspects of Tolkien's work — linguistic discoveries, individual sources and analogues, the poetics of the interpolated verse, the evolution of invented flora and fauna, the rich realms of the naming of things and creatures, and even a herd of hobbyhorses ridden by idiosyncratic interpreters — can provide insight into particular features of the novel. But the typical tendency in them is toward digression, and our intention was to choose the work of critics who kept their focus on the main chance, whose eyes were ever on the prize: general appreciation of Tolkien's narrative art. This decision may have cost us some intriguing slants upon the work, but it also shielded us from the onslaught of continuing allegorical interpretations and assumptions.

We were ever mindful of the need to avoid superficiality and redundancy. The final choices, however, should exemplify our standards of importance, timeliness, and the likelihood of enduring value. In other words, we have chosen essays that we believe already are, or are likely to become, classics of Tolkien criticism. The final selections speak for themselves. They all maintain focus on the central issues of the artistry of *The Lord of the Rings.* (Rose Zimbardo's headnotes to the essays provide precise indications of that focus and concise accounts of the context of each.)

We were faced, however, with a thorny problem in the presence of serious book-length studies of Tolkien's work. Those of Joseph Pearce, Patrick Curry, Verlyn Flieger, and, preeminently, Tom Shippey will come to mind. Of particular interest to us was Jane Chance's *Tolkien's Art,* originally published in 1979, for it persuasively argued two major points: that Tolkien's creative and scholarly work was all of a piece, a comprehensive, coherent, cohesive, interrelated corpus; and that the central intention of his art was to construct, in the phrase of her subtitle, "a mythology for England." The revised edition (2001) supports her argument with extensive documentation derived from work published in the decades since the first publication of her book, including Tolkien's letters. Chance's chapter on *The Lord of the Rings* can stand alone; we reprint it here, with minor adjustments, from the revised edition. It was rare in our experience to find a separable chapter that could be isolated and retain the integrity of its critical focus.

Let me demonstrate the essence of the problem. I studied Shippey's *Road to Middle-earth* and *J.R.R. Tolkien: Author of the Century* in an attempt to isolate passages that met our criteria. I found three that were tantalizingly close: from *Road,* the first fifteen pages of chapter 5, "Interlacements and the Ring," and from *Author,* the subsections "the ironies of interlace" and "the myth of Frodo" plus "Timeless poetry and true tradition." But the very presence of the word "interlace" in the titles of two of these selections identifies the problem, because a critical analyst attempting to do justice to Tolkien's work will inevitably produce works structured by *critical* interlace. And such excerpting as I contemplated would do great injustice to Shippey's accomplishment. It is the nature of great works of literature to attract critics of the first rank and criticism of the highest quality, which becomes essential accoutrement to the works themselves. Dostoevsky has found his Joseph Frank, James Joyce his Richard Ellmann and Stuart Gilbert, Nabokov his Brian Boyd, and Tolkien his Tom Shippey.

In the case of Flieger, while *Splintered Light: Logos and Language in Tolkien's World* and *A Question of Time: J.R.R. Tolkien's Road to Faërie* are justly admired books of Tolkien scholarship, we bridged the dilemma by reprinting her earliest published essay, "Frodo and Aragorn: The Concept of the Hero," which appeared in our *New Critical Perspectives*. In the case of Shippey, we found a most promising solution. We commissioned an original essay, the only one in the collection. "Another Road to Middle-earth: Jackson's Movie Trilogy" explores the process by which the screen version of the novel would lead to new generations of readers.

Here, then, in one volume, in addition to the Kocher, Chance, and Shippey pieces, is a great deal of material unavailable elsewhere now: essays by C. S. Lewis, Edmund Fuller, W. H. Auden, Patricia Meyer Spacks, Rose Zimbardo, Marion Zimmer Bradley, R. J. Reilly, J. S. Ryan, Verlyn Flieger, Patrick Grant, and Lionel Basney. Besides providing handily packaged availability, the book offers some happy unintended results of our criteria of selection. It contains works of criticism from Australia, Canada, the U.K., and the U.S. It contains works of criticism, not only by general critics, medievalist scholars, and another Inkling, but also by a world-class poet, an acclaimed writer of science fiction/fantasy, a prominent folklorist, a devoted environmentalist, and two esteemed scholars of eighteenth-century literature. And among its fourteen contributors are six who are no longer with us, so that part of their legacy lives on in their appreciation of yet another sub-created world.

We have passed from the "possibilities" of Tolkien criticism (now richly fulfilled but viably open to enrichment), through the "need" for Tolkien criticism (now satisfied by a commonly accepted recognition of *The Lord of the Rings* as a masterwork), to the "pleasures" of what is gathered here (with the promise of more to come). Enjoy.

C. S. LEWIS

The Dethronement of Power

With Tolkien, his Oxford colleague and close friend, C. S. Lewis was a founding member of the Inklings, a congenial group of intellectuals that also included Charles Williams and Owen Barfield. The friends met regularly but quite informally to enjoy good beer, good pipe tobacco, and, best of all, good talk. They often read to one another portions of works they were engaged in writing. At the time that Tolkien was writing The Lord of the Rings, *C. S. Lewis was engaged in writing the masterful* Oxford History of English Literature *volume* The Sixteenth Century *and his brilliant critical study* The Allegory of Love. *Lewis was also a writer of fantasy — or, more precisely, what J. S. Ryan in his essay included in this volume calls "Christian romanticism." Lewis's best-known work in this mode is the trilogy* Out of the Silent Planet, Perelandra, *and* That Hideous Strength.

When I reviewed the first volume of this work, I hardly dared to hope it would have the success which I was sure it deserved. Happily I am proved wrong. There is, however, one piece of false criticism which had better be answered: the complaint that the characters are all either black or white. Since the climax of volume I was mainly concerned with the struggle between good and evil in the mind of Boromir, it is not easy to see how anyone could have said this. I will hazard a guess. "How shall a man judge what to do in such times?" asks someone in volume II. "As he has ever judged," comes the reply. "Good and ill have not changed . . . nor are they one thing among Elves and Dwarves and another among Men" (II, 40–41).

This is the basis of the whole Tolkienian world. I think some readers, seeing (and disliking) this rigid demarcation of black and white, imagine they have seen a rigid demarcation between black and white people. Looking at the squares, they assume (in defiance of the facts) that all the pieces must be making bishops' moves which confine them to one color. But even such readers will hardly brazen it out through the two last volumes. Motives, even on the right side, are mixed. Those who are now traitors usually began with comparatively innocent intentions. Heroic Rohan and imperial Gondor are partly diseased. Even the wretched Sméagol, till quite late in the story, has good impulses; and, by a tragic paradox, what finally pushes him over the brink is an unpremeditated speech by the most selfless character of all.

There are two books in each volume, and now that all six are before us the very high architectural quality of the romance is revealed. Book 1 builds up the main theme. In book 2 that theme, enriched with much retrospective material, continues. Then comes the change. In 3 and 5 the fate of the company, now divided, becomes entangled with a huge complex of forces which are grouping and regrouping themselves in relation to Mordor. The main theme, isolated from this, occupies 4 and the early part of 6 (the latter part of course giving all the resolutions). But we are never allowed to forget the intimate connection between it and the rest. On the one hand, the whole world is going to the war; the story rings with galloping hoofs, trumpets, steel on steel. On the other, very far away, two tiny, miserable figures creep (like mice on a slag heap) through the twilight of Mordor. And all the time we know that the fate of the world depends far more on the small movement than on the great. This is a structural invention of the highest order: it adds immensely to the pathos, irony, and grandeur of the tale.

This main theme is not to be treated in those jocular, whimsical tones now generally used by reviewers of "juveniles." It is entirely serious: the growing anguish, the drag of the Ring on the neck, the ineluctable conversion of hobbit into hero in conditions which exclude all hope of fame or fear of infamy. Without the relief offered by the more crowded and bustling books it would be hardly tolerable.

Yet those books are not in the least inferior. Of picking out great moments, such as the cock-crow at the siege of Gondor, there would be no end; I will mention two general, and totally different, excellences. One, surprisingly, is realism. This war has the very quality of the war my generation knew. It is all here: the endless, unintelligible movement, the sinister quiet of the front when "everything is now ready," the flying civilians, the lively, vivid friendships, the background of something like despair and the merry foreground, and such heaven-sent windfalls as a cache of choice tobacco "salvaged" from a ruin. The author has told us elsewhere that his taste for fairy tale was wakened into maturity by active service; that, no doubt, is why we can say of his war scenes (quoting Gimli the Dwarf), "'There is good rock here. This country has tough bones'" (II, 137). The other excellence is that no individual, and no species, seems to exist only for the sake of the plot. All exist in their own right and would have been worth creating for their mere flavor even if they had been irrelevant. Treebeard would have served any other author (if any other could have conceived him) for a whole book. His eyes are "filled up with ages of memory, and long, slow, steady thinking" (II, 66). Through those ages his name has grown with him, so that he cannot now tell it; it would, by now, take too long to pronounce. When he learns that the thing they are standing on is a hill, he complains that this is but "a hasty word" (II, 69) for that which has so much history in it.

How far Treebeard can be regarded as a "portrait of the artist" must remain doubtful; but when he hears that some people want to identify the Ring with the hydrogen bomb, and Mordor with Russia, I think he might call it a "hasty" word. How long do people think a world like his takes to grow? Do they think it can be done as quickly as a modern nation changes its Public Enemy Number One or as modern scientists invent new weapons? When Tolkien began there was probably no nuclear fission and the contemporary incarnation of Mordor was a good deal nearer our shores. But the text itself teaches us that Sauron is eternal; the war of the Ring is only one of a thousand wars against him. Every time we shall be wise to fear his ultimate victory, after which there will be "no more songs." Again and again we shall have good evidence that "the wind is setting East, and the withering of all woods may be drawing near" (II, 76). Every time we win we shall know that our victory is impermanent. If we insist on asking for the moral of the story, that is its moral: a recall from facile optimism and wailing pessimism alike, to that hard, yet not quite desperate, insight into man's unchanging predicament by which heroic ages have lived. It is here that the Norse affinity is strongest: hammer-strokes, but with compassion.

"But why," some ask, "why, if you have a serious comment to make on the real life of men, must you do it by talking about a phantasmagoric never-never-land of your own?" Because, I take it, one of the main things the author wants to say is that the real life of men is of that mythical and heroic quality. One can see the principle at work in his characterization. Much that in a realistic work would be done by "character delineation" is here done simply by making the character an elf, a dwarf, or a hobbit. The imagined beings have their insides on the outside; they are visible souls. And man as a whole, man pitted against the universe, have we seen him at all till we see that he is like a hero in a fairy tale? In the book Éomer rashly contrasts "the green earth" with "legends." Aragorn replies that the green earth itself is "a mighty matter of legend" (II, 37).

The value of the myth is that it takes all the things we know and restores to them the rich significance which has been hidden by "the veil of familiarity." The child enjoys his cold meat, otherwise dull to him, by pretending it is buffalo, just killed with his own bow and arrow. And the child is wise. The real meat comes back to him more savory for having been dipped in a story; you might say that only then is it real meat. If you are tired of the real landscape, look at it in a mirror. By putting bread, gold, horse, apple, or the very roads into a myth, we do not retreat from reality: we rediscover it. As long as the story lingers in our mind, the real things are more themselves. This book applies the treatment not only to bread or apple but to good and evil, to our endless perils, our anguish, and our joys. By dipping them in myth we see them more clearly. I do not think he could have done it in any other way.

The book is too original and too opulent for any final judgment on a first reading. But we know at once that it has done things to us. We are not quite the same men. And though we must ration ourselves in our rereadings, I have little doubt that the book will soon take its place among the indispensables.

EDMUND FULLER

The Lord of the Hobbits: J.R.R. Tolkien

In this essay Fuller explores The Lord of the Rings *as an example of fictional "sub-creation." The "Other World," to use Tolkien's own description, shaped by this extraordinary literary work has a self-contained geography and condenses in its scope millennia of history. Its inhabitants are other-than-human species as well as distinctly different human communities, each group having a unique language, lore, and culture. Dwarves, Elves, Riders of Rohan, Ents — each has a particular excellence that it uses in the service of the whole. Moreover, it is in the diversity among its elements that the "Other World" maintains unity and coherence. E pluribus unum.*

The Lord of the Rings is a fairy tale in the highest aspect of its kind — which requires some discussion. "Fairy" is prominent in the long lexicon of words ruined by the nasty vulgarism of our time — at least in the American culture. It is probably irrecoverable for several generations because it has been made a sniggering, derisive synonym for homosexual. This unhappy association with effeminacy clearly came out of a saccharine sentimentality that previously had vulgarized an ancient and noble conception into a sickly-sweet, flutter-winged miniature image that flourished in Victorian times. To be fair, this corruption had earlier roots, and it has since reached its peak of nau-

16

seousness in the excruciating cutenesses of Walt Disney. What, then, was a fairy before this despoiling, and how is he to be restored to his lost stature and quality?

Here Tolkien has done a great rehabilitation, not only in the hobbit books, but in a long essay, "On Fairy-Stories," originally delivered as a lecture at St. Andrews University, in Scotland, and printed in the memorial volume *Essays Presented to Charles Williams*. Professor Tolkien deprecates his expertness, but it is the most profound and illuminating discussion of the subject I have ever seen.

"Faërie," in its essence, means "enchantment." As a place name, perhaps its best usage, Faërie is the realm or world of enchantment whether viewed as remote and separated in time and place or superimposed upon our own, for Faërie is wherever and whenever the enchantment is operable, when men have entered or fallen under it. A "fairy" is one of the denizens of that realm, the people of Faërie, the agents of its natural spells, the masters of its enchantments. A better name than fairy for such a being is Elf, and it is so used by Tolkien as it was by Spenser.

In Tolkien's story the Elven peoples are of major importance. It is before the separation of the ways of men and Elves, before the withdrawal (not the end) of the latter. The Elves are of an antiquity greater than man; are uncorrupted, of tall stature and handsome visage, bear themselves with dignity and joy, preserve their ancient tongue and songs, have rich arts and crafts, which men call enchantments. It is the character of their workmanship to "put the thoughts of all that we love into all that we make." They use their powers benevolently, are immortal but not unconquerable. In a few instances they have wedded with men, producing a race of the Half-elven, still a noble kind though their powers are less and in them immortality is diminished to long living. All this is in Tolkien's canon. Fairy tale at large has a tradition of bad fairies along with good, but I suspect that in primal origin, the relationship is not unlike that of the fallen angels to the good.

It is important to remember that this realm of Faërie encompasses all the natural phenomena and creatures known to us, augmented by much else in plants, animals, and intelligent beings. In Tolkien's world there are not only Elves and men, but hobbits, Dwarves, and some unique creatures, such as Ents, his oldest living species, a kind of walking, talking tree. There are Beornings — a sort of were-bear. We also meet an individual figure, unclassifiable other than as some primal nature spirit, Tom Bombadil. The passage about him is one of the most joyously lyrical and contains, too, one of the finest of the work's many poems.

There are wizards, also. The greatest of these, Gandalf, has profound aspects for further discussion. A wizard, as here drawn, is partly an enigma but seems to be in essence a man, but possessed of long life and magical powers. Following the lead of Tolkien, I have avoided the word "magic" in relation to Elves. Not that it may not be used, but that it may confuse a fine distinction. Enchantment is not a technique that Elves use; rather it is the total natural mode of their being and action. The wizard commands magic as an acquired technique and lore, consciously employed for specific effects, good or bad. From ancient times the lore of magic has known both the black magician and the white magician. Merlin was one of the latter, and even the poet Virgil was sometimes considered so.

Tolkien's world also has a variety of malevolent creatures. At the center are demonic powers, greatest of whom is Sauron, who is unmistakably a satanic figure, who might be nothing less than one of the fallen angelic host, and whose very name suggests the serpent. Orcs form the largest category of his mortal servants — goblin creatures of a debased order — but other mysterious powers, demonic or wraithlike, also are deployed under his command.

Here, then, is summarized the basic frame and cast. It seems wise not to attempt anything in the line of detailed synopsis. On this much we can attempt some examination of the story's meaning. In the first place, it is itself, at its face value, rich with inherent meaning, inescapably bonded with the events and characters. This is meaning of a sort that the reader translates into appropriate analogies for his own life, if he is so minded: as in the fact that courage and integrity, seen in any context, are enhancements and encouragements of those qualities wherever we have need of them. Beyond the inherent meaning lies the possibility of allegorical elements, in which there are many implications, subject to argument and disagreement among interpreters.

As to the inherent meaning, we are confronted basically by a raw struggle between good and evil. This contest offers a challenge and demands decisions of several kinds. The power of evil is formidable and ruthless. The initial decision, in which many of the characters participate, is whether or not to attempt to resist it at all. So great and discouraging are the odds involved in resistance that the possibility of surrender, terrible as it may be, seems only in degrees more terrible than the fight — unless the deciding element is the moral choice of rejecting evil regardless of consequences.

Before some of the great ones is dangled the old temptation "If you can't lick 'em, join 'em." A corrupted wizard seeks to persuade Gandalf:

> "A new Power is rising. Against it the old allies and policies will not avail us at all. . . . This then is one choice before you, before us. We may join with that Power. . . . Its victory is at hand; and there will be rich reward for those that aided it. . . . The Wise, such as you and I, may with patience come at last to direct its courses, to control it. We can bide our time . . . deploring maybe evils done by the way, but approving the high and ultimate purpose: Knowledge, Rule, Order. . . . There need not be . . . any real change in our designs, only in our means." (I, 272–73)

Tolkien pursues still further that most ancient and insidious moral dilemma, the problem of ends and means. If Sauron recovers his Ring, his power will be irresistible. The only means of assuring that he can never recover it is the awful one of carrying it right to the heart of his own realm and casting it into the volcanic fire in which it was first forged and that alone can destroy it. Yet an alternative constantly confronts the Fellowship in its resistance to Sauron. The Ring could be used to overthrow him by any one of several persons with advanced mastery of great powers. It is the nature of the Ring to give power according to the stature of its user — petty powers to the unknowing or inconsequential, vast ones to the strong and adept.

But the Ring and its potencies are evil, conditioned by its maker and his motives. It participates in the essence of its maker. At several crucial times the appeal arises: "Let the Ring be your weapon. . . . Take it and go forth to victory!" Each time that counsel is rejected, as here in the words of Elrond Halfelven:

> "We cannot use the Ruling Ring. . . . Its strength . . . is too great for anyone to wield at will, save only those who have already a great power of their own. But for them it holds an even deadlier peril. The very desire of it corrupts the heart. . . . If any of the Wise should with this Ring overthrow the Lord of Mordor, using his own arts, he would then set himself on Sauron's throne, and yet another Dark Lord would appear. And that is another reason why the Ring should be destroyed: as long as it is in the world it will be a danger even to the Wise. For nothing is evil in the beginning. Even Sauron was not so. I fear to take the Ring to hide it. I will not take the Ring to wield it." (I, 281)

Here we are brought to the classic corrupting quality of power in direct proportion to its approach to the absolute. Yet, of course, it is not simply the power, in itself, that corrupts, but the pride which power may engender, which in turn produces the swift corruption of the power. The primal nature of the sin of Pride, bringing the fall of angels before the seduction and fall of Man, is the wish to usurp the Primal and One source of Power, incorruptible in His nature because He *is* Power and Source and has nothing to usurp, in being All.

The Ring had found its way into the hands of the hobbit Bilbo, who, in his old age, at the advice of the wizard Gandalf, reluctantly entrusts it to Frodo. Upon the back of the younger hobbit descends this monstrous burden. None of the great dare lift it from him. Frodo's first response is that of anyone caught abruptly in a responsibility too great to contemplate. "I wish it need not have happened in my time."

> "So do I," said Gandalf, "and so do all who live to see such times. But that is not for them to decide. All we have to decide is what to do with the time that is given us." (I, 60)

Then, further, Frodo protests:

> "I wish I had never seen the Ring! Why did it come to me? Why was I chosen?"
>
> "Such questions cannot be answered," said Gandalf. "You may be sure that it was not for any merit that others do not possess: not for power or wisdom, at any rate. But you have been chosen and you must therefore use such strength and heart and wits as you have." (I, 70)

The merit of Frodo, then, is not any built-in endowment but the painfully, gradually ripening fruit of his response to the challenge set before him.

How Frodo fails or succeeds is the burden of the story — and it is not simple. Comparable tests are placed before other characters and are passed or failed in varying degrees, so that, in all, there are few aspects of challenge and response in the area of inexorable moral responsibility that Tolkien does not exemplify for us in this tale.

The next significant aspect involves the ability of the hobbits to cope with the actively malevolent Ring, so dreaded by greater and wiser than they. It is not to be assumed that the Ring does not work upon them, yet some circumstances help to shield them from its powers, at least at the outset. In the episode in *The Hobbit* when Bilbo acquired the Ring, he began his ownership with an act of pity which had an insulating effect. At the beginning of the trilogy he voluntarily gives it up — something which only he has ever done — though not without a wrench. In turn, Frodo, though subject to corruption like any creature, begins his guardianship of the Ring unwillingly and without ambition, accepting it as an obligation thrust upon him.

With so heavy odds, against so formidable an adversary, a significant factor provides one hopeful element in the grim web of Sauron's network of agents, tracking down the Ring. In Sauron's very nature, he is incapable of anticipating the policy adopted by his enemies. He cannot conceive that they would voluntarily relinquish the Ring and destroy it, for it would be incompatible with his nature to do so. Thus, the one move that he does not expect is that they would themselves convey it to his very threshold in an ultimate renunciation and destruction of its power.

Yet counterbalancing this small advantage is a demonstration of the fact that creaturely life does not always offer us clear choices of good or evil. Often we must choose between degrees of evil, and we are fortunate when we know that is what we are doing. Frodo, at times, is compelled to use the Ring for its power of invisibility as the immediate alternative to losing all. Yet every time he does so, two bad results are involved: the always baleful influence of the Ring gains perceptibly over Frodo, and Sauron is instantly aware of its use and his mind is able to grope, in a general way, toward its location, like a radio direction-fix. The expedient of employing it thus is doubly harmful each time momentary necessity forces it. In addition, the nearer Frodo gets to his destination, the heavier becomes the physical burden and the greater the influence of the Ring — consequences of its approach to its source. The question of endurance therefore is progressively acute.

At the outset, the Fellowship of the Ring comprises the wizard Gandalf; an Elf, Legolas; a Dwarf, Gimli; two men, Aragorn and Boromir; and four hobbits: Frodo, his servant Sam, and two others called Merry and Pippin. All the nonmalevolent rational species thus have a hand, as well as a stake, in the enterprise. The Fellowship is dispersed early. Frodo must make his grim attempt with the aid only of his loyal servant, Sam. In shuttling narrative patterns of the most prolific story spinning, the others play a variety of necessary roles in the widely dispersed secondary campaign against Sauron's far-ranging forces.

Now we shall shift to another level of meaning. In this story there is no overt theology or religion. There is no mention of God. No one is worshipped. There are no prayers (though there are invocations of great names of virtue). Yet implicit in the conflict between good and evil is a limited eschatology for the Third Age of Middle-earth. A theology contains the narrative rather than being contained by it. Grace is at work abundantly in the story.

In the Judeo-Christian scriptures, God is seen at work in history, taking an initiative, intervening in the affairs of his creatures. Even in the pagan Homeric literature (and in all other primitive literatures) the heroes are seen operating, as in the *Iliad* and the *Odyssey,* with the constant intervention and support of the gods, without which their enterprises and achievements would be impossible.

In Tolkien's Third Age an Ultimate Power is implicit. There is the possibility of Sauron gaining total sway over Middle-earth, but it is clear that there are other realms where his machinations are inoperable. The "Blessed Realm" lies in the mystery of the West, beyond the Sea, and certain characters sail toward it in an image akin to the passing of Arthur to Avalon.

It is a premise of Christian theology that man must cope with certain of his problems with all his own resources. There are things in which it is up to him to succeed or fail. Yet the Will of God, if not completed through one option, will complete itself through another, and in all contingencies there are helps of which a man may avail himself. The Christian rejects utterly the notion that God is dead, or will be mocked, or even that He has withdrawn Himself from human affairs.

In Tolkien's Third Age, the powers that Gandalf and the High

Elves can bring to bear against Sauron clearly are derived from the Prime Source, Who is in some way identified with the Blessed Realm. The great ancient names of men and Elves often invoked are on His side. Running through the story is a thread of prophecy being fulfilled, and Frodo is regarded as "chosen" for his heavy task.

Bilbo's acquiring of the Ring was not just a combination of chance and the power of the Ring itself to work its way back toward its master, Gandalf says to Frodo:

> "Behind that there was something else at work, beyond any design of the Ring-maker. I can put it no plainer than by saying that Bilbo was *meant* to find the Ring, and *not* by its maker. In which case you also were *meant* to have it." (I, 65)

A mysterious, overarching purpose is manifested, too, in the enigmas of the odd, repulsive, but fascinating creature called Gollum, who had treasured the Ring for a long time before Bilbo came upon him. He haunts the Ring through the whole chronicle. There are moments when he is spared only in remembrance of Gandalf's early words:

> "He is bound up with the fate of the Ring. My heart tells me that he has some part to play yet, for good or ill, before the end; and when that comes, the pity of Bilbo may rule the fate of many — yours not least." (I, 69)

The intricacy of Tolkien's web of cause and effect, of the interactions of motives and wills, natural and supernatural, is extraordinary and — notwithstanding the frame of fantasy — profoundly realistic. As for the choosing of Frodo, it is said:

> "This quest may be attempted by the weak with as much hope as the strong. Yet such is oft the course of deeds that move the wheels of the world: small hands do them because they must, while the eyes of the great are elsewhere." (I, 283)

There is no evading the problem of the Ring:

"They who dwell beyond the Sea would not receive it: for good or ill it belongs to Middle-earth; it is for us who still dwell here to deal with it." (I, 279)

And so it is that the hobbit, Frodo, quietly, reluctantly, in a sustained action, surely as brave as any recorded in imaginative literature, assents:

"I will take the Ring," he said, "though I do not know the way." (I, 284)

Thus, at its core, still leaving unreckoned all the wealth of its detailed unfolding, this wonder tale is rich with teaching for life as we lead it. This places it among the true elite of books that can claim to offer such rewards.

Yet so far we have dealt only with inescapable inherent meanings. Possible allegorical elements can be discerned in it, whether or not they were a part of Tolkien's conscious purpose. It is true that things can be got out of a work of art that its creator did not knowingly put in. Yet rather than say it *is* an allegory, which is too rigid for so large, free, and flexible a story, I will say that it has allegorical possibilities and suggestions underlying the face value of the narrative. It is some of these which suggest themselves to me that I put forward, rather than any complete and systematic scheme.

Tolkien vigorously rejects any formal allegorical or other elaborately schematized "interpretations" of his stories. These tend to proliferate even more in the wake of the immense surge in the popularity of the books since this essay was first published in 1962. Reluctantly he concedes the right of readers to find certain "correspondences" to the modern world, if they insist. The intent of this essay is no more than that. He really wishes we would read his work at its face value and keep quiet about it. One cannot blame him, or help feeling slightly guilty about such a discussion as this.

It has for me an allegorical relation to the struggle of Western Christendom against the forces embodied, successively but overlappingly, in Nazism and Communism. The work was conceived and carried forward when the darkest shadow of modern history was cast over the West and, for a crucial part of that time, over England in particular.

Although the notion of the Blessed Realm in the true West is an ancient motif, it is no simple association that also makes the Westernesse of Middle-earth — Númenor as he calls it (which suggests land of spirit) and its men — the hope for justice, peace, and order. In the story, men are the inheritors of earth and theirs is the new age coming. The other creatures are withdrawing, having completed their destinies, but a man is king again in the West and the future lies with his kind.

For those to whom Christianity — not any political or economic or military system — is the one possible counterpoise to the Communist doctrine of man, Tolkien's image of the West is a meaningful parable. He shows us a challenge that must be met, or to which surrender is the only other alternative. All the seductions and rationalizations are there, including that of accepting a "wave of the future," or of using power in such ways as to supplant the enemy with nothing better than ourselves corrupted into his own image. Though Tolkien could not have foreseen it, a natural analogy arises between the hydrogen bomb and the Ring of Power which by its nature could not be used to achieve anything that could be called good.

In both the Third Age and our world, evil is never defeated once for all. Even men who fight evil devotedly are not themselves free of its taint:

> "Always after a defeat and a respite, the Shadow takes another shape and glows again." . . . The evil of Sauron cannot be wholly cured, nor made as if it had not been. . . . Other evils there are that may come; for Sauron is himself but a servant or emissary.

Yet it is not our part to master all the tides of the world, but to do what is in us for the succor of those years wherein we are set, uprooting the evil in the fields that we know, so that those who live after may have clean earth to till. (I, 60; II, 154; III, 155)

If we survive the hydrogen crisis, we will find new technologically pressing moral dilemmas, from genetics to space colonization. There is never a hiding place, or a time when the perennial but Protean moral dilemma has been solved forever. Though we feel with Frodo, "I wish it need not have happened in my time" (I, 60), we must accept the fact that "The wide world is all about you: you can fence yourselves in, but you cannot for ever fence it out" (I, 92). We are faced with what Aragorn, foremost of the men in the story, sternly calls "the doom of choice. . . . There are some things that it is better to begin than to refuse, even though the end may be dark" (II, 36, 43).

"How shall a man judge what to do in such times?"

"As he ever has judged," said Aragorn. "Good and ill have not changed since yesteryear; nor are they one thing among Elves and Dwarves and another among Men." (II, 40–41)

So, likewise, one faces with Frodo the necessity that he expresses: "'It must often be so, Sam, when things are in danger: some one has to give them up, lose them, so that others may keep them.'"

The parallels for our world continue:

"In nothing is the power of the Dark Lord more clearly shown than in the estrangement that divides all those who still oppose him." (I, 362)

Part of this divisive power is the force with which everyone sometimes nurses the thought

that he was offered a choice between a shadow full of fear that lay ahead, and something that he greatly desired: clear before his mind it lay, and to get it he had only to turn aside from the road and leave the Quest and the war against Sauron to others. (I, 373)

We have seen enough to show that it is impossible not to be haunted by parallels between Tolkien's Middle-earth and our here and now. Greater than the samples that are offered is the cumulative effect of the whole tale. It is a moral fable on a scale commensurate with its narrative scope.

Other things remain unremarked. The blight of Mordor and the damage sustained as far away as The Shire are images of the blight which the first half-century of the industrial revolution laid upon fair lands, especially England. The sins of the Christian West in that era are directly visited upon the heads of the generations since in the warped and fragmentary version of the neglected Christian ethic which, since Marx, has been the ideological appeal of the adversary.

We have noted already the general harmony of the elements in this story with Christian theology. It is clear from the nature and powers of Sauron — not always evil, but become so, and not himself the greatest of his kind — that he is a type of the fallen Angels. In the era of the making of the twenty Rings of the runic rhyme, even certain of the subangelic High Elves were for a time deceived by him and, with biblical and Faustian parallels, ensnared by "their eagerness for knowledge" (I, 255). We learn that "it is perilous to study too deeply the arts of the Enemy, for good or for ill" (I, 276).

I shun a too-eager search for supposed Christ figures in literature, and excessively elaborate constructions in pursuit of them. But it is possible to say that both Gandalf and Frodo, each in his way, appear not as Christ equivalents but as partial anticipations of the Christ. With Frodo, quite simply and movingly, it lies in his vain wish that the cup might be taken from him, and since it may not, he goes his long, dolorous way as Ring-bearer — a type of the Cross-bearer to come. More mystically with Gandalf, indicative of the operation of an unexpressed Power behind the events, the wizard undergoes a harrowing prefiguring of the death, descent into Hell, and rising again from the dead. Also he experiences something of the temptation in the wilderness in his refusal of the Ring which he has power enough to wield.

In a conversation in June of 1962 Professor Tolkien was explicit about the nature of Gandalf. In response to my question he said, unhesitatingly, "Gandalf is an angel." He went on to explain that Gandalf had voluntarily accepted incarnation to wage the battle against Sauron. Gandalf the Grey does indeed die in the mortal flesh in the encounter with the Balrog in the Mines of Moria. Gandalf the White, who returns, is the angel in the incorruptible body of resurrection.

Professor Tolkien worked on the whole enterprise for more than fourteen years. He brought to it, apart from his great inventive gifts as what he nicely insists on calling a Subcreator, a background as an authority on Anglo-Saxon language and literature. He is richly steeped in an enormous lore — but it is not that he has pillaged it for his story. Rather he has so profoundly penetrated the spirit of a genre that he has created a modern work in its mode. Internal evidence indicates that *The Hobbit* was begun as a complete and self-sufficient tale. Somewhere in the stages of its growth, I believe the vision of the larger projection in the trilogy came upon him, and that the gathering darkness and gloom over the remnants of the West in the Third Age of Middle-earth grew from the darkness and threats looming over Western Christendom in the 1930s when *The Hobbit* was written. The trilogy was produced during and after the years of World War II, a circumstance which seems to support much of what I read into it.

The volumes of the trilogy appeared in 1954 and 1955 and were received with a critical acclaim so great as to carry in it the danger of faddism and an inevitable counterreaction — a natural hazard of any work unique in its time that kindles a joy by its very freshness. The names of Spenser, Malory, and Ariosto were immediately invoked in the search for comparisons. . . .

I think it safe to say that . . . this extraordinary imaginative feat in the making of an Other-world, meaningfully related to our own, is likely to be one of the most tenacious works of fiction in this present age of Middle-earth. It gives joy, excitement, a lift of spirits, and it contains the kind of wisdom and insight which, if applied to the world we inhabit, might help our sore-beset race to hang on through the present shadows of modern Mordor into yet another age.

W. H. AUDEN

The Quest Hero

At the very moment that such champions of modernism as Philip Toyn-bee and Edmund Wilson were mocking and maligning The Lord of the Rings *as "dull, ill written, whimsical, and childish," coarse fodder for those readers who have "a life-long appetite for juvenile trash," Auden, among the great modernist poets, wrote this admiring and penetrating analysis of Tolkien's great epic. Auden considered* The Lord of the Rings *to be the kind of work that shapes an enduring, universal mythic and psychological pattern in human culture and consciousness. It is, he says, a "literary mimesis of the subjective experience of becoming." Dismissing the left-wing paper warriors who attacked Tolkien as a fascist and a racist, Auden calls attention to the political and social ideals the novel upholds: a "benevolent monarchy," within which the Shire exists as "a kind of small-town democracy." It is Sauron's kingdom, which all the free peoples of Middle-earth abhor, that is "a totalitarian and slave-owning dictatorship."*

I. General Observations

To look for a lost collar button is not a true Quest: to go in quest means to look for something of which one has, as yet, no experience;

one can imagine what it will be like but whether one's picture is true or false will be known only when one has found it.

Animals, therefore, do not go on quests. They hunt for food or drink or a mate, but the object of their search is determined by what they already are and its purpose is to restore a disturbed equilibrium; they have no choice in the matter.

But man is a history-making creature for whom the future is always open; human "nature" is a nature continually in quest of itself, obliged at every moment to transcend what it was a moment before. For man the present is not real but valuable. He can neither repeat the past exactly — every moment is unique — nor leave it behind — at every moment he adds to and thereby modifies all that has previously happened to him.

Hence the impossibility of expressing his kind of existence in a single image. If one concentrates upon his ever open future, the natural image is of a road stretching ahead into unexplored country, but if one concentrates upon his unforgettable past, then the natural image is of a city, which is built in every style of architecture and in which the physically dead are as active citizens as the living. The only characteristic common to both images is a sense of purpose; a road, even if its destination is invisible, runs in a certain direction; a city is built to endure and be a home.

The animals who really live in the present have neither roads nor cities and do not miss them. They are at home in the wilderness and, at most, if they are social, set up camps for a generation. But man requires both. The image of a city with no roads leading from it suggests a prison; the image of a road that starts from nowhere in particular suggests, not a true road, but an animal spoor.

A similar difficulty arises if one tries to describe simultaneously our experience of our own lives and our experience of the lives of others. Subjectively, I am a unique ego set over against a self; my body, desires, feelings, and thoughts seem distinct from the *I* that is aware of them. But I cannot know the Ego of another person directly, only his self, which is not unique but comparable with the selves of others, including my own. Thus, if I am a good observer and a good mimic, it is conceivable that I could imitate another so accurately as to deceive his best friends, but it would still be I imitating him; I can never know what it would feel like to be someone else. The social relation of my Ego to my Self is of a fundamentally different kind from all my other social relations to persons or things.

Again, I am conscious of myself as becoming, of every moment being new, whether or not I show any outward sign of change, but in others I can only perceive the passage of time when it manifests itself objectively; So-and-so looks older or fatter or behaves differently from the way he used to behave. Further, though we all know that all men must die, dying is not an experience that we can share; I cannot take part in the deaths of others nor they in mine.

Lastly, my subjective experience of living is one of having continually to make a choice between given alternatives, and it is this experience of doubt and temptation that seems more important and memorable to me than the actions I take when I have made my choice. But when I observe others, I cannot see them making choices; I can only see their actions; compared with myself, others seem at once less free and more stable in character, good or bad.

The Quest is one of the oldest, hardiest, and most popular of all literary genres. In some instances it may be founded on historical fact — the Quest of the Golden Fleece may have its origin in the search of seafaring traders for amber — and certain themes, like the theme of the enchanted cruel Princess whose heart can be melted only by the predestined lover, may be distorted recollections of religious rites, but the persistent appeal of the Quest as a literary form is due, I believe, to its validity as a symbolic description of our subjective personal experience of existence as historical.

As a typical example of the traditional Quest, let us look at the tale in the Grimm collection called "The Waters of Life." A King has fallen sick. Each of his three sons sets out in turn to find and bring back the water of life which will restore him to health. The motive of the two elder sons is not love of their father but the hope of reward; only the youngest really cares about his father as a person. All three encounter a dwarf who asks them where they are going. The first two rudely refuse to answer and are punished by the dwarf, who imprisons them in a ravine. The youngest answers courteously and truthfully, and the dwarf not only directs him to the castle where the Fountain of the Waters of Life is situated but also gives him a magic wand to open the castle gate and two loaves of bread to appease the lions who guard the Fountain. Furthermore, the dwarf warns him that he must leave before the clock strikes twelve or he will find himself imprisoned. Following these instructions and using the magic gifts, the youngest brother obtains the Water of Life, meets a beautiful Princess who promises to marry him if he will return in a year, and carries away with him a magic sword which can slay whole armies and a magic loaf of bread which will never come to an end. However, he almost fails because, forgetting the dwarf's advice, he lies down on a bed and falls asleep, awakening only just in time as the clock is striking twelve; the closing door takes a piece off his heel.

On his way home he meets the dwarf again and learns what has happened to his brothers; at his entreaty the dwarf reluctantly releases them, warning him that they have evil hearts.

The three brothers continue their homeward journey and, thanks to the sword and the loaf, the youngest is able to deliver three kingdoms from war and famine. The last stretch is by sea. While the hero is asleep, his older brothers steal the Water of Life from his bottle and substitute seawater. When they arrive home, their sick father tries the water offered by the youngest and, naturally, is made worse; then the older brothers offer him the water they have stolen and cure him.

In consequence the King believes their allegation that the youngest was trying to poison him and orders his huntsman to take the hero into the forest and shoot him in secret. When it comes to the point, however, the huntsman cannot bring himself to do this, and the hero remains in hiding in the forest.

Presently wagons of gold and jewels begin arriving at the palace for the hero, gifts from the grateful kings whose lands he had delivered from war and famine, and his father becomes convinced of his innocence. Meanwhile the Princess, in preparation for her wedding, has built a golden road to her castle and given orders that only he who comes riding straight along it shall be admitted.

Again the two elder brothers attempt to cheat the hero by going to woo her themselves, but, when they come to the golden road, they are afraid of spoiling it; one rides to the left of it, one to the right, and both are refused admission to the castle. When the hero comes to the road he is so preoccupied with thinking about the Princess that he does not notice that it is made of gold and rides straight up it. He is admitted, weds the Princess, returns home with her, and is reconciled to his father. The two wicked brothers put to sea, never to be heard of again, and all ends happily.

The essential elements in this typical Quest story are six:

1. A precious Object and/or Person to be found and possessed or married.
2. A long journey to find it, for its whereabouts are not originally known to the seekers.
3. A hero. The precious Object cannot be found by anybody, but only by the one person who possesses the right qualities of breeding or character.
4. A Test or series of Tests by which the unworthy are screened out, and the hero revealed.
5. The Guardians of the Object who must be overcome before it can be won. They may be simply a further test of the hero's *arete*, or they may be malignant in themselves.
6. The Helpers who with their knowledge and magical powers as-

sist the hero and but for whom he would never succeed. They may appear in human or in animal form.

Does not each of these elements correspond to an aspect of our subjective experience of life?

1. Many of my actions are purposive; the *telos* toward which they are directed may be a short-term one, like trying to write a sentence which shall express my present thoughts accurately, or a lifelong one, the search to find true happiness or authenticity of being, to become what I wish or God intends me to become. What more natural image for such a *telos* than a beautiful Princess or the Waters of Life?

2. I am conscious of time as a continuous irreversible process of change. Translated into spatial terms, this process becomes, naturally enough, a journey.

3. I am conscious of myself as unique — my goal is for me only — and as confronting an unknown future — I cannot be certain in advance whether I shall succeed or fail in achieving my goal. The sense of uniqueness produces the image of the unique hero; the sense of uncertainty, the images of the unsuccessful rivals.

4. I am conscious of contradictory forces in myself, some of which I judge to be good and others evil, which are continually trying to sway my will this way or that. The existence of these forces is given. I can choose to yield to a desire or to resist it, but I cannot by choice desire or not desire.

Any image of this experience must be dualistic, a contest between two sides, friends and enemies.

On the other hand, the Quest provides no image of our objective experience of social life. If I exclude my own feelings and try to look at the world as if I were the lens of a camera, I observe that the vast majority of people have to earn their living in a fixed place, and that journeys are confined to people on holiday or with independent means. I observe that, though there may be some wars which can be called just, there are none in which one side is absolutely good and the other absolutely evil, though it is all too common for both sides to persuade themselves that this is so. As for struggles between man and the forces of nature or wild beasts, I can see that nature is unaware of being destructive and that, though there are animals which attack men out of hunger or fear, no animal does so out of malice.

In many versions of the Quest, both ancient and modern, the winning or recovery of the Precious Object is for the common good of the society to which the hero belongs. Even when the goal of his quest is marriage, it is not any girl he is after but a Princess. Their personal happiness is incidental to the happiness of the City; now the Kingdom will be well governed, and there will soon be an heir.

But there are other versions in which success is of importance only to the individual who achieves it. The Holy Grail, for example, will never again become visible to all men; only the exceptionally noble and chaste can be allowed to see it.

Again, there are two types of Quest Hero. One resembles the hero of Epic; his superior *arete* is manifest to all. Jason, for example, is instantly recognizable as the kind of man who can win the Golden Fleece if anybody can. The other type, so common in fairy tales, is the hero whose *arete* is concealed. The youngest son, the weakest, the least clever, the one whom everybody would judge as least likely to succeed, turns out to be the hero when his manifest betters have failed. He owes his success, not to his own powers, but to the fairies, magicians, and animals who help him, and he is able to enlist their help because, unlike his betters, he is humble enough to take advice, and kind enough to give assistance to strangers who, like himself, appear to be nobody in particular.

Though the subject of this essay is the Quest in its traditional form, it is worthwhile, perhaps, to mention, very briefly, some variants.

A. The Detective Story

Here the goal is not an object or a person but the answer to a question
— Who committed the murder? Consequently, not only is there no
journey, but also the more closed the society, the more restricted the
locale, the better. There are two sides, but one side has only one member, the murderer, for the division is not between the Evil and the
Good but between the Guilty and the Innocent. The hero, the detec-
tive, is a third party who belongs to neither side.

B. The Adventure Story

Here the journey and the goal are identical, for the Quest is for more
and more adventures. A classic example is Poe's *Gordon Pym.* More
sophisticated and subtler examples are Goethe's *Faust* and the Don
Juan legend.

The condition laid down in his pact with Mephisto is that Faust
shall never ask that the flow of time be arrested at an ideal moment,
that he shall never say, "Now, I have reached the goal of my quest."
Don Juan's Quest can never come to an end because there will always
remain girls whom he has not yet seduced. His is also one of the rare
cases of an Evil Quest which ought not to be undertaken and in
which, therefore, the hero is the villain.

C. Moby Dick

Here the Precious Object and the Malevolent Guardian are combined
and the object of the Quest is not possession but destruction. Another example of a Quest which should not have been undertaken,
but it is tragic rather than evil. Captain Ahab belongs in the company
of Othello, not of Iago.

D. The Kafka Novels

In these the hero fails to achieve his goal, in *The Trial* either to prove
himself innocent or learn of what he is guilty, in *The Castle* to obtain
official recognition as a land surveyor; and he fails, not because he is

unworthy, but because success is humanly impossible. The Guardians are too strong and, though Kafka avoids saying so I think one can add, too malevolent. What makes K a hero is that, despite the evidence that Evil is more powerful than Good in the world, he never gives up the struggle to worship the Prince of this world. By all the rules he ought to despair; yet he does not.

Any literary mimesis of the subjective experience of becoming is confronted by problems of form and limitations of subject matter. Like a man's life which has a beginning, birth, and an end, death, the Quest story has two fixed points, the starting out and the final achievement, but the number of adventures in the interval cannot but be arbitrary; for, since the flow of time is continuous, it can be infinitely divided and subdivided into moments. One solution is the imposition of a numerical pattern, analogous to the use of meter in poetry. Thus, in *The Waters of Life* there are three brothers, three kingdoms to be delivered from war and famine, and three ways of approaching the Princess's castle. There are two tests, the dwarf and the golden road, but the right and wrong behavior are symmetrically opposed; it is right to take notice of the dwarf but wrong to take notice of the road.

The hero twice nearly comes to disaster by falling asleep, on the first occasion in direct disobedience of the dwarf's instructions, on the second in neglect of the warning that his brothers are evil men.

To take a man on a journey is to cut him off from his everyday social relations to women, neighbors, and fellow workers. The only sustained relation which the Quest Hero can enjoy is with those who accompany him on his journey, that is to say, either the democratic relation between equal comrades-in-arms, or the feudal relation between Knight and Squire. Aside from these, his social life is limited to chance and brief encounters. Even when his motive for understanding the Quest is erotic, the lady has to remain in wait for him either at the start or the end of the road. Partly for this reason and partly because it deals with adventures, that is, situations of crisis in which a man behaves either well or badly, the Quest tale is ill adapted to subtle portrayals of character; its personages are almost bound to be archetypes rather than idiosyncratic individuals.

So much for general observations. I shall devote the rest of this essay to an examination of a single work, J.R.R. Tolkien's trilogy, *The Lord of the Rings.*

II. THE SETTING

Many Quest tales are set in a dreamland, that is to say, in no definite place or time. This has the advantage of allowing the use of all the wealth of dream imagery, monsters, magical transformations and translations, which are absent from our waking life, but at the cost of aggravating the tendency of the genre to divorce itself from social and historical reality. A dream is at most capable of allegorical interpretation, but such interpretations are apt to be mechanical and shallow. There are other Quest tales, a thriller like *The Thirty-Nine Steps,* for example, which are set in places which we can find in the atlas and in times we can read of in history books. This gives the Quest a social significance, but the moral ambiguities of real history clash with the presupposition which is essential to the genre, that one side is good and the other bad.

Even in wartime, the sensitive reader cannot quite believe this of the two sides which the writer of thrillers takes from real life. He cannot help knowing that, at the same time that John Buchan is making the heroes English and American and the enemies German, some German author may be writing an equally convincing thriller in which the roles are reversed.

Tolkien sets his story neither in a dream world nor in the actual world but in an imaginary world. An imaginary world can be so constructed as to make credible any landscape, inhabitants, and events which its maker wishes to introduce, and since he himself has invented its history, there can be only one correct interpretation of events, his own. What takes place and why is, necessarily, what he says it is.

But the construction of a convincing imaginary world makes formidable demands upon the imagination of its creator. There must be no question which, according to our interests, we ask about the real world to which he cannot give a convincing answer, and any writer who, like Tolkien, sets out to create an imaginary world in the twentieth century has to meet a higher standard of concreteness than, say, his medieval predecessor, for he has to reckon with readers who have been exposed to the realistic novel and scientific historical research.

A dream world may be full of inexplicable gaps and logical inconsistencies; an imaginary world may not, for it is a world of law, not of wish. Its laws may be different from those which govern our own, but they must be as intelligible and inviolable. Its history may be unusual but it must not contradict our notion of what history is, an interplay of Fate, Choice, and Chance. Lastly, it must not violate our moral experience. If, as the Quest generally requires, Good and Evil are to be incarnated in individuals and societies, we must be convinced that the Evil side is what every sane man, irrespective of his nationality or culture, would acknowledge as evil. The triumph of Good over Evil which the successful achievement of the Quest implies must appear historically possible, not a daydream. Physical and, to a considerable extent, intellectual power must be shown as what we know them to be, morally neutral and effectively real: battles are won by the stronger side, be it good or evil.

To indicate the magnitude of the task Tolkien set himself, let me give a few figures. The area of his world measures some thirteen hundred miles from east (the Gulf of Lune) to west (the Iron Hills) and twelve hundred miles from north (the Bay of Forochel) to south (the mouth of the River Anduin). In our world there is only one species, man, who is capable of speech and has a real history; in Tolkien's there are at least seven. The actual events of the story cover the last twenty years of the Third Historical Epoch of this world. The First Age is treated as legendary so that its duration is unknown, and its history is only vaguely recalled, but for the 3,441 years of the Second Age and the 3,021 years of the Third he has to provide a continuous and credible history.

The first task of the maker of an imaginary world is the same as that of Adam in Eden: he has to find names for everyone and everything in it and if, as in Tolkien's world, there is more than one language, he has to invent as many series of names as there are tongues.

In the nominative gift, Tolkien surpasses any writer, living or dead, whom I have ever read; to find the "right" names is hard enough in a comic world; in a serious one success seems almost magical. Moreover, he shows himself capable of inventing not only names but whole languages which reflect the nature of those who speak them. The Ents, for example, are trees which have acquired movement, consciousness, and speech but continue to live at the tempo of trees. In consequence their language is "slow, sonorous, agglomerated, repetitive, indeed long-winded." Here is only a part of the Entish word for hill:

a-lalla-lalla-rumba-kamanda-lind-or-burúmë.

The extremes of good and evil in the story are represented by the Elves and Sauron, respectively. Here is a verse from a poem in Elvish:

A Elbereth Gilthoniel,
silivren penna míriel
o menel alglar elenath!
Na-chaered palan díriel.
o galadhremmin ennorath,
   Fanuilos, le linnathon
    nef aer, sí nef aearon.

And here is an evil spell in the Black Speech invented by Sauron:

Ash nazg durbatulûk, ash nazg gimbatul, ash nazg thrakata-lûk,
agh burzum-ishi-krimpatul.

An imaginary world must be as real to the senses of the reader as the actual world. For him to find an imaginary journey convincing, he must feel that he is seeing the landscape through which it passes as, given his mode of locomotion and the circumstances of his errand, the fictional traveler himself saw it. Fortunately, Mr. Tolkien's gift for topographical description is equal to his gift for naming and his fertility in inventing incidents. His hero, Frodo Baggins, is on the road, excluding rests, for eighty days and covers over 1800 miles, much of it on foot, and with his senses kept perpetually sharp by fear, watching every inch of the way for signs of his pursuers, yet Tolkien succeeds in convincing us that there is nothing Frodo noticed which he has forgotten to describe.

Technologically, his world is preindustrial. The arts of mining, metallurgy, architecture, road and bridge building, are highly developed, but there are no firearms and no mechanical means of transport. It is, however, a world that has seen better days. Lands that were once cultivated and fertile have gone back to the wilderness, roads have become impassable, once-famous cities are now ruins. (There is one puzzling discrepancy. Both Sauron and Saruman seem to have installed heavy machinery in their fortresses. Why, in that case, are they limited to waging untechnological warfare?) Though without machines, some people in this world possess powers which our civilization would call magical because it lacks them; telepathic communication and vision are possible, verbal spells are effective, weather can be controlled, rings confer invisibility, etc.

Politically, the commonest form of society is a benevolent monarchy, but the Shire of the hobbits is a kind of small-town democracy, and Sauron's kingdom of Mordor is, of course, a totalitarian and slave-owning dictatorship.

Though the unstated presuppositions of the whole work are Christian, we are not told that any of the inhabitants practice a religious cult.

The Elves, the Wizards, and Sauron, certainly, and perhaps some others, believe in the existence of the One and the Valar, to whom He has entrusted the guardianship of Middle-earth, and a Land in the Uttermost West which I take to be an image of Paradise.

III. THE QUEST HERO

In our subjective experience, of which the Quest is, I have suggested, a literary mimesis, what we ought to become is usually dependent upon what we are; it is idle and cowardly of me if I fail to make the fullest use of any talent with which I have been endowed, but it is presumptuous of me to attempt a task for which I lack the talent it requires. That is why, in the traditional Quest story, the hero desires to undertake the quest and, even when to others he appears lacking in power, he is confident of success. This problem of vocation is specifically dealt with in one Quest tale, *The Magic Flute*. Prince Tamino is the typical hero, who must dare the trials by Fire and Water to attain wisdom and win the hand of the Princess Pamina.

But beside him stands Papageno, who is, in his own way, a hero too. He is asked whether he is prepared to endure the trials like his master, and he answers no, such dangers are not for the likes of him. "But," says the priest, "if you don't, you will never win a girl." "In that case," he replies, "I'll remain single." This answer reveals his humility, and he is rewarded with his mirror image, Papagena. In contrast to him stands the villain Monostatos. Like Papageno, he is incapable of enduring the trials, but unlike him, he lacks the humility to forego the rewards of heroism; he is even unwilling to accept an equivalent of Papagena and demands nothing less than the Princess.

But there is another kind of vocation which may be called religious. Not everybody experiences it, and even for those who do, it may concern only moments of their life. What characterizes the religious vocation is that it comes from outside the self and generally to the self's terror and dismay, as when God calls Abraham out of the land of Ur, or when a man, by nature physically timid, is called to enter a burning building to rescue a child because there is no one else around to do it.

Some of the characters in *The Lord of the Rings*, Gandalf and Aragorn, for instance, are expressions of the natural vocation of talent. It is for Gandalf to plan the strategy of the War against Sauron because he is a very wise man; it is for Aragorn to lead the armies of Gondor because he is a great warrior and the rightful heir to the throne. Whatever they may have to risk and suffer, they are, in a sense, doing what they want to do. But the situation of the real hero, Frodo Baggins, is quite different. When the decision has been taken to send the Ring to the Fire, his *feelings* are those of Papageno: "Such dangerous exploits are not for a little hobbit like me. I would much rather stay at home than risk my life on the very slight chance of winning glory." But his conscience tells him: "You may be nobody in particular in yourself, yet, for some inexplicable reasons, through no choice of your own, the Ring has come into your keeping, so that it is on you and not on Gandalf or Aragorn that the task falls of destroying it."

Because the decision has nothing to do with his talents, nobody else can or should try to help him make up his mind. When he stands up at the Council of Elrond and says: "'I will take the Ring though I know not the Way,'" Elrond replies: "'It is a heavy burden. So heavy that none could lay it on another. I do not lay it on you. But if you take it freely, I will say that your choice is right'" (I, 284).

Once he has chosen, Frodo is absolutely committed; the others who set out with him are not:

> "The Ring-bearer is setting out on the Quest of Mount Doom;
> on him alone is any charge laid — neither to cast away the Ring
> nor to deliver it to any servant of the Enemy, nor indeed to let

any handle it, save members of the Company and the Council, and only then in gravest need. The others go with him as free companions to help him on his way. You may tarry, or come back, or turn aside to other paths as chance allows. The further you go the less easy it will be to withdraw; yet no oath or bond is laid upon you to go further than you will. For you do not yet know the strength of your hearts and you cannot foresee what each may meet on the road."

"Faithless is he who says farewell when the road darkens," said Gimli.

"Maybe," said Elrond; "but let him not vow to walk in the dark who has not seen the nightfall."

"Yet sworn vow may strengthen quaking heart," said Gimli.

"Or break it," said Elrond. "Look not too far ahead. But go now with good hearts." (I, 294)

IV. The Conflict of Good and Evil

If it is a defect in the usual Quest tale that Good triumphs over Evil simply because Good is more powerful, this is not a defect that can be avoided by giving Good no power at all. Quite rightly, Tolkien makes the elves, dwarves, wizards, and men who are Sauron's opponents a formidable lot indeed, but in sheer strength, Sauron is, even without his Ring, the stronger. Yet their power has its part to play, as Gandalf points out:

> "Victory cannot be achieved by arms. . . . I still hope for victory, but not by arms. For into the midst of all these policies comes the Ring of Power, the foundation of Barad-dûr, and the hope of Sauron. . . . If he regains it, your valour is vain, and his victory will be swift and complete: so complete that none can foresee the end of it while this world lasts. If it is destroyed, then he will fall; and his fall will be so low that none can foresee his arising ever again. . . . This, then, is my counsel. We have not the Ring. In wis-

dom or great folly, it has been sent away to be destroyed, lest it destroy us. Without it we cannot by force defeat his force. But we must at all costs keep his Eye from his true peril. We cannot achieve victory by arms, but by arms we can give the Ring-bearer his only chance, frail though it be." (III, 154–56)

The Quest is successful, and Sauron is overthrown. One of Tolkien's most impressive achievements is that he convinces the reader that the mistakes which Sauron makes to his undoing are the kind of mistakes which Evil, however powerful, cannot help making just because it is Evil. His primary weakness is a lack of imagination, for, while Good can imagine what it would be like to be Evil, Evil cannot imagine what it would be like to be Good. Elrond, Gandalf, Galadriel, Aragorn are able to imagine themselves as Sauron and therefore can resist the temptation to use the Ring themselves, but Sauron cannot imagine that anyone who knows what the Ring can accomplish, his own destruction among other things, will not use it, let alone try to destroy it. Had he been capable of imagining this, he had only to sit waiting and watching in Mordor for the Ring-bearer to arrive, and he was bound to catch him and recover the Ring. Instead, he assumes that the Ring has been taken to Gondor where the strongest of his enemies are gathered, which is what he would have done had he been in their place, and launches an attack on that city, neglecting the watch on his own borders.

Secondly, the kind of Evil which Sauron embodies, the lust for domination, will always be irrationally cruel since it is not satisfied if another does what it wants; he must be made to do it against his will. When Pippin looked into the Palantír of Orthanc and so revealed himself to Sauron, the latter had only to question him in order to learn who had the Ring and what he intended to do with it. But, as Gandalf says: "'He was too eager. He did not want information only: he wanted *you*, quickly; so that he could deal with you in the Dark Tower, slowly'" (II, 199).

Thirdly, all alliances of Evil with Evil are necessarily unstable and untrustworthy since, by definition, Evil loves only itself and its alliances are based on fear or hope of profit, not on affection. Sauron's greatest triumph has been his seduction of the great wizard Saruman, but though he has succeeded in making him a traitor to the cause of Good, he has not yet completely enslaved him, so that Saruman tries to seize the Ring for himself.

Lastly, unforeseeable by either side, is the role played by Sméagol-Gollum. When Frodo first hears about him from Gandalf, he exclaims:

> "What a pity Bilbo did not stab that vile creature, when he had a chance!"
>
> "Pity? It was Pity that stayed his hand. Pity, and Mercy: not to strike without need. And he has been well rewarded, Frodo. Be sure that he took so little hurt from the evil, and escaped in the end, because he began his ownership of the Ring so. With Pity." . . .
>
> ". . . I cannot understand you. Do you mean to say that you, and the Elves, have let him live on after all those horrible deeds? . . . He deserves death."
>
> "Deserves it! I daresay he does. . . . [But] do not be too eager to deal out death in judgment. For even the very wise cannot see all ends. I have not much hope that Gollum can be cured before he dies, but there is a chance of it. And he is bound up with the fate of the Ring. My heart tells me that he has some part to play yet, for good or ill, before the end; and when that comes, the pity of Bilbo may rule the fate of many — yours not least." (I, 68–69)

Gollum picks up Frodo's trail in the Mines of Moria and follows him. When Frodo manages to catch him, he remembers Gandalf's words and spares his life. This turns out to his immediate advantage for, without Gollum's help, Frodo and Sam would never have found their way through the Dead Marshes or to the pass of Cirith Ungol.

Gollum's motives in guiding them are not wholly evil; one part of him, of course, is waiting for an opportunity to steal the Ring, but another part feels gratitude and genuine affection for Frodo.

Gandalf was right, however, in fearing that there was little hope of his being cured; in the end his evil side triumphs. He leads Frodo and Sam into Shelob's lair and, after their escape, pursues them to Mount Doom and attacks them. Once again they spare his life. And then the unexpected happens:

> There on the brink of the chasm, at the very Crack of Doom, stood Frodo, black against the glare, tense, erect, but still as if he had been turned to stone.
>
> "Master!" cried Sam.
>
> Then Frodo stirred and spoke with a clear voice, . . . it rose above the throb and turmoil of Mount Doom, ringing in the roof and walls.
>
> "I have come," he said. "But I do not choose now to do what I came to do. I will not do this deed. The Ring is mine!" And suddenly, as he set it on his finger, he vanished from Sam's sight. . . . Something struck Sam violently in the back, his legs were knocked from under him and he was flung aside, striking his head against the stony floor, as a dark shape sprang over him. . . .
>
> Sam got up. He was dazed, and blood streaming from his head dripped in his eyes. He groped forward, and then he saw a strange and terrible thing. Gollum on the edge of the abyss was fighting like a mad thing with an unseen foe. . . . The fires below awoke in anger, the red light blazed, and all the cavern was filled with a great glare and heat. Suddenly Sam saw Gollum's long hands draw upwards to his mouth; his white fangs gleamed, and then snapped as they bit. Frodo gave a cry, and there he was, fallen upon his knees at the chasm's edge. But Gollum, dancing like a mad thing, held aloft the Ring, a finger still thrust within its circle. . . .

"Precious, precious, precious!" Gollum cried. "My Precious! O my Precious!" And with that, even as his eyes were lifted up to gloat on his prize, he stepped too far, toppled, wavered for a moment on the brink, and then with a shriek he fell. . . .

"Well, this is the end, Sam Gamgee," said a voice by his side. And there was Frodo, pale and worn, and yet himself again; and in his eyes there was peace now, neither strain of will, nor madness, nor any fear. His burden was taken away. . . .

"Yes," said Frodo. ". . . Do you remember Gandalf's words: *Even Gollum may have something yet to do?* But for him, Sam, I could not have destroyed the Ring. The Quest would have been in vain, even at the bitter end." (III, 223–25)

V. The Fruits of Victory

"And so they lived happily ever after" is a conventional formula for concluding a fairy tale. Alas, it is false and we know it, for it suggests that, once Good has triumphed over Evil, man is translated out of his historical existence into eternity. Tolkien is much too honest to end with such a pious fiction. Good has triumphed over Evil so far as the Third Age of Middle-earth is concerned, but there is no certainty that this triumph is final. There was Morgoth before Sauron and, before the Fourth Age ends, who can be sure that no successor to Sauron will appear? Victory does not mean the restoration of the Earthly Paradise or the advent of the New Jerusalem. In our historical existence even the best solution involves loss as well as gain. With the destruction of the Ruling Ring, the three Elven Rings lose their power, as Galadriel foresaw:

"Do you not see now wherefore your coming is to us as the footstep of Doom? For if you fail, we are laid bare to the Enemy. Yet if you succeed, then our power is diminished, and Lothlórien will fade, and the tides of Time will sweep it away. We must depart into the West, or dwindle to a rustic folk of dell and cave, slowly to forget and be forgotten." (I, 380)

Even Frodo, the Quest Hero, has to pay for his success:

> "But," said Sam, and tears started from his eyes, "I thought you were going to enjoy the Shire . . . for years and years, after all you have done."
>
> "So I thought too, once. But I have been too deeply hurt, Sam. I tried to save the Shire, and it has been saved, but not for me. It must often be so, Sam, when things are in danger: some one has to give them up, lose them, so that others may keep them." (III, 309)

If there is any Quest Tale which, while primarily concerned with the subjective life of the individual person as all such stories must be, manages to do more justice to our experience of social-historical re-alities than *The Lord of the Rings*, I should be glad to hear of it.

PATRICIA MEYER SPACKS

Power and Meaning in
The Lord of the Rings

In this essay Spacks distinguishes Tolkien from the two writers with whom he is most usually associated, C. S. Lewis and Charles Williams. The two latter, she argues, are architects of archetypal Christian fables wherein the soul battles evil and wins a heavenly home. In contrast, Tolkien's ethos is pagan Anglo-Saxon. The hero in Anglo-Saxon litera-ture struggles against monsters, and ultimately in the turning wheel of time, he must be defeated. That is his Fate; as the Beowulf poet puts it, "Wyrd bit ful anræd" (Fate is fully determined). The particular excel-lence of the Anglo-Saxon hero is "naked will and courage." Those agents of good freely choose to act for good in the time that Fate allows them.

As a writer of fiction, J.R.R. Tolkien has often been thought of in con-nection with the excursions of C. S. Lewis and Charles Williams into the "serious" supernatural. Both Williams and Lewis, formerly fellow members with Tolkien of an Oxford discussion group in which por-tions of their fiction were read aloud for criticism, have received re-cent critical attention in this country as Christian "mythmakers." Tolkien, however, has been neglected ever since Edmund Wilson, in a review in *The Nation,* informed us that he was not to be taken seriously.[1]

Yet in a fuller sense than Lewis or Williams, Tolkien is a modern mythmaker. In *The Lord of the Rings,* his epic trilogy, he virtually created a new genre: one possessing obvious affinities with folk epic and mythology, but with no true literary counterpart. The novels of Williams and Lewis gain from their Christian teleology an effect of cosmic scope and depth; the novels of Tolkien possess, in addition to enormous physical scope, a mythic structure of yet more subtle complexity.

In "Oo, Those Awful Orcs!" Wilson remarked of Tolkien's trilogy: "The hero has no serious temptations, is lured by no insidious enchantments, perplexed by few problems. What we get is a simple confrontation in more or less the traditional terms of British melodrama — of the Forces of Evil with the Forces of Good" (313). But the confrontation of the Forces of Evil with the Forces of Good is the basic theme also of tragedy, epic, and myth. Tolkien's presentation of this theme is by no means so simple as Wilson suggests. Indeed, the force and complexity of its moral and theological scheme provide the fundamental power of *The Lord of the Rings.*

For this scheme there are no explicit supernatural sanctions: *The Lord of the Rings* is by no means a Christian work. An anonymous early review in the *Times Literary Supplement*[2] remarked on the fact that throughout the trilogy no character, good or bad, performs an act of worship. Although supernatural powers abound, no deity is evident on the side of the good or of the evil. A clear ethos rules the virtuous, but its derivation is unclear.

The principles of that ethos are simple, embodied primarily in the hobbit-heroes, members of a Tolkien-created race essentially human in characteristics, gnomelike in appearance. The first important representative of the hobbit is Bilbo Baggins, eponymous hero of *The Hobbit,* a children's book which was an offshoot along the way of Tolkien's trilogy. Its events immediately antedate those of *The Lord of the Rings;* its hero closely resembles Frodo Baggins, Bilbo's nephew, who is the central character of the trilogy. Both hobbits possess the same morality, share the same virtues. They are unfailingly loyal, to companions and to principles. They are cheerful in the face of adversity, persistent to the point of stubbornness in pursuit of a goal, deeply honest, humble in their devotion to those they consider greater than they. And as their most vital attributes they possess "naked will and courage."

The quotation is from Tolkien in reference to quite different heroes, and its context is significant. In 1936, Tolkien published one of the most important pieces of *Beowulf* criticism of the past several decades. Entitled "*Beowulf:* The Monsters and the Critics," it defends the Anglo-Saxon poem's structural dependence on encounters with nonhuman monsters, Grendel, his dam, and the dragon. The defense could stand equally well for Tolkien's own fiction, which, even in the comparatively slight children's book *Farmer Giles of Ham,* centers characteristically on encounters between human beings — or such symbolic representatives of humans as the hobbits — and inhuman monsters. In connection with *Beowulf,* Tolkien points out the difference between the Christian imagination and the northern mythological imagination. The archetypal Christian fable, he observes, centers on the battle between the soul and its adversaries. (This, of course, is the battle which preoccupies Williams and Lewis.) In this struggle, the Christian is finally triumphant, in the afterlife if not on earth. But northern mythology takes a darker view. Its characteristic struggle between man and monster must end ultimately, within Time, in man's defeat. Yet man continues to struggle; his weapons are the hobbit-weapons: naked will and courage.

These are the basic virtues of most epic heroes. Their opposites are apparent in Tolkien's representatives of evil, who are characteristically disloyal, whose courage depends on numbers, whose wills are enslaved. The conflict between good and evil appears, in this trilogy, to be a contest between representatives of opposed ethical systems.

The opposed forces also differ in their relation to nature. Goodness is partly equated with understanding of nature, closeness to the natural world. The Rangers, important forces on the side of Good, understand the languages of beasts and birds. Tom Bombadil, who rescues the hobbits from evil in the forest, whose natural power for good is so great that he can see the wearer of the Ring which makes men invisible to all other eyes and he does not become invisible himself when wearing it, is in the most intimate communion with natural forces; he has the power of "the earth itself" (I, 279). The power of the noble Elves gives Frodo new awareness of trees: "It was the delight of the living tree itself" (I, 366). The most potent force in the destruction of the realm of Saruman, a corrupted sorcerer, is provided by the Ents, guardians of the forest so closely involved with its life that their form is that of giant trees. The progress toward the heart of evil, toward the Crack of Doom into which, in the trilogy's central fable, the Ring-bearer must throw his Ring of Power, is from natural fertility to the desolation of nature. The Enemy's territory, even its outskirts, is physically and morally a wasteland; the implication is strong that the barrenness of nature here is a direct result of the operations of evil. "We see that Sauron can torture and destroy the very hills" (I, 279). And, later, "What pestilence or war or evil deed of the Enemy had so blasted all the region even Aragorn could not tell" (I, 396).

It is characteristic of the Enemy to depend upon machinery rather than natural forces. Saruman's city has smithies, furnaces, iron wheels revolving endlessly, hammers thudding, steam rising; Treebeard, the great Ent, describes Saruman as having "a mind of metal and wheels" (II, 76). The Dark Tower, which looms above the Crack of Doom and is the very heart of Sauron's power, is described as "that vast fortress, armoury, prison, furnace of great power" (II, 161) — the reverse of the natural.

As a corollary of their different relations to nature, the representatives of Good tend to be vegetarian, to rely on the simplest of food — bread and honey, mushrooms, compressed grain cakes — whereas the evil powers eat corrupt flesh, drink intoxicating beverages compounded of dreadful, nameless ingredients.

On this level the difference between good and evil seems rather simple. The good possess the Boy Scout virtues; the evil are treacherous and cowardly. The good love nature, the evil destroy it. The good eat good food, the evil eat bad food. If this were all, one might agree with Wilson in his condemnation of Tolkien's trilogy for impotence of imagination, superficiality of conception.

But the simplicity of this ethical system is redeemed by the philosophic complexity of its context: simplicity does not equal shallowness. The pagan ethos which that of *The Lord of the Rings* most closely resembles is redeemed from superficiality by the magnitude of the opposition it faces. The Anglo-Saxon epic hero operates under the shadow of fate; his struggle is doomed to final failure — the dragon, at last, in some encounter, will win. His courage and will alone oppose the dark forces of the universe; they represent his triumphant assertion of himself as man, his insistence on human importance despite human weakness. Even the classic hero, Achilles or Odysseus, operates always in the face of the possibility of motiveless malignance. His gods are arbitrary and unpredictable; they do not necessarily reward courage and loyalty. Chance and fate are almost equivalent — for the classic hero as for Beowulf.

Frodo's steadfast adherence to virtue, too, achieves importance first of all in being maintained in maximum adversity, unwaveringly upheld even against the most dreadful supernatural opposition — the pursuit, for example, of the faceless Black Riders, the Ringwraiths, who are faded into physical nothingness by their devotion to evil, possessed of enormous spiritual power for evil, the bringers of unearthly cold, the cold of the deepest reaches of Dante's Hell. But Frodo's virtue is more significant because it operates in a context of total free will: he is *not* the creature of chance and fate in the same way as Beowulf.

A theological scheme is implied though not directly stated in *The Lord of the Rings,* and it is of primary importance to the form and meaning of the work. The fact of freedom of the will implies a structured universe, a universe like the Christian one in that only through submission to the Good can true freedom be attained — willing acceptance of evil involves necessary loss of freedom; a universe like the Christian one, further, in that it includes the possibility of Grace.

The repeated emphasis on the importance of free will and on Fate which is not chance is one aspect in which *The Lord of the Rings* differs from its simpler predecessor, *The Hobbit*. In *The Hobbit*, freedom of the will is not an issue, and there is only one faint suggestion of pattern in the universe. That appears on the final page, after Bilbo is safely returned from his adventures, the dragon killed, although not by his hand. Gandalf, the good sorcerer, says to him then: "'Surely you don't disbelieve the prophecies, because you have a hand in bringing them about yourself? You don't really suppose, do you, that all your adventures and escapes were managed by mere luck, just for your sole benefit? You are a very fine person, Mr. Baggins, and I am very fond of you; but you are only quite a little fellow in a wide world after all!'" (315).

In *The Lord of the Rings*, on the other hand, references to these two themes — freedom of will and order in the universe, in the operations of fate — are so strongly recurrent that it is remarkable that they have not been noted before in discussions of the work. Early in *The Fellowship of the Ring*, after Gandalf has told Frodo the dreadful nature of his Ring (it partakes of too much power and brings about the "fading" of its wearer into final submission to evil), the wizard comments that always after defeat the Shadow takes another shape and grows again. "'I wish it need not have happened in my time,'" says Frodo. "'So do I,' said Gandalf, 'and so do all who live to see such times. But that is not for them to decide. All we have to decide is what to do with the time that is given us'" (I, 60). The necessity for free decision is thus early affirmed: it is to become a central issue of the trilogy. In the same chapter, a few pages later, comes the first hint of plan in the universe. Gandalf has just finished the narrative of the Ring; he has been speaking of the Ring's attempt to get back to its master, an attempt foiled by Bilbo's picking it up. But there is no chance in Bilbo's apparently fortuitous discovery. As Gandalf explains, "'there was something else at work, beyond any design of the Ring-maker. I can put it no plainer than by saying that Bilbo was *meant* to find the Ring, and *not* by its maker. In which case you also were *meant* to have it'" (I, 65). The italics are Tolkien's — and his point is worth emphasizing.

When Gandalf speaks of Gollum, the slinking creature from whom Bilbo first obtained the Ring, Frodo wonders why Bilbo did not kill him at once. Gandalf is even more emphatic in his reply: he praises Bilbo for his pity and explains that it is because he began his ownership of the Ring with an act of mercy that he was able to escape its power at last. Gollum, he says, "'is bound up with the fate of the Ring. My heart tells me that he has some part to play yet, for good or ill, before the end; and when that comes, the pity of Bilbo may rule the fate of many — yours not least'" (I, 69). An act of virtue has become a part of Fate; by Fate — for lack of a better word — Frodo has been *chosen:* "'I am not made for perilous quests,'" he cries, and Gandalf replies, "'You have been chosen, and you must therefore use such strength and heart and wits as you have'" (I, 70).

The theme of responsibility, so closely linked with free will, is also reiterated — by the Elves, who know that their meeting with Frodo is more than chance; by Strider, who insists that even an innkeeper must do what little he can against the Shadow in the East, who feels strongly his own responsibility to protect the simple folk; by the Lady Galadriel, who offers Frodo the chance to look into a magic mirror and observes solemnly, "'For the fate of Lothlórien you are not answerable, but only for the doing of your own task'" (I, 380). Frodo himself comes to realize that he must not refuse the burden that is laid on him; this realization is his weapon against the temptations of Boromir, the member of his company who would steal the Ring for his own purposes. This is also what sustains him in his dreadful journey across the Land of Mordor toward the Crack of Doom, and what sustains his hobbit companion, Sam, when he thinks Frodo killed and knows he must go on. The responsibility involved here, and throughout the epic, is not simply to one's individual integrity; it is cosmic responsibility, justified by the existence of some vast, unnamed power for good. Gandalf's most sweeping statement of the nature of responsibility, although it makes no reference to any such power, strongly implies the existence of an ordering force in the universe: "'Other evils there are that may come; for Sauron is himself but a servant or emissary. Yet it is not our part to master all the tides of the world, but to do what is in us for the succour of those years wherein we are set, uprooting the evil in the fields that we know, so that those who live after may have clean earth to till. What weather they shall have is not ours to rule'" (III, 155).

Both Gandalf and Aragorn, the great King, speak repeatedly of *purpose* in the operations of apparent chance; the source of that purpose is never identified. The existence of one ordering power in the universe, however, is explicitly indicated in the appendices which recount the history of all the races involved in the quest for the Ring's destruction. There we find repeated mentions of "the Valar, the Guardians of the World" (e.g., III, 314, 315, 316, 317). In a moment of cosmic crisis, we are told, "the Valar laid down their Guardianship and called upon the One, and the world was changed" (III, 317). Again, death is referred to as "the gift of the One to Men" (III, 343). This sort of reference to "the One" is all we have as precise evidence that Tolkien's universe has a Ruler, but it is sufficient, when combined with the repeated mentions of cosmic purpose, of beings "sent" for some particular mission. If the trilogy, as has been said, deals with a "prereligious" age, an age in which worship was confined to adherence to a special ethos, the fact remains that its author includes in it all the necessary materials for religion.

So it is that the Fate which governs all here is not arbitrary. Indeed, as has been hinted already in relation to Bilbo's act of mercy, it is to some extent determined by individual acts of will. "'Now we have chosen,'" says the Lady Galadriel, "'and the tides of fate are flowing'" (I, 381). In the Council of Elrond, in which the final decision that the Ring must be destroyed is taken, Elrond says, "'That is the purpose for which you are called hither. Called, I say, though I have not called you to me, strangers from distant lands. You have come and are here met, . . . by chance as it may seem. Yet it is not so. Believe rather it is so ordered that we, who sit here, and none others, must now find counsel for the peril of the world'" (I, 255). The theme is constant throughout the trilogy: over and over we find similar statements denying the existence of mere chance, insisting on some plan governing the activities of all. Tom Bombadil implies that his appearance for the rescue of the hobbits was no accident; Galadriel tells the company that their paths are laid out, although not apparent to them; Frodo feels that a way will be found for him to reach the Dark Tower because such is his "doom"; he speaks to Gollum of a fate moving them both. And, although all participants in the Quest realize that the Shadow repeatedly rises again, far more forceful is the affirmation made by Frodo — "'in the end the Shadow was only a small and passing thing: there was light and high beauty forever beyond its reach'" (III, 199).

The universe of Tolkien, unlike that of the Anglo-Saxons, is ultimately affirmative. Within the vast affirmative context, however, there are enormous possibilities for immediate evil: the individual exists in a realm where choice is always necessary. The freedom of that choice, for the virtuous, is of paramount importance. "'I count you blessed, Gimli, son of Glóin,'" says Legolas the Elf to a Dwarf member of the Ring-bearer's company: "'for your loss you suffer of your own free will, and you might have chosen otherwise'" (I, 395). When Aragorn meets the Riders of Rohan, their leader asks him what doom he brings out of the north. "'The doom of choice,'" replies Aragorn (II, 36): all men must now choose good or evil. Sam, Frodo's closest companion, realizes how many opportunities they have had of turning back, and understands that heroism, in legend and in fact, consists of making repeatedly and freely the choice of good (II, 321).

In his moment of crisis, he knows that destiny has put him in this dilemma, and that his most important responsibility is to make up his own mind (II, 341).

In this world as in the Christian one, the result of repeated choices of good is the spiritual growth of the chooser. Frodo's stature increases markedly in the course of his adventures, and the increase is in the specifically Christian virtues. When Gandalf first tells him of Gollum, he feels no pity and rejects the pity that Bilbo has felt. But by the time he has his own first encounter with the creature, he himself makes the choice of pity and mercy: he does not kill Gollum when he has him in his power. When they reach the depths of Mordor, Sam watches while Frodo sleeps. He notes in Frodo's face that a light seems to be shining within. "Now the light was even clearer and stronger [than when he first noticed it a few months earlier]. Frodo's face was peaceful, the marks of fear and care had left it; but it looked old, old and beautiful, as if the chiselling of the shaping years was now revealed in many fine lines that had before been hidden, though the identity of the face was not changed" (II, 269). Finally, Frodo has mercy even on Saruman, who has been far more definitely than Gollum an active agent of evil, an agent who, indeed, has just tried to murder Frodo. Saruman looks at him with "mingled wonder and respect and hatred. 'You have grown, Halfling,' he said. 'Yes, you have grown very much. You are wise'" (III, 299). And, at the very end, it is Frodo who asserts the necessity and value of sacrifice. "'When things are in danger,'" he says to Sam, "'some one has to give them up, lose them, so that others may keep them'" (III, 309). So he gives up his beloved Shire and goes into the unknown West, to a land equivalent to Arthur's Avalon. He has become heroic in mind as well as in action; heroic in mind as a direct result of his action.

The course of the evil beings is equally well defined. By using their freedom to choose evil, the wicked destroy freedom: emphasis is consistently upon the essential *slavery* of the servants of Sauron, who can no longer accept freedom when it is offered them. Pride and self-will, here as in so many great works, are often the sources of evil. Saruman has been corrupted through pride; even the trees of the forest which attempt to capture the hobbits are said to have become evil by the growth of pride in them. Denethor, the Steward of the King, kills himself, as a direct result of pride and that other great Christian sin, despair. It is pride that leads Boromir to want the Ring — pride, indeed, that lures all toward the Ring: Sam is able to resist its pull solely because of his humility, the fact that he is content with his own garden (III, 177).

Saruman and Gollum provide the main case histories of the gradual destructive effect of willing submission to evil wills, but Gandalf makes it clear that the result of such submission must always be the same, even for one predominantly virtuous at the outset. Even Frodo began his ownership of the Ring with a lie intended to make his claim on it more secure. If a mortal often uses the Ring, says Gandalf, he "'*fades:* he becomes in the end invisible permanently, and walks in the twilight under the eye of the dark power that rules the Rings. Yes, sooner or later — later, if he is strong or well-meaning to begin with, but neither strength nor good purpose will last — sooner or later the dark power will devour him'" (I, 56). The Ring represents power: and Frodo the hobbit is no more capable than Tamburlaine the Great of controlling unlimited power without himself being destructively controlled by it. Not even Gandalf can wield such force. Frodo offers him the Ring because he is already "wise and powerful," but he rejects it vehemently. "'And over me the Ring would gain a power still greater and more deadly. . . . Do not tempt me! For I do not wish to become like the Dark Lord himself. Yet the way of the Ring to my heart is by pity, pity for weakness and the desire of strength to do good. Do not tempt me! I dare not take it, not even to keep it safe, unused. The wish to wield it would be too great for my strength. . . . With that power I should have power too great and terrible (I, 70–71).'"

Indeed, Saruman began from precisely the position of Gandalf, and even without possession of the Ring, pride and the lust for power destroy him. In one of the most dramatic scenes of the trilogy, Gandalf confronts Saruman in his ruined stronghold and offers him the choice of complete freedom — "'free from bond, of chain or command: to go where you will, even, even to Mordor, Saruman, if you desire'" (II, 188) — or continued slavery to Sauron. But the sorcerer, too corrupted to choose, is forced by the decay of his own will to remain in a slavery resulting from free choice made long before.

So too with Gollum, a far more pitiable creature, essentially amoral, but degraded to the uses of evil: amorality is not really possible in Tolkien's scheme. Gandalf tells the story of his slow destruction through possession of the Ring: "'All the 'great secrets' under the mountains had turned out to be just empty night: there was nothing more to find out, nothing worth doing, only nasty furtive eating and resentful remembering. He was altogether wretched. He hated the dark, and he hated light more: he hated everything, and the Ring most of all. . . . He hated it and loved it, as he hated and loved himself. He could not get rid of it. *He had no will left in the matter*" (I, 64; italics mine). As Frodo's Quest nears its end, Faramir advises him against trusting — as he is — to Gollum's leadership. Faramir is convinced that Gollum is wicked; Frodo maintains that the creature is not altogether wicked. "'Not wholly, perhaps,'" agrees Faramir, "'but malice eats it like a canker, and the evil is growing'" (II, 301). And this is apt: the progress of evil in an individual cannot be reversed without a specific conscious act of will, an act that Gollum, like the other characters devoted to evil, is quite incapable of performing.

Yet this same Gollum, even more corrupted by lust for the Ring, his "Precious," becomes finally the instrument of Grace for Frodo in one of the most perplexing episodes of *The Lord of the Rings*. At the very end of his Quest, having struggled against hideous adversity to reach the Crack of Doom — at the very end, Frodo "changes his mind." "'I have come,' he said. 'But I do not choose now to do what I came to do. I will not do this deed. The Ring is mine!'" (III, 223). He uses still the language of free will — "I do not choose" — but the speech and the act which accompanies it (he puts on the Ring) represent rather a crucial failure of will. For "he was come to the heart of the realm of Sauron and the forges of his ancient might, greatest in Middle-earth; *all other powers were here subdued*" (III, 222; italics mine). Strong as it is, Frodo's will here succumbs.

Yet still he is saved — not by an act of will but by an act of Fate. Gollum, whose corruption is complete at this moment, leaps on Frodo, bites off the finger which wears the Ring, waves it aloft in triumph, and — falls into the Crack of Doom with it: the Quest is thus accomplished.

Dramatically, this final twist is quite unnecessary. It prolongs the suspense by barely a page; the dilemma raised by Frodo's failure is immediately resolved. Thematically it is essential. In the presentation of this event, the idea of free will intimately involved with fate receives its most forceful statement. The same idea has been suggested before; now it becomes inescapable. Free choice of good by the individual involves his participation in a broad pattern of Good; individual acts become a part of Fate. Frodo has repeatedly chosen to behave mercifully toward Gollum, even in the face of treachery on the other's part. His merciful acts determine his fate, and because he has, by his acceptance of his mission, come to hold a symbolic position, they determine also the fate of the world he inhabits. Gollum, on the other hand, though he is comparatively weak in evil, has become the symbolic representative of evil. His original acceptance of evil has made him will-less; it is appropriate that at the last he should be merely an instrument of that essentially benevolent fate through which, as Sam realizes, "his master had been saved; he was himself again, he was free" (III, 225) — free at the cost of physical maiming, the emblem of his human (or hobbit) weakness — like Lewis's hero, Ransom, who is in *Perelandra* successful in physical struggle with the Devil but emerges from it with an unhealable wound in the heel.

So, although *The Lord of the Rings* is by no means allegorical, it gains much of its force from its symbolic concentration on the most basic human concerns: the problems of man's relation to his universe. The fact that Tolkien's cosmos seems at first totally alien to our own might mislead us into thinking that his trilogy has no more right than ordinary science fiction to be considered as serious literature, that it is really the "juvenile trash" that Wilson thinks it. Yet Tolkien removes his fiction from the realm of "real life," only to be enabled to talk more forcefully about reality. A serious reading of *The Lord of the Rings* must produce the realization that its issues are profoundly relevant to human problems. Tolkien's method of communicating that relevance differs markedly from that of Lewis and Williams, who write always with the clear and specific purpose of Christian apologetics. If they create weird and alien worlds, worlds of science fiction, of the ghost story, it is with the basic intent of demonstrating the engulfing power of Christianity. Their primary referents are Christian and (especially in Lewis) classic myth, and didacticism lurks always behind their tales: the ultimate success of *That Hideous Strength* or *All Hallows' Eve* would be the conversion of its readers.

Tolkien's apparent moral purpose is more subtle, less specific. The force of his trilogy comes from its mythic scope and imagination, its fusion of originality with timelessness. *The Lord of the Rings* is a more widely popular work than any adult fiction by Lewis or Williams; it has become, indeed, the center of a cult. . . . One reason why *The Lord of the Rings* captivated readers so diverse as W. H. Auden and Edmund Wilson's eight-year-old daughter is that it creates a compellingly detailed and authentic imaginary universe which seems an appealing alternative to our own chaotic world. It is not the never-never land of science fiction or of James Bond but a realm in which moral problems are taken seriously and in which it is possible — not easy, but possible — to make right decisions. Tolkien lavishes such loving detail on his world that he encourages the willing suspension of disbelief.

But paradoxically the richness of detail which makes the world

of Frodo and Gandalf convincing also weakens the literary effective-
ness of the trilogy by detracting from its mythic authenticity. The
fiction of Lewis and Williams occasionally suffers from its simplicity
and constancy of didactic purpose. Tolkien tends rather to overcom-
plicate — not in purpose, but in detail. His elaboration of the minu-
tiae of his imagined world seems sometimes an end in itself; it diminishes the essential moral weight of his fable. The action of *The Lord
of the Rings*, in the Aristotelian sense, is at times obscured by the dec-
oration. Although that action is both powerful and significant, the
reader can lose consciousness of it in a mass of detail which is itself
vibrant with imaginative energy.

A second aspect of the trilogy which makes it difficult to take seriously in literary terms is its language, an important basis of Mr.
Wilson's objections to it. Like the richly imagined unreal world, the
language appeals to the child side of its readers; it evokes memories of
fairy tales and of legends of chivalry. "The grey figure of the Man,
Aragorn son of Arathorn, was tall, and stern as stone, his hand upon
the hilt of his sword; he looked as if some king out of the mists of
the sea had stepped upon the shores of lesser men. Before him
stooped the old figure, white, shining now as if with some light kin-
dled within, bent, laden with years, but holding a power beyond the
strength of kings" (II, 104). The simple vocabulary recalls traditional
material of romance: sword hilts, kingliness, the mists of the sea,
shining light, the ancient man of mysterious power. But its rhetoric
and its references seem automatic. Tolkien repeatedly employs the
same imagery of mysterious inner light as an index of spiritual
power; such imagery sometimes substitutes for demonstration of
that power. All too often, Tolkien asserts rather than demonstrates
character. By self-conscious alliteration and deliberately simple metaphor he may hope to recall the technique of primitive northern epic,
but there is an inevitable and disastrous gap between the primitive
and the pseudoprimitive. One is unavoidably conscious of Tolkien's
artifice, and it does not seem sufficiently skillful to be self-justifying.

A critic who demands verbal complexity, integrity, richness, subtlety, will find little to attract him in Tolkien's fiction. The language of the books is entirely an instrument of the story. When it demands attention in its own right, it is unlikely to justify the attention it receives. The depth and subtlety of imagination, both fictional and moral, which control the fable find no counterparts in the language of the trilogy, derivative and often impoverished or pretentious.

Yet the power of the fable remains, and remains important: other modes of criticism besides the verbal are relevant here. Although Tolkien's achievement is far outside the central modes of twentieth-century fiction, it is nonetheless significant. It demonstrates how even a framework of fantasy can provide a context for the exploration of serious concerns, how moral energy can animate far-fetched fiction, how a tale of other worlds than ours can incorporate and be enriched by a complex ethical structure. Its linguistic limitations may prevent its assuming a high position in recognized literary canons, but it will surely continue to exercise compelling power over its readers.

ROSE A. ZIMBARDO

Moral Vision in
The Lord of the Rings

This essay envisions The Lord of the Rings *as romance, in the Renaissance use of the term. Within the framework of the whole there is an order that stretches from wizards, who work in sheer energy, to dwarves, whose work is deep below the earth. Each order of being has its particular excellence, its unique way of creating "the Beautiful." The elves make the beautiful in song, the dwarves in rare metals, the men in heroic action. Each is distinctly different from all the others, yet each finds the fullest expression of itself in relation to the others. However, the singularity of each creature presents a moral choice: to sacrifice the demands of self to the good of the whole fellowship of creatures, as Galadriel and Gandalf do, or to subject all creatures to my Self, my will, as Sauron would do. The choice for good requires that one must assume the burden of individual existence and then use it for the welfare of all.*

The Lord of the Rings expresses the vision of Romance: "theme rather than fable is the central structural element."[1] The theme shaped in this structure centers on the problem of the All versus the Self in human consciousness. To qualify further: tragedy concerns itself with the division in human nature and describes the arc wherein a man aspires toward identification with the transcendent ideal and inevitably falls back down into the confines of his limited self. Romance, too, is concerned with the self and the other, but it envisions the other not as other but as All, a wholeness or harmony to the operation of which man's unique nature contributes. Moreover, while tragedy insists upon the *impossibility* of man's identification with the other, romance insists upon the absolute necessity of his identification with the All, and while tragedy stresses the duality, the conflict between the metaphysical and physical aspects of man's nature, romance insists upon the harmony of human being. The physical nourishes the metaphysical in man because in human nature as in the cosmos, physical and metaphysical are complementary parts of an embracing whole. In *The Lord of the Rings*, for instance, the heroes in every courageous enterprise, those who against all expectation prove to be most durable in the face of evil, are hobbits, beings who operate best *within* physical nature, who prefer to live in snug dugouts and eat six meals a day.[2] Evil in the romance vision is not an aspect of human nature but rather is the perversion of human will. It results when a being directs his will inward to the service of the self rather than outward to the service of the All. The effect of such inversion is the perversion of nature, both man's nature and the greater nature of which it is a part.

The All in *The Lord of the Rings* is a chain of being, a scale of creatures, differing from one another in the degree to which substance combines with form in their natures, each degree necessary to the composition of the whole, and contributing to the formation of a *discordia concors*. Good is the cooperation of all levels of being, a harmony but not an interpenetration of kinds, for each kind of being has its particular excellence and consequently its peculiar contribution to make to the order of the whole.

The wizards are nearest to essence — they are sheer powers or colors: Radagast the Russet, Saruman the White, Gandalf the Grey, who becomes Gandalf the White by an act of sacrifice he makes in the service of the Fellowship. In encountering the Balrog, he falls into the fiery center of the earth, where he undergoes a mighty contest of will, and triumphing, is resurrected. After his sacrifice he comes to embody the white, or positive principle, the fellowship of beings.

The elves comprise the next level of being. They are associated with light, as Gandalf is, but theirs is a softer light, starlight. They are not powers, as the wizards are, but they are not groundlings either. Their nature is airy; they hover in trees, and they are conceived as an aura, a halo that has surrounded the earth but that is fading from it. Their wisdom is neither the supernatural power of the wizards nor the practical intelligence of natures below theirs on the scale. It is rather a mantic and bardic wisdom. Light of substance, fading in time, they transform experience into essence in poetry.

The creatures that follow the elves on the scale of being, as their age will follow the Age of the Elves in the cycle of time, are the Men. But these are the Men of Middle-earth, the giants that *were* in the earth. They are kings, and their peculiar virtue is heroic courage and statecraft. Theirs is the *bios politikos* that forges out of beautiful deeds and the materials of the earth the foundations of civilization.

After them come the hobbits, a linking kind, halflings between kingly nature and animal nature. Furry-footed, they are nearer to the earth than the men and more animal the nearer they get. If the cycles of time have continued to revolve since the days of Middle-earth and if the kings have faded as the elves before them were destined to fade, then we may assume that our age is the age of the hobbits. The hobbits are the common man, who does not seek out the opportunity for great deeds, who prefers his bounded life in the Shire. Yet the hobbits are the heroes. From Frodo the knightly Ring-bearer and Sam his faithful squire to Merry, who dares battle with the Nazgûl, they unexpectedly transcend themselves in selfless action. Their peculiar excellence is not heroic honor but love. Frodo is finally saved because he has pitied Sméagol. Sam is moved to deeds of heroic exploit out of love for Frodo. Merry and Pippin are transformed into thanes out of love for the kings they serve. They comprise the core of the fellowship, and in the end, as in the beginning, it is love that binds them. It is significant that Tolkien makes them heroes in every enterprise, because the virtue they embody is the idea of good that *The Lord of the Rings* shapes. *Caritas* is the virtue that sustains the fellowship of being, that makes a concordant whole of the discordant parts that comprise it.

But the hobbits are not the last beings on the scale. The harmony does not extend merely from the surface of the earth outward, for the physical is not damned for its physicality. Last on the scale are the beings under the earth, the dwarves.

They are as heavy of substance as the elves are light. Their peculiar excellence is craft, and as the elves forge substanceless language into beauty in poetry, the dwarves shape elemental metal into beautiful things. The potentiality for beauty exists even in the bowels of matter, but the creation of beauty depends upon the proper use of being. The operation of the harmony of being is expressed emblematically in the relation between Legolas and Gimli. The dwarves and elves are opposite in nature, that is, in the proportions of form and substance that each nature combines. When each holds the good of his *own* people above the good of the whole, they war, and warring, they endanger the whole. Yet they are drawn into harmony by love. Gimli's love for Galadriel prepares him to love Legolas, and Legolas is in turn drawn into love for Gimli. Out of hostility grows loving competition, and at last each is led to the desire to see the beautiful through the eyes of the other. But though Legolas may visit the caves and Gimli the forests in token of their fellowship, neither can become the other, for their fellowship depends on the maintenance of separate identity.

For each of the classes of creatures on the chain there exists a perverse counterpart. Treebeard says that the creations of the Enemy are perversions, mockeries, or counterfeits (II, 89). For Gandalf, who sacrifices himself for the fellowship, there is Saruman, who falls self-tempted and who tempts others to fall to the service of self. For the elves there are the orcs, made by the Enemy as imitation elves. Because of their maker's nature they turn out to be the antithesis of elvish-ness. As the elves are refined almost to essence, the orcs are grotesquely gross. As the elves float above the earth, the orcs ferret under it. As the elves worship the light, the orcs fear it. (The response of the Enemy, characteristic of *his* nature, is to breed a more efficient orc who will even withstand light in the urge to destroy.) As the elves glory in their elvish nature and tradition, the orcs fall upon each other in their spite.

The dark counterpart of men is the Ringwraiths, the dark riders whose lust for the Ring's power has deprived them of that which is most characteristic of the men, heroic identity. The Ringwraiths have lost any identity beyond the hollow malevolent force that drives them. At this level of being, as at the wizards' level, the creature cooperates in the perversion of his own nature so that there is no need for the Enemy to create an imitation of him. We are given some insight into the process by which the will of men is misdirected in the contrasting fates of Théoden and Denethor. With the help of Gandalf, Théoden is able to shake off the paralysis of will to which Wormtongue's temptations have brought him. Exercising his will to the service of fellowship, he reasserts his natural excellence, kingly courage, and leadership. In contrast, Denethor, having chosen to keep to his own use a power too great for him, a power beyond his stewardship, lusts for more. He mourns his son Boromir less than he does the loss of the power that Boromir would have brought him. Consequently, not only does the particular virtue of his kind, courage and loyalty, wither in him, but ultimately his nature itself is corrupted and, mad, he attempts to destroy his faithful son, Faramir.

Finally, the perverse counterpart of the heroic hobbits, more exactly the counterpart of Frodo, the Ring-bearer, is Sméagol, who was himself a hobbit until desire for the Ring moved him to kill a fellow hobbit. Under the torment of his lust for the Ring, every aspect of his hobbit nature has been distorted to parody. It is significant that the final destruction of the Ring occurs when Frodo and Sméagol are fighting for it. Frodo must conquer his own dark counterpart; the Ring-bearer must prevail over his own image turned Ringwraith before the destruction of that shadow-image, and with it the destruction of the Ring, can be accomplished.

As the fellowship of love is the ultimate positive power, the negation of fellowship, the rejection of the other and subjection of the All to the self, is the ultimate negative power. As in St. Augustine's, so in Tolkien's vision nothing is created evil. Evil is good that has been perverted. Good in its nature, a creature, by *inverting* its vision and making itself its only object, turns the good into nothingness. Sin, as one sixteenth-century thinker said, is "naughty nothing that makes all things nought." Gandalf tells us that even Sauron had to fall from goodness. Moreover, the power of darkness cannot see into the heart of light. It must depend for its power upon a failure in the will to good. Yet the vulnerability of each creature to such a failure is built into his very nature. The singularity, the one-ness of each creature, leaves him open to the temptation of asserting the demands of self above those of the All and finally of attempting to subject the All to the demands of self.

> *One* Ring to rule them all, *One* Ring to find them,
> *One* Ring to bring them all and in the darkness bind them.

The Ring is all that we see of Sauron because Sauron has no other identity but that for which the Ring stands. He has only negative identity. He is a dark shadow, the negation of positive being itself. He has become the very principle of misdirected, self-directed will. His power, expressed in the power of the Ring, is the power to separate oneself from the community of positive being. The wearer of the Ring becomes invisible, and the more often he chooses to use the power, the more the power wears away his substance. Even after the Ring has been destroyed, the effects of having exercised its power remain. Frodo, who has endured the full temptation of the Ring's power and who has had to war with himself before it could be destroyed, has become, as Sam tells us, almost transparent. Even Bilbo has lost a great deal of his hobbit nature. Both have lost something of their substance and have moved off their own position on the scale of being toward a more elvish nature. It is significant that neither can live among hobbits; Bilbo lives among the elves, and at last they both must embrace the fate of the elves. In losing their hobbit nature they have changed their position in being as well as in time; they become part of the elvish aura that must fade from the earth.

This brings us to a second property of the Ring, the quality that makes it almost irresistible. It arrests time. Both Bilbo and Frodo are more youthful for having worn the Ring, and Bilbo has lived beyond the time allotted to hobbit nature. Galadriel in refusing the Ring must resist not merely the demands of self but also the demands of kind, for she is aware that possession of the Ring would prevent the passing of the elves. The Ring, then, takes its wearer not only out of the community of positive being, but out of the cycle of time to which all earthly being is subject. The permanence of the whole harmony consists in change. Each age must pass, but in every age, if the inhabitants of the world set right the balance of a time that may seem to their eyes to be "out of joint," if they capture the past in poetry — as the elves do — and if they plant seeds for coming generations — as Sam Gamgee and the High King do — they can insure a new birth and can contribute in their turn of time to the cycle of endless renewal.

The age of the elves must end in order that the age of men can grow. And all that the elves can legitimately do to preserve their experience is to cast it into poetry. Their songs, full of the glory of their past and the sorrow of their decline, freeze into the permanence of art their having been. But it is because the individual, and even his age, must die that the urge to preserve one's own time at the cost of the cycle of time is so great. Individuation makes one open to the temptation of the Ring. Only Tom Bombadil can wear it without disappearing because, as he says of himself,

> "Eldest, that's what I am. . . . Tom was here before the river and the trees. . . . He knew the dark under the stars when it was fearless — before the Dark Lord came from Outside." (I, 142)

When Frodo asks Gandalf why Tom cannot be one of the fellowship of the Ring, he is told that Tom would not remember the Ring nor be able to recognize its importance. He has neither history nor memory because change for him is only seasonal change. He is the permanence at the heart of change, the force of life itself that was present when "the dark . . . was fearless," before the principle of self came. Tom Bombadil can restore the hobbits when they have been frozen by the Barrow-wight. He can reawaken life from death, but he cannot belong to the fellowship of love because his love is only to Goldberry, the nature he enlivens. The fellowship of love, the exercise of will in the service of an order that transcends the self, is moral action. It is possible only for those self-reflexive creatures who are subject to individuation and time, that is, those who are conscious of the division between the self and the other.

However, the nearer a creature is to nature, to the pattern that Tom Bombadil embodies, the greater his ability to resist the demands of self. Sam Gamgee is the only character in the book who is able to wear the Ring and yet to give it up without a struggle. He is not, like Tom, impervious to the Ring's power. Even Sam experiences the temptation to subject the All to himself, but because he is a gardener, the very nature of his vision restores his balance. For an instant he wants the whole world to be his garden alone, but because his particular excellence has been promoting and sustaining nature's life, he sees at once the folly of a small creature in nature trying to consume the whole that embraces him. In Sam's momentary dream of power we are given a flash of comic insight into a human being's moral dilemma. In Sam's response, love for and faithful service to another creature like himself, we are given the resolution of that dilemma that the vision of romance affords.

Men, Halflings, and Hero Worship

Marion Zimmer Bradley was herself a sub-creator of "Other Worlds"
and a traveler in the realm of Faërie. Her best-known trilogy, The Forest House, The Mists of Avalon, *and* The Lady of Avalon, *revivifies the*
Arthurian legends, casting them from the perspective of their female
characters: Morgan le Fay, The Lady of the Lake, etc. We call her twenty-
five Darkover novels science fiction or fantasy only for want of a better
term; she writes much in the mode of Tolkien. In this essay she examines
the varieties and dimensions of "heroic love," which, she argues, is the
dominant emotion in The Lord of the Rings. *Carefully examining the*
subtle complexities of what we often carelessly name "hero worship,"
Bradley uncovers its true nature. Although she sheds new light on char-
acters whom critics often neglect, like Merry and Pippin, her most pro-
found analysis is of the love between Sam and Frodo. It is devoutly to be
wished that this essay may finally put to rest the cliché, upstairs-down-
stairs interpretations of that relationship that some lesser critics have
proposed.

Love is the dominant emotion in *The Lord of the Rings,* and love in
the form of hero worship is particularly evident in the relationship
between Aragorn and the other characters and between Frodo and
Sam. Other forms of love are also apparent; the most important of
these is heroic love, which includes love of honor and love of coun-

try; additionally there is Gandalf's paternal and Goldberry's and Galadriel's maternal love. Relatively little romantic love is depicted, and what is appears to follow the chivalric, although not courtly, love convention. Underlying all of these is the love of the fellowship — that of one man for another; this love extends beyond the initial fellowship as the original members extend their relationship to serve and battle with others.

It should be noted, briefly and in passing, that Tolkien's self-consistent world, along with an alien geography and ecology, has its own appropriate manners, in general those of the heroic ages; they are *not* the stiff-upper-lip unemotional ones of the modern English-speaking peoples. Affectionate and emotional displays are permitted not alone to women and children, but to men; thus Legolas trembles with terror and wails aloud before the Balrog without his courage or manliness (if this word may be used of an Elf) being suspect; Boromir weeps in passionate repentance after his attack on Frodo, and when he is slain, Aragorn kneels at his side so "bent with weeping" that Legolas and Gimli are dismayed, fearing he too has "taken deadly hurt." The men display affection freely, e.g., Faramir parts from Frodo with an embrace and kiss; this is simply a pattern of manners and does not in itself merit mention as ballast for the thesis that the major emotional threads of the story are drawn between men.

The prevalent emotion in general is the hero worship of a young man for one older, braver, and wiser. All the company treat Gandalf as an exalted Father-figure, but the major object of *hero* worship, as opposed to paternal veneration, is Aragorn himself. With the single exception of Boromir, the actual leadership is resigned to him by all; Frodo, a hero in his own right, immediately yields to him:

> "Yes, it was Strider that saved us. Yet I was afraid of him at first. Sam never quite trusted him, I think. . . ."
>
> Gandalf smiled. "I have heard all about Sam," he said. "He has no more doubts now."
>
> "I am glad . . . for I have become very fond of Strider. Well,

fond is not the right word. I mean he is dear to me; though he is strange, and grim at times . . . he reminds me often of you." (I, 232)

Éomer and Faramir, too, quickly fall under Aragorn's spell. The only one who does not is Boromir, and one of the subtlest threads of the story is Boromir's competition for Aragorn's place. In many small episodes he attempts persistently to maneuver things his way, not Aragorn's — not in petty jealousy nor, at first, for any base motive. He is brave and valiant and well worthy of the admiration he gets from the young hobbits; he fights for them and defends them, and at least in Pippin's case, he partially succeeds (and this is very carefully, deftly studied, for Pippin is the persistent rebel against Gandalf). Slain in the first chapter of volume II, Boromir is nevertheless a compelling force of emotional motivation throughout the book. He is emotionally present in Frodo's meeting with Faramir and Pippin's with Denethor; further it is Pippin's memory, his admiration for Boromir, that lies behind his service to Denethor, which ultimately saves the life of Faramir.

If Gandalf plays the ideal father, and Aragorn the heroically loved elder brother — and there is some hint of the sullen rivalry between Achilles and Agamemnon in Boromir's jealousy of Aragorn — then Peregrin Took, the hobbit Pippin, is most emphatically the spoiled youngest child. Here we reemphasize the peculiar chronology of fantasy, for Peregrin is twenty-nine years old, but four years short of his "coming of age," and thus equivalent to a boy in his teens. He is literally treated like a child. He falls asleep and is carried to bed while Frodo talks with the Elves. Elrond's "heart is against his going" on the dangerous Quest. Gandalf, who lets him come, nevertheless, in Pippin's words "thinks I need keeping in order" and singles him out, several times, for testy rebuke. He is in fact the childish mischief-maker of the company, yet even Gandalf treats him indulgently when he is not squelching his bubbling spirits. This subtle study of Pippin as the "naughty rebel" against Gandalf's kind authority culminates in his logical resentment against being treated as a child; so that his theft of the *Palantír* — which is treachery in essence — is motivated and at last understood simply as an act of purely childish mischief and devilry. We should note that Gandalf fears and refuses the challenge of the *Palantír*, pointing out that Pippin's folly helped prevent him from daring to use it himself. He cautions Aragorn against looking into it (II, 200), but Aragorn later makes up his own mind. And the "moral" of this seems to be that the young, as they grow toward independence, sometimes have their own answers for what their elders fear. However, this father-son relationship remains; during the sequence of the Great Ride, when Gandalf flees on the wings of the wind of war, he bears Pippin with him on Shadowfax quite literally as a small child: "Aragorn lifted Pippin and set him in Gandalf's arms, wrapped in cloak and blanket" (II, 201). Volume III opens with the passage "Pippin looked out from the shelter of Gandalf's cloak. He wondered if he were awake or still sleeping, still in the swift-moving dream in which he had been wrapped . . . since the great ride began." As Pippin slowly recovers, Gandalf first scolds, then lectures, and finally forgives him in true father fashion. Their relationship in Minas Tirith continues to be that of loving, if stern, father and willful, but no longer rebellious, child.

The character evolution of Meriadoc (Merry), the other of the young hobbits, is less obvious and takes place at a somewhat deeper level. Merry, older than Pippin, more sensible and quieter, seems less vital at first and, until Pippin draws attention to himself by the theft of the *Palantír*, seems to have remained in the background. Yet on second evaluation it becomes obvious that Merry, like a perfectly cast supporting actor, performs his quiet background activities in a perfectly consistent way. It comes slowly to the reader's notice that Merry has, in fact, played a very quiet part in all their adventures. It is Merry who provided ponies for their flight, who led them into the Old Forest, and after the attack on Weathertop, it is consistently and logically

Merry on whom Aragorn calls for help to bring them, quietly and without credit, through dangers — Frodo is wounded and too burdened, Sam too hostile and absorbed in Frodo, Pippin too irresponsible.

After Pippin's escapade, while the others show concern, Merry simply turns away; he shows all the earmarks of the neglected "good" child resenting the kindness shown to the naughty one who has drawn attention to himself; as Gandalf rides away, his bitter comment to Aragorn is virtually his clearest utterance:

> A beautiful, restful night! Some people have wonderful luck. He didn't want to sleep, and he wanted to ride with Gandalf — and there he goes! Instead of being turned into a stone himself to stand here forever as a warning. (II, 201)

And it seems significant that after the two are separated, they follow paths similar on the surface but differing greatly in emotional motivation. Both offer their sword and service to a mighty King. "In payment of [his] debt" to Boromir, slain defending him and Merry, Pippin impetuously enters the service of Denethor; Gandalf is astonished, saying:

> "I do not know what put it into your head, or your heart, to do that. . . . I did not hinder it, for generous deed should not be checked by cold counsel." (III, 32)

But Merry's choice, though equally impulsive, is not motivated by pride:

> Filled suddenly with love for this old man, he knelt on one knee, and took his hand and kissed it. "May I lay the sword of Meriadoc of the Shire on your lap, Théoden King?" he cried. "Receive my service, if you will!"
>
> "Gladly will I take it," said the king; and laying his long old hands upon the brown hair of the hobbit, he blessed him. . . .

"As a father you shall be to me," said Merry. (III, 50–51)

When ordered later to remain behind, Merry reacts with almost childish desperation. "'I won't be left behind, to be called for on return! . . . I won't be left, I won't'" (III, 73). And he disobeys with the connivance of the other "disobedient son," Éowyn in her male disguise as Dernhelm.

Together Éowyn and Merry face and slay the Nazgûl, both striking an enemy far beyond their strength for the love of a father, Théoden. Later Faramir, Éowyn, and Merry all lie in the shadow of the Black Breath, and additionally Faramir lies in the shadow of a father's displeasure. Gandalf has had to counsel him when he goes in desperation on his last mission: "'Do not throw your life away rashly or in bitterness. . . . Your father loves you, . . . and will remember it ere the end'" (III, 90). When he is recalled by Aragorn, it is apparent that Merry has been through a profoundly maturing experience:

> "I would like supper first, and after that a pipe. No, not a pipe. I don't think I'll smoke again." At that his face clouded.
>
> "Why not?" said Pippin.
>
> "Well," answered Merry slowly. "He is dead. It has brought it all back to me. He said he was sorry he had never had a chance of talking herb-lore with me. Almost the last thing he ever said. I shan't ever be able to smoke again without thinking of him, and that day, Pippin, when he rode up to Isengard and was so polite."
>
> "Smoke then, and think of him!" said Aragorn. "For he was a gentle heart and a great king and kept his oaths. . . . Though your service to him was brief, it should be a memory glad and honourable to the end of your days."
>
> Merry smiled. "Well then," he said, "if Strider will provide what is needed, I will smoke and think." (III, 145–46)

This scene between Aragorn and Merry evidences not only warmth but also Aragorn's humanness; he consoles the grieving Merry, teases him, then confesses weariness, and for the first time

Merry speaks in realization of Aragorn's real stature: "'I am frightfully sorry. . . . Ever since that night at Bree we have been a nuisance to you'" (III, 146). And this change in Merry is made more emphatic when, left alone with Pippin, the irresponsible younger hobbit says: "'Was there ever anyone like him? . . . Except Gandalf, of course. I think they must be related,'" and of course, spiritually, they are. Then he adds: "'Dear me! We Tooks and Brandybucks, we can't live long on the heights'" (III, 146). And here it is apparent that, if Pippin has changed from a rebellious child to a loving one, Merry has been far more deeply affected by his service to a beloved king: "'No, . . . I can't. Not yet, at any rate. But at least, Pippin, we can now see them, and honour them. It is best to love first what you are fitted to love, I suppose. . . . Still there are things deeper and higher. . . . I am glad that I know about them, a little'" (III, 146). Few clearer statements could be made of the way in which the young come to the simple but deeply affecting discovery of worlds far outside their own small selfish concerns and events greater than the small patterns of their lives. The experience is universal, even though Tolkien has cast it into heroic mold and scorned obvious moral or allegory.

Whatever hobbit chronology, neither Merry nor Pippin quite achieves full adult stature until they return to the Shire to set their own country in order; Gandalf resigns his authority, saying in effect, "You do not need me . . . you have grown up." Then Merry's firmness and Pippin's courage show echoes of Théoden, of Aragorn, even of Denethor and Gandalf. They have to some extent become what they admired. And it is Merry who perceives why Éowyn belongs to the story and Arwen does not. For Éowyn, too, achieves the passing of the "Heroic Age" — the age in which girls rebel against their sex and their limitations and dream of male deeds. Gandalf says with pity:

> "She, born in the body of a maid, had a spirit and courage at least the match of yours. . . . Who knows what she spoke to the darkness, alone, . . . when all her life seemed shrinking, and the walls

of her bower closing in about her, a hutch to trammel some wild thing in?" (III, 143)

She does indeed achieve great deeds in male disguise and chafes at her "imprisonment" in the Houses of Healing. When she meets Faramir she is abashed, after she complains to him, thinking that he might see her as "merely wayward, like a child" (III, 328), yet it is Faramir who sees Éowyn most clearly. He describes her love for Aragorn in unmistakable terms — simple hero worship on a masculine level: "'And as a great captain may to a young soldier he seemed to you admirable. For so he is.'" And Éowyn, suddenly understanding, accepts what she is, and is not: "'I will be a shieldmaiden no longer, nor vie with the great Riders. . . . I will . . . love all things that grow and are not barren. . . . No longer do I desire to be a queen'" (III, 242–43). In other words, no longer does she desire to be a *king*, i.e., not to identify with Aragorn, but to be a woman. This is not a new theme — Wagner, at the end of *Siegfried*, puts such words into the mouth of Brunhilde — but it is apt to the picture of the passing of the Heroic Age.

I have reserved for last, because most intense, the strong love between Frodo and Samwise, and the curious part played in it by the creature Gollum. Toward the end of the third book Frodo and Sam reach classical "idealized friendship" equivalent in emotional strength to the ardor of Achilles and Patrocles or David and Jonathan: "passing the love of women." Wilson speaks with some contempt of the "hardy little homespun hero" and the "devoted servant who speaks lower-class and respectful and never deserts his master,"[1] thus displaying a truly cataclysmic ignorance of the pattern of heroic literature. Both Frodo and Sam display, in full measure, the pattern of the Hero in Quest literature, although of another order than the shining gallantries of Aragorn.

Aragorn of course is the "born hero" — son of a long line of kings, born to achieve great deeds in his time. Frodo is the one who has heroism thrust upon him, and to complete and fulfill the analogy we might say that Sam achieves heroism undesired and unrecognized. Frodo accepts the charge of the accursed Ring because it has come to him by chance and because the great ones — Elrond, Gandalf, Galadriel, and even Aragorn — are afraid to trust themselves to the lure of its power. Sam cares even less for heroic deeds; he simply wishes to guard and remain with Frodo. Elrond realizes this even before they set out. "'It is hardly possible to separate you from him, even when he is summoned to a secret council and you are not'" (I, 284). It is in Elrond's house that the intensity which will eventually enter this relationship is first shown:

> Sam came in. He ran to Frodo and took his left hand, awkwardly and shyly. He stroked it gently and then he blushed and turned hastily away. (I, 237)

Frodo, as a hero in his own right, displays slightly less helpless hero worship for Aragorn than do the others, though while Aragorn is with them, he bows to his judgment. Sam, during this time, is little more than, as he calls himself, "luggage in a boat," and at first appears to provide little more than comic relief. This early element of comedy is doubtless what misled Edmund Wilson and caused others to identify him with the type made immortal by Sancho Panza.

It is also traditional in Quest literature that the Hero should have a comic-relief satellite. But Sam, though occasionally witty, is not really a figure of comedy — not in the sense that Papageno in *The Magic Flute* is a comic figure. He is blunt of speech, and there is the humor of incongruity when he faces down the wise and valorous, e.g., when he defies Faramir, twice his size. But he is far less a comic figure than Butterbur, or even Pippin.

Frodo makes his own choice and proclaims his emancipation from the others at the end of volume I — as Aragorn clearly realizes when he says: "'Well, Frodo, . . . I fear that the burden is laid upon you. . . . I cannot advise you'" (I, 412). Frodo is cognizant both of

Aragorn's offer to guide him to Mordor and Aragorn's commitment to his word: "'If by life or death I can save you, I will'" (I, 183). Yet Frodo realizes that Aragorn's quest is not really his: "'I will go alone. Some I cannot trust, and those I can trust are too dear to me: poor old Sam, and Merry and Pippin. Strider, too: his heart yearns for Minas Tirith, and he will be needed there'"(I, 418).

But it is Sam who has courage to speak up and to explain Frodo even to Aragorn, to read Frodo's heart, to disobey Aragorn (the only time *any* one does so), and to slip off alone with Frodo.

In the second volume Sam has begun to foreshadow the eventual conflict and denouement. Still insensitive, seeing only his own fear for Frodo, he wishes to kill Gollum. Frodo, having come through his own first sufferings to compassion, protects the wretched creature from Sam. And from that moment Sam's love and Gollum's hate become the millstones between which Frodo is eventually broken — both victor and vanquished.

Sam's emotional growth is spotlighted briefly the second time he watches the sleeping Frodo, not helplessly as in Elrond's house. He muses that he loves him "whether or no," though this is still shown in terms appropriate to the simplicity of the character, as when he coaxes-threatens Gollum into finding better food for Frodo, and then cooks it for him. As Frodo is weakened by the cursed Ring and his doom, Sam grows ever more fiercely protective; this curious, triangular relationship reaches its apex in Gollum's treachery at Cirith Ungol.

In very strong emotional relationships, particularly among the weak, hatred and love are very much akin. Gandalf, describing Bilbo's first encounter with the wretched, lonely, miserable old Gollum, says:

> "Even Gollum was not wholly ruined. . . . There was a little corner of his mind that was still his own, and light came through it, as through a chink in the dark. . . . It was actually pleasant, I think, to hear a kindly voice again bringing up memories of

wind, and trees, and sun on the grass, and such forgotten things. But that, of course, would only make the evil part of him angrier in the end — unless it could be conquered. Unless it could be cured." (I, 64)

Gandalf points out too that Gollum loved and hated the Ring, much as he loved and hated himself, and in this fearful ambivalence, Gollum — like a terrible shadow of Frodo himself — comes to have dual love and hate for Frodo as well.

To me the most poignant moment in the three books is that in which Gollum comes on the two friends sleeping: Frodo with his head in Sam's lap, Sam himself fast asleep. And anyone who has noted the small threads running through the story will be reminded of a time very obviously present to Gollum when he, then Sméagol, had a trusted and loved friend, Déagol, who shared his wanderings and searches, whom he called "my love," and whom he killed for the sake of the cursed thing he later came wholly to love and hate. And in this ambivalent sway of emotions, "an old starved pitiable thing," he touches Frodo humbly, fleetingly, "almost the touch was a caress" (II, 324), but Sam, startled awake, uses rough words to him. And Gollum's momentary softening is once more overcome by a blasting hurricane of hate and rage equal to the pitiable impulse of despair which it displaces.

Sam too is cheated by his own hate. Later because he delays in trying to kill Gollum, Shelob has a chance to attack Frodo. Gollum escapes, and Frodo lies apparently dead. Here at the apparent bitter end of this relationship, Sam's anguish is difficult to read without emotion. So compelling is it that only in retrospect has it become apparent how Sam's choices here foreshadow his final status. One by one he forsakes the other possibilities: vengeance; suicide, "that was to do nothing, not even to grieve!" (II, 341); return for wiser counsel; take the Ring and complete the Quest. Although knowing its full terrible power, Sam chooses the last possibility. Even Aragorn and Gandalf had feared this test. Elrond would not take the Ring, even to guard it. Galadriel, confessing temptation, finally renounced it. Frodo, when he took it, had no knowledge of its awful power. Sam knew but accepted. This is the decisive moment in character development.

In essence the Quest from this moment is Sam's. It is significant that when he believes Frodo dead, for the first time he drops the formal "Mr. Frodo" and cries out "Frodo, me dear, me dear" (II, 340), although after rescuing him he returns to the old deferential speech; the "Mr. Frodo" partially restores his sense of security. Sam has become, not the devoted dogsbody of volume I, nor the sometimes fierce but simple and submissive watchdog of volume II, but the "tall, towering elf-warrior" of the orc's vision. He renounces the temptation to use the Ring for his own, then flings his defiance against the shadows: "I will not say the Day is done, nor bid the Stars farewell" (III, 185). When he finds Frodo, beaten, naked and unconscious in the orc-tower, their reunion sets the tone of their relationship from that moment:

> Frodo . . . lay back in Sam's gentle arms, closing his eyes, like a child at rest when night-fears are driven away by some loved voice or hand.
>
> Sam felt that he could sit like that in endless happiness; but it was not allowed. (III, 186–87)

Instead he gently takes on himself the task of bringing Frodo to the end of his Quest. And here again Sam achieves what no one else has been able to do. Except for Tom Bombadil, only Bilbo has ever given up the Ring of his free will, and Bilbo, who did not know its power, achieved this only with Gandalf's help. Yet Sam, after momentary hesitation ("reluctant . . . to burden his master with it again" [III, 188]), immediately takes the chain from around his neck and hands it over; he is wounded but not angry when Frodo, maddened by the thing that is destroying him, turns on him and calls him "thief."

The surrendered-sword symbolism returns when Frodo allows Sam to keep his Elvish sword Sting, saying that though he has an orc-knife, "'I do not think it will be my part to strike any blow again'" (III, 204). From this point he places himself unreservedly and passively in Sam's hands, allowing Sam to clothe him, to deal out their food, to choose their road. As his will and endurance are sapped by the destructive, tormenting power of the Ring he speaks of himself as "naked in the dark" (III, 215) while every thought and movement of Sam's reaches an almost religious devotion and tenderness toward easing Frodo's path, even though he cannot share his torment or even his burden.

This lessening distance and growing devotion, increasing as Frodo weakens, continues to the end of the Quest. When they cast away their arms and gear, Frodo throws away even the orc-knife, saying, "'I'll bear no weapon, fair or foul'" (III, 214), and lets Sam clothe him in the grey Lórien cloak. But Sam, even at that edge of desperation and despair, retains some spark of hope; and though casting away his own treasures, he retains the gifts of Galadriel and the Elvish sword which Frodo had given him. Once again, watching awake for the last time while Frodo sleeps, Sam fights his own battle with despair and gives up his own last hopes. Realizing that all he can do is to accompany Frodo to the Crack of Doom and die with him there, he fights the temptation to abandon the Quest, knowing that without his insistent courage Frodo cannot complete it either. In his own unguarded moment of despair he shows how he now regards their death: "'You could have lain down and gone to sleep together days ago, if you hadn't been so dogged'" (III, 216). This last stage, where nothing matters and they may never return, is significantly the first time that his thoughts turn to Rosie Cotton — *who has never been mentioned before* — but "'the way back, if there is one, goes past the Mountain'" (III, 216). And at the very end of their Quest, Sam held no more debates with himself — "he knew all the arguments of despair" and had absorbed them. He takes Frodo in his arms, trying to comfort him "with his arms and body" so that "the last day of their quest found them side by side"(III, 217).

This growth in intensity, this closing the distance between the two, each change documented and studied, is surely one of the most compelling analyses of heroic friendship.

Sam's emotional growth is shown at the final meeting of love and hate, when Gollum appears at the last moment. Frodo, far past all pity or humanity (in Sam's vision only a tall figure, with a wheel of fire at its breast), only curses Gollum and threatens him with the Fire of Doom; and here it is Sam the inarticulate who achieves the height of pity and compassion for Gollum's agony, and in his own rough, painful manner, says:

> ". . . you stinking thing! . . . Go away! Be off! I don't trust you, not as far as I could kick you; but be off. Or I *shall* hurt you, yes, with nasty cruel steel." (III, 222)

Even at this moment of desperate danger he still mocks Gollum's whining speech.

Frodo at the end cannot destroy the Ring and fulfill his Quest; Gollum's tormented love and hate effects what even the Dark Lord could not do. He tears Ring and finger from Frodo — but his fall into the Crack of Doom, glossed as an accident of his exaltation, is more, far more, than accidental. It has been too carefully prepared by this studied hate and love. Gollum loved the thing which destroyed him and destroyed it in revenge. In "saving" his "Precious" from destruction, he genuinely saves Frodo, whom he loves as much as he hates, from destruction too; in seeking to save and destroy what he loves and hates, he saves himself and Frodo by bringing the accursed Ring and his own long agony to an end; Frodo, rather than meeting the total destruction of his own curse, loses only his Ring finger.

When the Quest is finally completed and it seems that nothing remains but death, Sam's attitude is still distinct from Frodo's: "in all that ruin of the world for the moment he felt only joy, great joy. The burden was gone. His master had been saved; he was himself again, he was free." But even so, it is Sam who does not abandon himself to despair. "'Yes, I am with you, Master,' said Sam, laying Frodo's wounded hand gently to his breast. 'And you're with me. . . . But after coming all that way I don't want to give up yet. It's not like me, some-how. . . .'" And Frodo replies: "'But it's like things are in the world. Hopes fail. An end comes. . . . We are lost in ruin . . . and there is no escape.'" Nevertheless he allows Sam to lead him out of the Crack of Doom. Although even there Sam makes jokes, asking if some day they will sing the song of Nine-fingered Frodo and the Ring of Doom, "'to keep fear away till the very last,'" still his eyes search the sky to the north, from whence their rescuers finally come (III, 228–29).

When Sam and Frodo are led before Aragorn it is to Sam, not Frodo, that Aragorn says, "'It is a long way, is it not, from Bree, where you did not like the look of me? A long way for us all, but yours has been the darkest road'" (III, 232).

As indeed it has. Frodo has known torment and agony and ter-ror, but Sam has endured them voluntarily, with no great cause to strengthen his will; rather it was only for the sake of one he loves be-yond everything else.

Edmund Wilson has said in his critical review that Frodo is "un-changed" by the Quest. This is manifestly ridiculous. If nothing else, the compassion he shows to Saruman, even at the moment when Saruman has attempted to stab him, is in great contrast to his insensi-tivity when Gandalf first told him the Gollum story and he cried out, "'What a pity that Bilbo did not stab that vile creature'" (I, 68). Saruman recognizes this; he says, "'You have grown, Halfling. . . . You have robbed my revenge of sweetness'" (III, 299).

Frodo shares for a time in the rewards of their labors, but he bears forever the three wounds: the knife-wound of Weathertop, for folly; the sting of Shelob, for overconfidence; and the finger torn away with the Ring, for pride.

The recoil of the wounded hero is mainly, however, on Sam. He longs to stay with Frodo forever, but Sam has achieved true maturity; and as the Heroic Age passes, he longs to put down roots into the soil of the Shire and raise a family. It has been said that significantly this dream comes, first, during the dreadful last stage of the Quest, when

Sam, denying himself water so that Frodo may drink, daydreams of the pools of Bywater, and of Rosie and her brothers.

Aragorn, the eldest and the classic Hero, wins his Lady as the reward of all his labors, but Sam is the only one of the characters who truly passes *out* of the Heroic Age into the world of today. Aragorn becomes a King, but it is aptly Sam who is shown making the actual, personal *choice*, at the end, between that early flame of true, single devotion which burns up the whole soul in a passion for heroic deeds and the quiet, manful, *necessary* compromise to live in a plain world and to do ordinary things. Merry, too, has achieved high adult stature; for him, the return to the Shire is like "a dream that has slowly faded," but for Frodo it is like "falling asleep again." Yet Frodo's quiet dream of peace is never achieved; he has given too much of himself to the struggle to cast away the curse, suffered too much in the achieving of this peace for others. He has won through to nobility and compassion, but hardly.

Sam is torn by divided loyalties: to raise his family or to remain always with Frodo. For Frodo there is no real return, while Sam has returned in heart and soul. It is partly this as well as the "memory of fear and darkness," which Arwen has foreseen would continue to trouble him (III, 253), that brings Frodo to his final choice. To me one of the most beautiful and poetic symbols is Arwen's white jewel; even though she lies outside the story, it has a dreamlike coherence, the fantasy of inner understanding. Arwen has given him another gift — the gift she herself has foregone for Aragorn's sake. Frodo chooses the course which Arwen cannot: "'Someone has to give [things] up . . . so that others may keep them'" (III, 309). How many young, young men had that choice forced on them, in the desperate England of Dunkirk and the Blitz, though the allegory is nowhere that crude?

At their last parting, Frodo shows how clearly he understands the nature of Sam's growth, his change and his conflict: "'You cannot always be torn in two. You will have to be one and whole, for many years'" (III, 309). He departs with the others and removes the need for Sam to feel "torn in two" by his divided loves and loyalties; and Sam, though grieving and in pain, returns to Rose and his children, to make the Shire even more "blessed and beloved." Sam can be compared neither to Jurgen, who also endures adventures and renounces them, nor to another famous adventurer who decides in the end to "cultivate his garden," for Jurgen and Candide belong to anti-Quest, rather than Quest, literature. A truer parallel would be to Papageno in *The Magic Flute;* Tamino achieved his quest and stood with Pamina before the sun, but Papageno asked only for a nice little wife and his birds. Yet Sam is a true figure of the Age. He recognizes that Rivendell, the Refuge, had "'something of everything here, if you understand me: the Shire and the Golden Wood and Gondor and kings' houses and inns and meadows and mountains all mixed'" (III, 264–65). Gandalf, too, after his return from death, has said: "'Indeed I *am* Saruman, one might almost say, Saruman as he should have been'"(II, 98). Sam, in becoming Frodo's heir, retains and passes on and keeps alive the memories of the days that are gone. He retains also in himself much of what he has become and known; enriched by the Heroic Age through which he has passed, he retains some — though sadly not all — of its glory. He has become, in a way, the beauty of the Elves, the hardiness of the Dwarves, the wisdom of the wizards, the gallantry of men, and the sound staunchness, at the root, of the halflings. And so this final relationship, even its failure (for all of Sam's selflessness and love could not save Frodo from his destiny, any more than the downfall of evil in Sauron could save the good things achieved by Elrond and Galadriel), reflects the symbolism of life, and the passing of the Heroic Age. Sam's heroism and devotion are in curious contrast to the humdrum marriage and life he accepts and desires ("one small garden . . . was all his need and due, not a garden swollen to a realm" [III, 177]). The only way to achieve maturity is to leave behind the Third Age with its dreams and desires, its emotions and needs and glories; the only way to remain forever young is to die young. Yet Sam names his daughter for the flowers of Lórien, and the Golden Tree blooms, forever, in the Shire.

R. J. REILLY

Tolkien and the Fairy Story

In this essay Reilly lays open for us the nature of "sub-creation" as a method of literary composition by examining what Tolkien had to say about the process in "On Fairy-Stories." He finds the source of Tolkien's thinking on the matter in Coleridge's theory of "Secondary [or "esemplastic"] Imagination." Using this faculty the writer creates a "Secondary World," which, in turn, the reader enters by using his own "Secondary Belief." As Coleridge did before him, Tolkien believes that it is precisely because fantasy deals with things that do not exist in the "Primary World" that it is a higher form of art. A work of art that can command a reader's Secondary Belief rewards him with three great gifts: Escape, Consolation, and Recovery. The escape it offers is that of a prisoner from a cell, the binding enclosure of "reality." Consolation stems from the work's ability to satisfy our "primordial desire" for wholeness. Recovery is of "true sight," a joyful recognition of the goodness of the world and our place in it.

Tolkien's essay attempts to determine the nature, origin, and use of fairy stories. As to the nature of them, no definition can be arrived at on historical grounds; the definition instead must deal with "the nature of Faërie: the Perilous Realm itself, and the air that blows in that country."[1] But this is exactly what cannot be either defined or accurately described, only perceived. Faërie may be roughly translated as

"Magic," but not the vulgar magic of the magician; it is rather magic "of a particular mood and power," and it does not have its end in itself but in its operations. Among these operations are "the satisfaction of certain primordial human desires" such as the desire "to survey the depths of space and time" and the desire "to hold communion with other living things." Travelers' tales are not fairy stories, and neither are those stories which utilize dream machinery to explain away their marvels. If a writer attaches his tale of marvels to reality by explaining that it was all a dream, as in the medieval tradition, "he cheats deliberately the primal desire at the heart of Faërie: the realization, independent of the conceiving mind, of imagined wonder."

Now these remarks throw much light on the trilogy. It is a fairy story in the sense just described: it concerns itself with the air that blows through the Perilous Realm of Faërie. It attempts to satisfy "certain primordial human desires." It surveys the depths of time, as Lewis's interplanetary trilogy surveys the depths of space, and in Tolkien's sense, Lewis's trilogy is thus a fairy story. The story itself is of the Third Age, but the story is full of echoes out of the dim past; in fact, the trilogy is in great part an attempt to suggest the depths of time, "which antiquates antiquity, and hath an art to make dust of all things." The Third Age is, for the reader, old beyond measure, but the beings of this age tell stories out of ages yet deeper "in the dark backward and abysm of time," and in fact often suggest that these stories recount only the events of relatively recent times and that the oldest things are lost beyond memory. All this is to satisfy that primordial desire to explore time, for "antiquity has an appeal in itself." Fairy stories, Tolkien's among them, "open a door on Other Time, and if we pass through, though only for a moment, we stand outside our own time, outside Time itself, maybe."

And the trilogy attempts to satisfy the other desire, "to hold communion with other living things" again, as Lewis's trilogy does. The Ents, for example, the great trees of the Third Age, are among the oldest living things. They speak to the hobbits in a language as old, as slowly and carefully articulated, as the earth itself. And when Tom Bombadil speaks, it is as if Nature itself — nonrational, interested only in life and in growing things — were speaking. The elves, the dwarves, even Gollum and the orcs, are gradations — either up or down — from the human level; they are "other living things" with whom the reader holds communion in the trilogy world of imagined wonder.

Readers of Lewis will recall that he has had much to say of the stories of Beatrix Potter: it was in these that he found the early glimpses of the thing he called Joy. And Tolkien finds something in them of Faërie. They are mostly beast fables, he thinks, but they "lie near the borders of Faërie" because of the moral element in them, "their inherent morality, not any allegorical *significatio*." And here is a partial answer to the question which . . . all the critics of the trilogy have dealt with: the relevance of the work to human life. It is not only through allegory that invented characters and actions may have significance. Allegory is ultimately reducible to rational terms; and in this sense there is no allegory in *The Lord of the Rings*. But there runs throughout the work an "inherent morality" which many critics have discerned and which some have tried to reduce to allegory. It is the element of the numinous that is to be found throughout the work of George Macdonald and in Lewis's novels. It is the sense of a cosmic moral law, consciously obeyed or disobeyed by the characters, but existing nowhere as a formulated and codified body of doctrine. Patricia Spacks has commented that Tolkien has included in the trilogy "all the necessary materials for religion." It is even more accurate to say that he has included conscience, which may be defined, for the purposes of the trilogy, as an awareness of natural law. But it is not a rational awareness; that is, rationality plays almost no part in it. It is an emotional or imaginative awareness; the doctrine does not exist, but the feeling normally attached to the doctrine does. The value of this inherent morality, as we will see, comes under Tolkien's heading of "Recovery," which is one of the uses of the fairy story.

Fairy stories, then, are those which utilize Faërie, the "realization of imagined wonder," and which have, or may have, an inherent morality. Their nature is "independent of the conceiving mind," or, as Lewis said of Macdonald's mythmaking, it comes to us on a level deeper and more basic than that of the conceptual intellect, and must be perceived with the imagination.[2]

Tolkien's views of the origin of fairy stories take us a step closer to the heart of the matter. The history of fairy stories is "as complex as the history of human language." In this history three elements have figured in the creation of "the intricate web of Story": invention, diffusion, and inheritance. The latter two lead ultimately back to the first and do nothing to clear up the mystery of invention. For diffusion is merely "borrowing in space" from an inventor, and inheritance is merely "borrowing in time." Both presuppose an inventive mind, and it is the nature of the inventive mind that concerns Tolkien:

> The incarnate mind, the tongue, and the tale are in our world coeval. The human mind, endowed with the powers of generalization and abstraction, sees not only *green-grass*, discriminating it from other things but sees that it is *green* as well as being *grass*. But how powerful, how stimulating to the very faculty that produced it, was the invention of the adjective: no spell or incantation in Faërie is more potent. And that is not surprising: such incantations might indeed be said to be only another view of adjectives, a part of speech in a mythical grammar. The mind that thought of *light, heavy, grey, yellow, still, swift*, also conceived of magic that would make heavy things light and able to fly, turn grey lead into yellow gold, and the still rock into swift water. If it could do the one, it could do the other; it inevitably did both. When we can take green from grass, blue from heaven, and red from blood, we have already an enchanter's power — upon one plane; and the desire to wield that power in the world external to our minds awakes. It does not follow that we shall use that power well on any plane. We may put a deadly green upon a man's face and produce a horror; we may make the rare and ter-

rible blue moon to shine; or we may make woods to spring with silver leaves and rams to wear fleeces of gold, and put hot fire into the belly of the cold worm. But in such "fantasy," as it is called, new form is made; Faërie begins; Man becomes a sub-creator. (pp. 50–51)

Clearly, behind this description of the inventive mind is the romantic doctrine of the creative imagination. Faërie is a product of the "esemplastic" imagination, a product of Coleridge's Secondary Imagination, which is an echo of the Primary Imagination that creates and perceives the world of reality.

Nor is the creative imagination to be taken lightly or metaphorically in Tolkien's theory of the fairy story. The writer of the story is really a sub-creator; he creates a "Secondary World" which the mind of the reader really enters. Further, the reader's state of mind is not accurately described in the phrase "willing suspension of disbelief," which indicates a kind of tolerance or tacit agreement. When the story is successful, the reader practices "Secondary Belief," which is an active and positive thing. So long as the writer's art does not fail him, "what he relates is 'true': it accords with the laws of that world. You therefore believe it, while you are . . . inside."

Tolkien elaborates, and slightly qualifies, the doctrine of the creative imagination in his discussion of the use of fairy stories. He begins with a dictionary distinction between the Fancy and the Imagination. According to this distinction, the Fancy is the image-making faculty, what Coleridge called "a mode of memory emancipated from the order of time and space," while the Imagination is "the power of giving to ideal creations the inner consistency of reality." Coleridge thought of the two capacities as wholly distinct faculties, the Fancy being analogous to the Understanding, and the Imagination analogous to Reason. Tolkien would combine them because he believes "the verbal distinction philologically inappropriate, and the analysis inaccurate. The mental power of image-making is one thing, or aspect; and it should appropriately be called Imagination. The perception of the image, the grasp of its implications, and the control, which are necessary to a successful expression, may vary in vividness and strength; but this is a difference of degree in Imagination, not a difference in kind." What gives "the inner consistency of reality" or Secondary Belief is not properly Imagination but Art, which is "the operative link between Imagination and the final result, Sub-creation." Needing a term to express both the "Sub-creative Art" and "a quality of strangeness and wonder in the expression, derived from the Image," he chooses to use the word "Fantasy." For the term in the sense in which he means it "combines with its older and higher use as an equivalent of Imagination the derived notions of 'unreality' (that is, of unlikeness to the Primary World), of freedom from the domination of observed 'fact,' in short of the fantastic."

He is aware of the implications of the word "fantastic," that it implies that the things with which it deals are not to be found in the "Primary World." In fact he welcomes such implications, for that is exactly what he means by the term, that the images which it describes are not extant in the "real" world. That they are not "is a virtue not a vice." We recall Shelley's lines: "Forms more real than living man, / Nurslings of immortality." Just because Fantasy deals with things which do not exist in the Primary World, Tolkien holds, it is "not a lower but a higher form of Art, indeed the most nearly pure form, and so (when achieved) the most potent." It is relatively easy to achieve "the inner consistency of reality" in realistic material. But good Fantasy is very difficult to write. Anyone, Tolkien points out, can say "the green sun," but

> to make a Secondary World inside which the green sun will be credible, commanding Secondary Belief, will probably require labour and thought, and will certainly demand a special skill, a kind of elvish craft. Few attempt such difficult tasks. But when they are attempted and in any degree accomplished then we have

a rare achievement of Art: indeed narrative art, story-making in its primary and most potent mode. (p. 68)

The fairy story, then, of which the trilogy is an example, uses Fantasy, and so far as it is successful is "story-making in its primary and most potent mode." That is to say, in dealing with fantastic things rather than with real ones it attempts the purest form of narrative art, and succeeds to the extent that it induces in the reader the state of mind called Secondary Belief. In short, invented stories, if successful, are better and on a higher level than stories which merely manipulate the materials of the Primary World. Here we are reminded of Coleridge's distinction between the Reason and the Understanding, the latter manipulating the "counters" of the real world. Now Fantasy is a higher form than Realism not only because such invented stories are harder to make but because they offer to the reader certain things which realistic stories do not offer, or do not offer to the same degree. These things Tolkien calls Recovery, Escape, and Consolation.

"'Recovery' (which includes return and renewal of health) is a re-gaining — re-gaining of a clear view." Recovery is a means of "seeing things as we are (or were) meant to see them." All things become blurred by familiarity; we come to possess them, to use them, to see them only in relation to ourselves. In so doing we lose sight of what the things themselves really are, *qua* things — and "things" here includes people, objects, ideas, moral codes, literally everything. Recovery is a recovery of perspective, the old Chestertonian lesson which Tolkien calls "*Mooreeffoc,* or Chestertonian fantasy," the lesson of *Manalive.* Fantasy provides the recovery necessary to those of us who do not have humility; the humble do not need fantasy because they already see things as not necessarily related to themselves; their vision is not blighted by selfishness or egotism. Lewis defends the trilogy's relevance to life, and he does so in terms of what Tolkien means by "Recovery." He has said that the book has some of the qualities of myth:

The value of the myth is that it takes all the things we know and restores to them the rich significance which has been hidden by "the veil of familiarity." . . . By putting bread, gold, horse, apple, or the very roads into a myth, we do not retreat from reality: we rediscover it. As long as the story lingers in our mind, the real things are more themselves. This book applies the treatment not only to bread or apple but to good and evil, to our endless perils, our anguish, and our joys. By dipping them in myth we see them more clearly.[3]

Applying the theory of Recovery to the trilogy, then, we rediscover the meaning of heroism and friendship as we see the two hobbits clawing their way up Mount Doom; we see again the endless evil of greed and egotism in Gollum, stunted and ingrown out of shape by years of lust for the Ring; we recognize again the essential anguish of seeing beautiful and frail things — innocence, early love, children — passing away as we read of the Lady Galadriel and the elves making the inevitable journey to the West and extinction, and see them as Frodo does: "a living vision of that which has already been left far behind by the flowing streams of Time." We see morality *as* morality by prescinding from this or that moral act and watching the "inherent morality" to which all beings of the Third Age — the evil as well as the good — bear witness. And, perhaps, the devouring nature of time itself is borne in on us, as it was on the Elizabethan sonneteers, and we learn again from the trilogy that all things are Time's fools, that all comes within the compass of his bending sickle.

If Tolkien is right, if Recovery is what he claims it is, and if Fantasy provides Recovery, then it follows that Fantasy, far from being irrelevant to reality, is in fact extremely relevant to moral reality. And the trilogy, so far as Tolkien's art does not fail him, is an example of the dictum, so favored by the Renaissance critics, that literature is both *dulce* and *utile*, that Spenser can be a better teacher than Aquinas.

Finally, Tolkien holds that the fairy story, by the use of Fantasy, provides Escape and Consolation, two elements which are very closely related. In fact, Escape brings about Consolation as its end or effect. Now the fact that the fairy story is "escapist" is the very crux of the accusations brought against it, as we have seen in regard to the trilogy. But Tolkien will not admit that escape is a bad thing. The word, he thinks, has fallen into disrepute because its users too often confuse "the Escape of the Prisoner with the Flight of the Deserter."

> Why should a man be scorned, if, finding himself in prison, he tries to get out and go home? Or if, when he cannot do so, he thinks and talks about other topics than jailers and prison walls? The world outside has not become less real because the prisoner cannot see it. (p. 76)

Thus escape from Hitler's Reich was not desertion; it was really rebellion, a refusal to be identified with Hitler. And, Tolkien thinks, this is often the nature of escape. A man may refuse to write about the world in which he lives not out of cowardice — the usual accusation — but because to write about it is in a sense to accept it. He may, like Thoreau, simply secede. And this is not desertion; it is war; it is "real Escape, and what are often its companions, Disgust, Anger, Condemnation, and Revolt."

But fairy stories, Tolkien thinks, provide other escapes, and these bring about consolations of various kinds. Fairy stories, like other kinds of literature and like many other things as well, can provide a kind of solace in a world of "hunger, thirst, poverty, pain, sorrow, injustice, death." And this kind of solace or respite is necessary; it is not refusal to face reality; it is a time needed to regroup one's forces for the next day's battle. Thus the poets talk of care-charmer sleep and the sleep that knits up the ravelled sleeve of care, but they do not advocate sleeping one's life away. Further, fairy stories, as we have seen, provide a kind of consolation in their satisfaction of "primordial human desires."

But the major consolation that the fairy story has to offer is one which it contains to a degree that no other kind of literature can equal. It is "the Consolation of the Happy Ending":

> Almost I would venture to assert that all complete fairy-stories must have it. At least I would say that Tragedy is the true form of Drama, its highest function; but the opposite is true of Fairy-story. Since we do not appear to possess a word that expresses this opposite — I will call it *Eucatastrophe*. The *eucatastrophic* tale is the true form of the fairy-tale, and its highest function. (p. 81)

What the fairy story preeminently presents is "the joy of the happy ending," and it is in this respect that the fairy story, for Tolkien, is related to reality. But the reality is not the reality of this world, the world of flux and opinion: rather the eucatastrophe "denies . . . universal final defeat and in so far is *evangelium*, giving a fleeting glimpse of Joy, Joy beyond the walls of the world, poignant as grief." The good fairy story, by means of its eucatastrophe, gives the reader "a catch of the breath, a beat and lifting of the heart, near to (or indeed accompanied by) tears," for in the eucatastrophe the reader gets "a piercing glimpse of joy, and heart's desire, that for a moment passes outside the frame, rends indeed the very web of story, and lets a gleam come through." The relevance of the fairy story to reality lies in this gleam, which is a "sudden glimpse of the underlying reality of truth."

Thus there are two answers to the question, Is the fairy story true? The first and obvious answer is, It is true if it induces Secondary Belief, if the art has successfully translated the image of the "created wonder." But that is merely a question of art. The nature of the eucatastrophe suggests that the second answer is infinitely more important, for "in the 'eucatastrophe' we see in a brief vision that the answer may be greater — it may be a far-off gleam or echo of *evangelium* in the real world." It is in this second truth that the fairy story, for Tolkien, ceases to be merely literature and becomes explicitly a vehicle for religious truth.

God has redeemed man in all man's capacities, and one of his capacities is that of telling stories, especially fairy stories. As Redemption has once more made man in the image and likeness of God, so the capacities of man to some degree echo the capacities of God. In this sense, this second truth of the fairy story is "only one facet of a truth incalculably rich," for in all spheres of human activity there is necessarily something like the signature of God. The eucatastrophic fairy story, a product of redeemed man, echoes the Gospels, which contain a story "which embraces the essence of all fairy-stories." For the Gospels contain not only marvels, as the fairy story does; they contain the birth of Christ, which is "the greatest and most complete conceivable eucatastrophe," "the eucatastrophe of Man's history." And they contain the Resurrection, which is "the eucatastrophe of the Incarnation."

The joy which the happy ending of the fairy story gives, says Tolkien, is of the same quality, though not the same degree, as the joy which we feel at the fact that the great fairy story of the Gospels is true in the Primary World, for the joy of the fairy tale "has the very taste of primary truth." This is the justification of the fairy story — and thus of the trilogy — that it gives us in small, in the beat of the heart and the catch of the breath, the joy of the infinite good news. For "Art has been verified. God is the Lord of Angels, and of men — and of elves. Legend and history have met and fused."

It is not too much to say that Tolkien's view of the fairy story has made explicit Coleridge's claim for the worth of the creative imagination. The Secondary Imagination, which created literature, was for Coleridge an "echo" of the Primary Imagination, which is "the living Power and prime Agent of all human Perception, and . . . a repetition in the finite mind of the external act of creation in the infinite I AM."[4] For the fairy story — and the trilogy — are sheer creation, the making of a Secondary World out of, and by means of, the Imagination.

That is the special activity of the fairy story maker, and one by which he becomes, not a writer, but a sub-creator of a kind of literature analogous — or more than analogous — to the universe created ex nihilo by the divine Creator. In his degree he creates Joy — or creates what gives Joy — as God, in the purposeful drama of creation, has created what also gives Joy, the world with the Christian happy ending. Speaking of Blake's definition of poetry, Northrop Frye has commented:

> We live in a world of threefold external compulsion: of compulsion on action, or law; of compulsion on thinking, or fact; of compulsion on feeling, which is the characteristic of all pleasure whether it is produced by the *Paradiso* or by an ice cream soda. But in the world of imagination a fourth power, which contains morality, beauty, and truth but is never subordinated to them, rises free of all their compulsions. The work of imagination presents us with a vision, not of the personal greatness of the poet, but of something impersonal and far greater: the vision of a decisive act of spiritual freedom, the vision of the recreation of man.[5]

Tolkien's defense of Fantasy and, I would add, of the trilogy, in verse in which there is perhaps more truth than poetry, is also a defense and, it may be, the last defense, of the doctrine of the creative imagination, which brings the making of God and the making of man so close that they nearly touch:

> Although now long estranged,
> Man is not wholly lost nor wholly changed.
> Disgraced he may be, yet is not de-throned,
> and keeps the rags of lordship once he owned:
> Man, Sub-creator, the refracted Light
> through whom is splintered from a single White
> to many hues, and endlessly combined
> in living shapes that move from mind to mind.

Though all the crannies of the world we filled
with Elves and Goblins, though we dared to build
Gods and their houses out of dark and light,
and sowed the seed of dragons — 'twas our right
(used or misused). That right has not decayed:
we make still by the law in which we're made. (pp. 71–72)

J. S. RYAN

Folktale, Fairy Tale, and the Creation of a Story

Like R. J. Reilly, J. S. Ryan is concerned to examine Tolkien's conceptions of myth, fairy tale, and "sub-creation." Therefore, this essay may profitably be read in conjunction with that which precedes it. Ryan's focus, however, is upon Tolkien's criticism. The seminal essay "Beowulf: The Monsters and the Critics," according to Ryan, illuminates Tolkien's conception of the nature of folktale and its function in designing the "mythical mode of imagination." Ryan also explores Tree and Leaf, *which, in addition to containing the important essay "On Fairy-Stories," provides a useful example of what a fairy tale should be, "Leaf by Niggle." In considering the crucial significance of Tolkien's work as a philologist in the formation of his art, Ryan examines as well the place of language in Tolkien's conception of tale and its role within the whole realm to which mythical imagination gives access. Tolkien thought of classes of languages as trees and of particular languages as their branches. For instance, Germanica is a tree and English one of its branches. A story is a leaf on the tree, a "net of words" that attempts to catch Faërie; the tree is a mass of tales; and the whole forest is a manifestation of time's continuous unfolding.*

In a form more compact than that of Williams, and with a simpler, more consistently presented philosophy than that of C. S. Lewis, Tolkien has explained for us his views of the function of myth. At the same time he has shown himself the best critic of his own major work¹ — a feat all the more illuminating of his consistency of thought when we realize that his theories appear to have been fully evolved when he had just begun the trilogy; original versions of his "On Fairy-Stories" and "Leaf by Niggle" were "written in the same period (1938–1939) when *The Lord of the Rings* was beginning to unroll itself and to unfold prospects of labour in yet unknown country."²

Although they are not as specific as one might like, it is best to note first the various comments Tolkien made in 1936 when he was lecturing on *Beowulf*, in a paper now widely recognized as a turning point in *Beowulf* criticism, stressing as it did the tragedy of the human condition and showing that tragedy is set forth in artistic terms as "a balance of ends and beginnings," "the moving contrast of youth and age," with the monsters, embodying the forces of evil and chaos, appropriately placed in the center of the poem. In his remarks Tolkien indicates that he is in sympathy with the poet for using afresh ancient and largely traditional material and for giving something nearer to mythical allegory than the folktale. He warns that formal intellectual snobbishness should not blind us to this:

> I will not . . . attempt at length a defence of the mythical mode of imagination. . . . Folk-tales . . . do often contain much that is far more powerful, and that cannot be sharply separated from myth . . . capable in poetic hands of . . . becoming largely significant — as a whole, accepted unanalysed. The significance of a myth is not easily to be pinned on paper by analytical reasoning. It is at its best when it is presented by a poet who feels rather than makes explicit what his theme portends: who presents it incarnate in the world of history and geography . . . ; myth is alive at once and in all its parts, and dies before it can be dissected. It is possible, I think, to be moved by the power of myth and yet to misunderstand the sensation, . . . [to] refuse to admit that there can be an interest for *us* . . . in ogres and dragons.³

He goes on to stress the impact of *draconitas,* lust for power over possessions and people, a large symbolism of malice, greed, and destruction, here walking in history and incarnate in time, and he underscores the inevitable overthrow of man in Time, for *lif is læne,* a theme which in its deadly seriousness begets the dignity of tone. He notes that the poem is by a great Christian just over the threshold of religious change, who has the uplifting hope which was denied his heroic ancestors.

Interestingly, Tolkien regrets that we do not know more "about pre-Christian English mythology" (p. 70), a gap which, it has often been felt, this scholar has been concerned to fill in his own creative writings. He is also here determined to stress the impact of the story from its cosmic dimension: "It is just because the main foes in *Beowulf* are inhuman that the story is larger and more significant. . . . It glimpses the cosmic and moves with the thought of all men concerning the fate of human life and efforts; it stands amid but above the petty wars of princes, and surpasses the dates and limits of historical periods. . . . During its process we look down as if from a visionary height upon the house of man in the valley of the world" (pp. 87–88). In his conclusion Tolkien notes that the poet is concerned to use materials then plentiful but from a day already passing, a time now forever vanished; using them for a new purpose, with a wider sweep of the imagination, and achieving a peculiar solemnity so that for all those of northern races "it must ever call with a profound appeal — until the dragon comes" (p. 88).

As his better-known minor writings indicate,[4] Tolkien's imagination was nourished on the materials of Old Norse and Old English literature, and on certain other texts from the Middle English period; therefore, it comes as no surprise to find that the strands and themes that are woven into the fabric of the major works are rich in Germanic associations. Yet early indications of certain concepts (e.g., that both in process and in nature man's imagination is like a tree) seem to have been overlooked. His 1924 essay in *The Year's Work in*

English Studies ended this way: "This study . . . is fired by the two emotions, love of the land of England and the allurement of the riddle of the past, that never cease to carry men through amazing . . . labours to the recapturing of fitful and tantalizing glimpses in the dark — 'Floreant Philologica et Archaeologica.'"[5] In 1925, he began his survey with lines which are a startling anticipation of "Leaf by Niggle," as well as of Aragorn and others in the woods of Lothlórien. Interestingly, they echo Dante and Frazer's *The Golden Bough:* "It is merry in summer when the 'shaws be sheen and shrads full fair and leaves both large and long.' Walking in that wood is full of solace. Its leaves require no reading. There is another and a denser wood where some are obliged to walk instead, where saws are wise and screeds are thick and the leaves too large and long. These leaves we must read (more or less), hapless vicarious readers, and not all we read is solace."[6]

Yet it was the need to clarify his comments on *Beowulf* about "the mythical mode of imagination" which may be assumed to have prompted the essay wherein he is concerned to describe the genre fairy tale in a way that does not relate well to many examples of the form but which does apply very closely to his own writing (and is accepted by Lewis, who uses it, without acknowledgment, when defending his friend's three volumes).[7] While it is possible to trace the lines of Tolkien's thought back through Chesterton's "The Ethics of Elf-land,"[8] and earlier to George Macdonald's "Imagination, Its Functions and Its Culture,"[9] and thence to Coleridge, in the *Biographia Literaria,* it will be enough here to analyze what is a substantially new piece of work which goes much further than its predecessors and argues its case with greater cogency and fuller development than they.

While both Chesterton and Tolkien are pointedly unconcerned about the origin of the fairy tale, they are alike attentive to its meaning and purpose. Chesterton had become disillusioned about "practical politics" but was committed to "vision," "ordinary things," and "the sense of the miracle of humanity." "Ordinary things are more valuable than extraordinary things. . . . Man is something more awful than men. . . . The mere man on two legs, as such, should be felt as something more heart-breaking than any music" (pp. 67–68). He goes on to stress that "a legend . . . ought to be treated more respectfully than a book of history"; "tradition means giving votes to the most obscure of all classes, our ancestors"; "I would always trust the old wives' fables against the old maids' facts"; "Fairyland is nothing but the sunny country of common sense"; "the test of fairyland . . . is the test of imagination"; "we all like astonishing tales because they touch the nerve of the ancient instinct of astonishment"; or "wonder has a positive element of praise."

Tolkien in "On Fairy-Stories" finds that no definition of them can be arrived at on historical grounds, and it must rather come from "Faërie," "the realm or state in which fairies have their being," "the Perilous Realm itself" which holds "the seas, the sun, the moon, the sky, and the earth and all the things that are in it: tree and bird, water and stone, wine and bread, and ourselves, mortal men, when we are enchanted" (p. 9).

Further, most good "fairy-stories" are about the *aventures* of men in that realm. Perhaps the best translation of "Faërie" is Magic "of a peculiar mood and power" which operates to give us "the enchantment of distance" and "the satisfaction of certain primordial human community with other living things" (p. 13).

The trilogy in its story is full of echoes of the dim past, the earlier ages and the ancient forces, and makes much use of borrowing in time. As is stated early on, "we stand outside our own time, outside Time itself, maybe." As well as "opening a door onto other time," there the language of the trees is a function of the story, as are the alien tongues of birds and horses, while the reader, through the hobbits, is able to communicate with many different rational species, from the Orcs and trolls, and eagles and horses, to the Elves and the High Elves who do not normally commune in words.

All of these processes satisfy the primal desire, of "imaginary wonder," which emotion we experience vicariously through the hobbits, as they behold with "wonder" the variety of Middle-earth: Goldberry (I, 134); the "silence of the heavens" (I, 14); or Strider, as one of the line of the old kings (I, 233). Throughout the trilogy we see people bigger than we existing in a world filled with marvels both horrifying and beautiful, so that, like the hobbits, we can only gaze with wonder. The men of Gondor marvel at the races of hobbits and Dwarves, while the Elves themselves have this attitude toward Númenor and the Far West.

In his section on the fairy story's origins, Tolkien acknowledges the validity of the investigation of story elements as an exercise for folklorists but stresses that "it is precisely the colouring, the atmosphere, the unclassifiable individual details of a story, and above all the general purport that informs with life the undissected bones of the plot, that really count" (pp. 18–19).

In words that both recall his comments on philology cited above and anticipate much later writing, he links several of his own yearnings: "Of course, I do not deny, for I feel strongly, the fascination of the desire to unravel the intricately knotted and ramified history of the branches on the Tree of Tales. It is closely connected with the philologists' study of the tangled skein of Language, of which I know some small pieces" (p. 19). In a change of symbol he argues that the reader should be content with the "soup" as presented, or "the story as it is served up by its author or teller," and not with the bones that went into the mix.[10]

In the making of the fairy story he sees three important ingredients — *invention, inheritance,* and *diffusion.* By the first he probably means collecting knowns in medieval fashion, while the second is "borrowing in time," and the third "borrowing in space," usually from another inventor. At the center is an inventive mind, the nature of which Tolkien (in a manner similar to that of Owen Barfield),[11] would explore. This leads to his analysis of the creative imagination, a theory that utilizes and goes beyond Coleridge's use of Platonic concepts to an implicitly Christian romanticism. "Faërie" is a product of the "esemplastic imagination" of the Secondary World, and this "Secondary Belief" is much more than the "willing suspension of disbelief."

Folktales, like all cosmologies, were once myths, or allegories "of the greater elemental . . . processes of nature" and only gradually became localized and humanized. Tolkien disagrees with the view of his friend Christopher Dawson (1889–1970) that they were once separate.[12] Indeed he stresses that they always were together "there, in the Cauldron of Story, waiting for the great figures of Myth and History, and for the yet nameless He or She, waiting for the moment when they are cast into 'the simmering stew'" (p. 29). After considering history and myth, and the power of many stories which "open a door on Other Time," he draws attention to the taboos in stories and has this to say of tales that are good enough: "What really happens is that the story-maker proves a successful 'sub-creator.' He makes a Secondary World which your mind can enter. Inside it, what he relates is 'true': it accords with the laws of that world. You therefore believe it, while you are, as it were, inside. The moment disbelief arises, the spell is broken; the magic, or rather, art, has failed. You are then out in the Primary World again, looking at the little abortive Secondary World from outside" (p. 37). This is the distinction between the outer, objective, or Primary World and the inner world of myth, the Secondary World produced by the "sub-creator." Tolkien in writing the trilogy has imaged an entire world and told the story of certain events which took place during its imagined history.

He is also concerned to underscore in stories the element of desire. From the tales he read as a child, he says, came a "wholly unsatisfied desire to shoot well with a bow" and "glimpses of an archaic mode of life, and, above all, forests." His taste for these stories, he tells us, was "wakened by philology . . . and quickened to full life by war."

Later, when commenting on the difficulties of being a successful sub-creator, he notes the difficulties involved in commanding Secondary Belief and comments that few attempt such difficult tasks:

"But when they are attempted and in any degree accomplished then we have a rare achievement of Art: indeed narrative art, story-making in its primary and most potent mode" (p. 49). It is just this craft and fusion, it may be contended, which produces the peculiar power of *The Lord of the Rings.*

Coleridge always appealed to Tolkien, and the *Biographia Literaria* was much discussed in various Oxford groups. Indeed, an early paper of Tolkien's[13] influenced a paper by L. A. Willoughby on Coleridge as philologist:

> He . . . even thought, for a moment, of turning to philology as his profession. . . . His linguistic inquiries took on a psychological bent. . . . His approach was philosophical, aesthetic, religious, and only rarely philological in the stricter sense. . . . His linguistic observations and suggestions bear witness to the sharpness of his intellect, and the penetration of his intuition. He showed particular insight in the cultural aspects of language and a keen sense of aesthetic values. But his chief strength was the way in which linguistic training was put to the service of literary criticism.[14]

The influence of Coleridge is to be found in Tolkien's discussion of the concept of the creative imagination. Finding a need for a term other than "Fancy" "which shall embrace both the Sub-creative Art in itself and a quality of strangeness and wonder in the Expression . . . a quality essential to fairy-story," he proposed "to use Fantasy for this purpose" (p. 47). In this mode, the images are of things not of the Primary World but possessed of "arresting strangeness," and the attack on them is that they are "Dreaming," in which, as Tolkien admits, "there is no Art," or like Drama, which "is naturally hostile to Fantasy" and which "has, of its very nature, already attempted a kind of bogus, or shall I say at least substitute magic. . . . For this precise reason — that the characters, and even the scenes [are] not imagined but actually beheld — Drama is . . . an art fundamentally different from narrative art" (p. 51).

"Fantasy" is an acceptable term to Tolkien for he is concerned to stress the peculiar ingredients which invented stories offer more fully than "adult" naturalistic ones do: Fantasy, Recovery, Escape, and Consolation. Needing a new term to express both "Sub-creative Art" and "a quality of strangeness and wonder," he used "Fantasy" in a thesis more elegant than Chesterton's: "We all like astonishing tales because they touch the nerve of the ancient instinct of astonishment" (*Orthodoxy*, p. 80). His conclusion suggests a motive for this urge in men, which he likens to the imagining of gods: "Fantasy remains a human right: we make in our measure and in our derivative mode, because we are made: and not only made, but made in the image and likeness of a Maker" (55). Recovery, which includes return and renewal of health, is the "regaining of a clear view." It is a means of "seeing things as we are (or were) meant to see them." For although all things once attracted us, "we locked them in our hoard, acquired them, and acquiring ceased to look at them." Seeing them only in relation to ourselves, we lose sight of their true nature, but by Recovery we attain again, "dangerous and potent . . . free and wild," a fresher and a brighter vision.

As Lewis observed, the method has been used in the trilogy to considerable effect:

> The value of the myth is that it takes all the things we know and restores to them the rich significance which has been hidden by "the veil of familiarity." . . . If you are tired of the real landscape, look at it in a mirror. By putting bread, gold, horse, apple, or the very roads into a myth, we do not retreat from reality: we rediscover it. As long as the story lingers in our mind, the real things are more themselves. This book applies the treatment not only to bread or apple but to good and evil, to our endless perils, our anguish, and our joys. By dipping them in myth we see them more clearly.[15]

One might add that the method had been applied to hospitality and courtesy, friendship and heroism, the operations of greed and the inexorable movement of time — from the passage of seasons, marked by "holiday and dancing in the Party Field" (III, 390), to "mortal summers that flicker and pass upon this Middle-earth" (III, 303).

Closely related to Recovery is Escape, the positive, even heroic, process of getting away from ordinary and drab surroundings, which is, in effect, the escape of the prisoner. As Tolkien says, "The world outside has not become less real because the prisoner cannot see it."[16] He answers one of the common critical charges against fantasy when he asks why a man should be scorned for thinking of topics other than prisons, that is, for transcending the limits of the actual world. He escapes the world because he will not accept it; his action . . . is rebellion compounded of "Disgust, Anger, Condemnation, and Revolt." It is a response to the distortion that leads us to say, "How real, how startlingly alive is a factory chimney compared with an elm-tree." The need for rebellion to restore one's perspective is well illustrated in the "scouring of the Shire," where the returning hobbits find a wilderness of hideous buildings, including just such a chimney stack. Having come "back again"[17] from a world where they have gained in moral fiber, they proceed to set the Shire to rights by first fighting and routing their enemies and then rebuilding and replanting the devastated areas. The lesson of the value in Escape does not need underscoring; in the trilogy it is seen in action, in the revitalizing of Minas Tirith, the rousing of Théoden and the scouring of Orthanc, and above all, in the destruction of the Ring, the actuality of Evil.

The vital element in Escape, however, is Consolation, the consolation of the happy ending, the eucatastrophe, which, by its very fantastic quality, the fairy story affords as solace for the evils of the world. The eucatastrophe is the opposite of tragedy, and in its sudden joyous "turn" gives "a sudden and miraculous grace: never to be counted on to recur. It does not deny the existence of *dyscatastrophe*, of sorrow and failure; the possibility of these is necessary to the joy of deliverance" (p. 68). Sorrow and evil can be as keenly felt as in any other literary form and perhaps more because of the clear outline of the fairy story; however "[fairy story] denies . . . universal final defeat and in so far is *evangelium,* giving a fleeting glimpse of Joy, Joy beyond the walls of the world, poignant as grief" (p. 68). And so it is that, by means of its eucatastrophe, fairy story gives the reader a lifting of the heart, "a piercing glimpse of joy . . . [that] . . . passes outside the frame, rends indeed the very web of story" (p. 70).

The relevance of the fairy story to reality lies in the "sudden glimpse of the underlying reality or truth," an "*evangelium* in the real world." This is what the fairy story offers to Tolkien and to other Christians. The Christian view of the happy ending of the world is significantly reflected in the fairy story. For Tolkien (who specifically states his faith) Christianity is a matter of historical fact and a philosophical interpretation of the universe as well as a religion. It is also the archetypal myth of which all others are confused images: "The Birth of Christ is the eucatastrophe of Man's history. The Resurrection is the eucatastrophe of the Incarnation" (p. 72).

The conclusion to be drawn is that Tolkien has advanced Coleridge's claim for the true value of the imagination. For him the Secondary Imagination is to be seen as an "echo" of the Primary Imagination, which Coleridge had regarded as "the living Power and prime Agent of all human Perception, and as a repetition in the finite mind of the eternal act of creation in the infinite I AM" (*Biographia Literaria,* chap. 13). The fairy story, the making of a Secondary World,[18] is a construct of the Imagination for Tolkien, just as the world is the creation of God the Creator. Thus all stories of "Faërie," and the trilogy is a notable example, look "forward or backward . . . to the Great Eucatastrophe" and partake of its epic and symbolic character. Since for Tolkien the Gospel story is true, by a transference of the transcending validity of the happy issue to the individual's battle with the world of evil, he declares that "God is the Lord of Angels, and of men — and of elves. Legend and history have met and fused" (p. 72).

The many legends referred to in the essay — the magic land of

Hy Breasail in the West; Layamon's story of King Lear in his *Brut;* the *Thrymskvitha* in the Elder Edda; the Shield-Kings of Denmark; the tale of Ingeld and his love for Freawaru; Sigurd of the Volsungs — are desperately serious for Tolkien, and so, he argues, should they be for us. They are, in a very literal sense, required "to be understood." Magic must be taken seriously in medieval story (e.g., *Sir Gawain and the Green Knight*), in eastern tale (e.g., the Egyptian *Tale of the Two Brothers*), or in modern fairy tale. And Tolkien chides Sir George Dasent for forbidding children to read two of his more "adult" tales, and quotes with approval the anecdote of Chesterton's concerning children who were dissatisfied with Maeterlinck's *Blue Bird* "because it did not end with a Day of Judgment" (p. 43).

These thoughts indicate the moral and theological concern which Tolkien posited for a fairy story, and they are underscored by his view that Elf-land depends on keeping promises and, ideally, on fulfillment of the "oldest and deepest desire . . . the Escape from Death." It is finally made clear that ideally "every writer making a Secondary World, . . . every sub-creator, wishes in some measure to be a real maker," to touch on "the serious and dangerous matter . . . the Christian story," for it "has long been my feeling (a joyous feeling) that God redeemed the corrupt-making creatures [by] the Great Eucatastrophe[,] the Christian Joy." The religious and literary conclusion is that story or art, the "Primary Art, that is, of Creation," are all come together in "the eucatastrophe of Man's history," the Birth of Christ (pp. 70–72). Thus it is made clear that it was Tolkien's artistic purpose in his own sub-creating to provide an analysis for his own generation, and those to follow, of the point of fusion of all creation and of its implications for the duty and destiny of humanity.

Tolkien insisted that to be complete the fairy tale or myth must have the eucatastrophe, since in its highest form myth dealt with universal or cosmic reality, and that there must be a progression, since myth is meant to tell the whole story of its world from the beginning to end. With the eucatastrophe comes Joy, and that is really the beginning.[19] While the formal and earthly historical process was brought to an end in Lewis's Narnia, and it was the reality of the afterlife which was beginning, the end for Tolkien's Middle-earth is still remote in time and space. As Gandalf says, "There are other men and other lives, and time still to be" (III, 87). Yet we are given to understand that the end is there and that Elves and Ring-bearers await it in the Undying Lands. Already the process of history has removed whole civilizations,[20] and even now, "much that was fair and wonderful shall pass for ever out of Middle-earth" (II, 155). Lewis neatly summed up the attitude of his friend: "All romantics are vividly aware of mutability, but most of them are content to bewail it: for Macdonald [and, we might add, for Tolkien] this nostalgia is merely the starting point — he goes on and discovers what it was made for."[21]

Although he does not discuss it in the expository essay, Tolkien is aware of the related problem of the apparent conflict between destiny and free will if the fruition of God's purposes is the true goal of man. This issue, like that of the recurrence of evil (and the task of every generation to attempt to remove it to the realm of future possibility, rather than present actuality), is not discussed in Tolkien's critical work, but is allowed to make its own impact in the writing itself.

Because of the refusal of critics to accept the trilogy on its own terms as myth, there has been considerable confusion about its genre, and this doubtless explains the 1964 reissue of the fairy story essay, as well as the Oxford discussion sermons which Tolkien gave at various times, particularly at Pusey House in the decade following the publication of the trilogy. It may easily be shown that Tolkien's aim was not to produce a naturalistic novel so much as to restore the Hero to modern fiction, and Christianity to a central position in men's thoughts. There is contained in the trilogy all the necessary material for religion. Conscience is presented in the form of an awareness of natural law, as the sense of fitness in the hobbits, and this in a form that is intuitive and emotional rather than rational. Lewis, elaborating on his friend's theory, was right to stress that "our victory is impermanent" and that the moral is "a recall from facile optimism and wailing pessimism alike, to that hard, yet not quite desperate, insight into Man's unchanging predicament by which heroic ages have lived."[22] In his review of the first volume, Lewis most neatly summarized the position Tolkien posited for modern man: "There was sorrow then too, and gathering dark, but great valour, and great deeds that were not wholly vain. *Not wholly vain* — it is the cool middle point between illusion and disillusionment."[23]

In the year in which he revised the text of the Andrew Lang lecture as "On Fairy-Stories" (1947), Tolkien published a most subtle story which is meant to be regarded as an allegorical exemplum for the essay and may be related to it, since both were written in the same period as the early stages of *The Lord of the Rings*. Although it can be understood as an illustration of the writer's "wholly unsatisfied desire . . . [for] forests," it is also related to his account of the student of fairy stories "collecting only a few leaves, many of them now torn or decayed, from the countless foliage of the Tree of Tales, with which the Forest of Days is carpeted. It seems vain to add to the litter. Who can design a new leaf? The patterns, from bud to unfolding, and the colours from spring to autumn were all discovered by men long ago. But that is not true. The seed of the tree can be replanted in almost any soil, even in one so smoke-ridden (as Lang said) as that of England" (p. 56). The passages also remind us of his 1924 chapter in *The Year's Work in English Studies* in which he referred to *Germanica* as a "tree of altogether larger girth and bigger branches."

But it is to his essay on fairy stories that we need to refer for illumination of his attitude toward trees. The awe and reverence he has for them is part of "the wonder of things." It is clear that the hierarchy of the imagination is to be found in the growing world. While a leaf is a new story, an attempt to catch "Faërie"[24] in a net of words (although this is never quite successful in this world, for the sought-after is "indescribable, though not imperceptible," p. 10), a tree is the mass of tales which the mind can take in. The forest is the continuous manifestation of time itself. As Tolkien the theorist observed: "Each leaf, of oak and ash and thorn, is a unique embodiment of the pattern, and for some eye this very year may be *the* embodiment, the first ever seen and recognized, though oaks have put forth leaves for countless generations of men" (p. 56).

And yet further dimensions of the little tale should perhaps be put aside for the moment, as Tolkien lets it slowly unravel. The opening and certain of the details inevitably suggest C. S. Lewis's *The Great Divorce* (1946), a kind of Harrowing of the Hell which man makes of his own world. Some have seen the text as a rebuttal of George Santayana's conception of immediate joy, our direct pleasure in beautiful objects wherein the human spirit is freed from "supernatural interference." (See, for instance, *The Realm of Essence* [1927] and *The Realm of Matter* [1930], or the 1936 collection, *The Philosophy of Santayana*.) . . .

[See Tolkien, "Leaf by Niggle" in *Tree and Leaf,* which Ryan summarizes here, citing it as an exemplum of Tolkien's theories of what a fairy story should be.]

"Leaf by Niggle" is, more than anything else Tolkien wrote, an allegory of his own and the artist's creative exercise on earth, of its function in helping him and others . . . on the spiritual journey towards the higher state represented by the Mountains.[25] The early part of the story, like the curious epilogue with its conversation between unimaginative, practical men in civil authority on the subject of Niggle's life, presents the conflict between those who are of the spirit, represented on earth by imagination, and those who are not. The man of creative intellect is often bothered by what appear to be extraneous influences which retard his attempts to realize his vision.

In terms of the story, even as the (potential) artist has responsibilities toward his fellows, so the practical man of affairs needs to have sympathy toward his imaginative brother, without whose help he will never leave the Workhouse[26] [of this grim world], let alone see the Forest [the trees of tale], or be introduced to the Mountains [the world of the spirit, Faërie].

The story is also important in showing that Tolkien at this time was actively engaged in putting his ideas into allegorical form. The critic is the safer in the assumption that he might have been doing the same in *The Lord of the Rings,* particularly in the challenge which the imagination poses to the plain everyday existence of the hobbits. . . .

The story, more than the essay, is an exploration of the difference between the states of life lived prosaically, life with imagination, and life after death, for, by an intensification of some aspects of earthly life, the individual is translated to a different plane. While for "Leaf" "one of its sources was a great-limbed poplar tree that . . . was suddenly lopped and mutilated by its owner," this has surely been transmuted into the "Tree of Tales" which every man of vision can glimpse, even if it is not in his earthly power to give actuality to the leaf which is the testimony to the value of the seed planted in the most arid soil, the soul of "a very ordinary little man."

VERLYN FLIEGER

Frodo and Aragorn: The Concept of the Hero

Because of her broad knowledge and rich understanding of medieval literature, Verlyn Flieger does not assign The Lord of the Rings *to a particular genre — fairy tale, epic, or romance — but rather speaks of the "soup" of story from which it emerges, which has been simmering since human beings first told tales. She argues that the motifs that recur in all mythologies — the hero, the quest, the . . . monstrous force of evil — whenever they are used put the reader in touch with what is timeless. The word hoard of Northern myth upon which Tolkien drew provides two traditional kinds of hero: the extraordinary man whose mighty deeds give epic sweep to great events (Aragorn) and the common man whose trials lend to his actions a poignancy that draws the reader into the text to experience events with him (Frodo). Aragorn is the epic/romance hero — a leader, warrior, lover, healer-king; we admire him. Frodo is the little man of fairy tale, the youngest, weakest, unexpectedly valiant little brother, who doubts, fears, and makes mistakes; we recognize ourselves in him. Each of the heroes throws the other into relief. Each undertakes a dangerous journey and undergoes terrible ordeals. The epic hero is in quest of a kingdom and a princess, and he wins both. The fairy-tale hero is an ordinary man on a most unusual quest. He goes not to win but to lose: to throw away the Ring of Power and to lose all that he holds dear. The two motifs cross and recross, each enriching the other. The balance between the two heroes, Aragorn and Frodo — each carrying a rich medieval heritage, one expressing the passing of the old, the other the emergence of the new — widens and deepens the meaning of Tolkien's tale and lifts it into the timeless realm that W. B. Yeats called "the artifice of eternity."*

J.R.R. Tolkien once said that his typical response to the reading of a medieval work was the desire not so much to make a critical or philological study of it as to write a modern work in the same tradition. In *The Lord of the Rings* he has done exactly that. The book is a modern work, but in style and content it is certainly in the medieval tradition.[1] I do not propose to assign *The Lord of the Rings* to a particular genre, such as fairy tale, epic, or romance. The book quite clearly derives from all three, and to see it as belonging only to one category is to miss the essential elements it shares with the others. More to the point is the way in which Tolkien has used these elements.

What precisely is the appeal of a modern work in a medieval tradition? What is the value of such a book to the common reader? Why not offer him a bona fide medieval work, *Beowulf* or *Sir Gawain and the Green Knight,* and leave the twentieth century to the modern novel? An answer may be found in Tolkien's essay "On Fairy-Stories." Borrowing a term from G. W. Dasent, Tolkien speaks in this essay of the "soup" of story,[2] that rich mixture which has been simmering since man first told tales, from which stories have been ladled out to nourish the imagination in every age, including our own. Although the soup is a blend of many morsels, certain elements, certain flavors, stand out and evoke immediate response. These are the basics, the raw stuff of myth out of which folktale, fairy tale, epic, and romance are fashioned. They are the motifs which recur in all mythologies and which tale-tellers have used time out of mind — the hero, the quest, the struggle with monstrous forces of evil, the ordeal and its outcome. They recur because they work, because they move the reader and put him in touch with what is timeless. A modern use of these motifs reaffirms their value as a vital part of literature in an age when only scholars and children (and too few of those) read the story of King Arthur, or of Jack the Giant-Killer, or the adventures of Sigurd dragon-slayer.

The conventional medieval story, whether epic, romance, fairy tale, or some combination of these, most often focuses on one figure — the hero of the tale. If it is romance or epic the hero will be of great stature, a larger-than-life Beowulf, or Galahad, or Arthur, or Sigurd. If it is a fairy tale he may be a common man like ourselves, the unlikely hero who stumbles into heroic adventure and does the best he can — Jack, who trades a cow for beans, or the miller's youngest son who inherits only Puss-in-Boots. Larger-than-life heroes are rare in twentieth-century literature; they do not fit comfortably in an age which seems preoccupied with the ordinary. But the little man is always with us, as alive in the films of Chaplin as he is in Chaucer.

In *The Lord of the Rings* Tolkien has written a medieval story and given it both kinds of hero, the extraordinary man to give the epic sweep of great events, and the common man who has the immediate, poignant appeal of someone with whom the reader can identify.

Aragorn is a traditional epic/romance hero, larger than life, a leader, fighter, lover, healer. He is an extraordinary hero who combines Northrop Frye's romance and high mimetic modes. He is above the common herd. We expect him to be equal to any situation. We are not like him, and we know it. We admire him, but we do not identify with him.

Frodo, on the other hand, is a fairy-tale hero. He is a little man both literally and figuratively, and we recognize ourselves in him. He is utterly ordinary, and this is his great value. He has the characteristics also of Frye's low mimetic hero, the hero of realistic fiction. He has doubts, feels fear, falters, makes mistakes; he experiences, in short, the same emotions we experience. He is a low mimetic hero thrown by circumstances not of his making into high mimetic action. The ways in which he deals with that action — coping with burdens that are too great, events that move too swiftly, trials that are too terrible — draw the reader into the narrative, so that he lives it with Frodo as he never could with Aragorn.

A look at the two side by side shows that each throws the other into greater relief, providing contrast and enriching and expanding the dimensions of the story. Having provided his book with an essentially epic hero and an essentially fairy-tale hero, Tolkien combines, and sometimes crosses, the characteristic motifs of each. Each hero has an extraordinary beginning. Each undertakes a dangerous quest and undergoes ordeals. But the parallels serve to heighten the contrast between the two. Aragorn's is a true quest to win a kingdom and a princess. Frodo's is rather an anti-quest. He goes not to win something but to throw something away, and in the process to lose all that he holds dear. In simplest terms, Aragorn's is a journey from darkness into light, while Frodo's is a journey from light into darkness — and out again. Aragorn derives from the pattern of the youthful hero, while Frodo has the characteristics of the hero come to the end of his adventures. Tolkien gives Aragorn the fairy-tale happy ending — the princess and the kingdom. To Frodo come defeat and disillusionment — the stark, bitter ending typical of the *Iliad*, *Beowulf*, the *Morte Darthur*.

This crossing of motifs is not uniform, since Tolkien allows each hero enough of his typical characteristics to be recognizable. The motifs do cross, however, at crucial points in the narrative and at psychologically important moments in the unfolding of each character. I hope to show that this crossing of motifs adds an appeal which few modern readers find in conventional medieval literature, and that by exalting and refining the figure of the common man, Tolkien succeeds in giving new values to a medieval story.

Let us begin, however, with Aragorn, the larger-than-life hero. William Ready calls him "almost too good to be human," implying that his goodness somehow impairs his believability.[3] The fact is that

many readers lack the background to recognize an Aragorn. Strider
— silent, watchful, road weary — is an attractive figure. His steely
presence, his air of being someone dangerous to cross, his resource-
fulness in crisis, evoke a character out of the mythic American West
— the stranger in town — cool, alert, alone. He has that quiet tough-
ness we associate with our folk heroes. But in the transition from
Strider to Aragorn much of that folk-hero quality is lost, and with it
his hold on our imagination. Paradoxically, the more we know him,
the less familiar he becomes.

He is in truth the traditional disguised hero, the rightful king, in
medieval romance terms the "fair unknown" who steps from the
shadows into the limelight when his moment comes. He is in the tradition of the young Beowulf, the young Galahad, the boy Arthur,
all the heroes whose early years are spent in obscurity but who are
destined for greatness and whose birth or origin foreshadows that
destiny.

A few examples will clarify the point. The medieval account of
the hero frequently includes his *compert*, or conception. The conception episode almost always involves some element of magic or the supernatural. Precedent for this comes from classical myth, where the
hero usually has one human and one divine or semidivine parent.
Achilles, Heracles, Theseus, and even so demonstrably real a figure as
Alexander the Great have divine heritage.

The best-known story of the hero's *compert* is undoubtedly that
of Arthur in Malory's retelling of the Arthurian legend, wherein Merlin by his magic gives King Uther access to Igraine's bed. From this
meeting Arthur is conceived. Thus the supernatural plays a part in
Arthur's conception, even though both his parents are mortal. The
conception of Galahad, later in the same book, is a parallel. The sorceress Brusen contrives to enchant Lancelot and bring him to the bed
of King Pelles's daughter, Elaine, in the belief that she is Guenevere.
Here again immortal ancestry is replaced by the use of magic in the
conception of the hero. We find the same convention in Celtic and

Scandinavian myth. The Irish hero Cuchulainn was fathered on a mortal woman by the god Lugh. The Norse heroes Sigmund and Sigurd were descended from the god Odin. And on a more mundane level, the genealogies of kings in the Anglo-Saxon Chronicle begin with Woden, the Germanic counterpart of Odin.

We will look in vain for any similar episode in Tolkien's account of Aragorn. No god's intervention, no magic, enchantment, or supernatural events are to be found. But Aragorn has immortal ancestry. It is not immediate, as in the medieval narratives, but must be traced back through many generations to an early union of elves and men. In appendix A at the end of the trilogy, titled "Annals of the Kings and Rulers," Tolkien makes the following statement: "There were three unions of the Eldar [elves] and the Edain [men]: Lúthien and Beren; Idril and Tuor; Aragorn and Arwen. By the last the long-sundered branches of the Half-elven were reunited and their line was restored" (III, 314). It is clear that Aragorn and Arwen each represent a branch of the half-elven. They are descended from two brothers, Elrond and Elros, grandsons of the aforementioned Idril, an elf, and Tuor, a man. Elrond, the father of Arwen, elected to remain with the elves. Elros chose to go with men, and became the first king of Nú-menor. His descendants, through many generations, were Elendil and Isildur, whose descendant and heir is Aragorn. In Tolkien's cosmology Aragorn's half-elven ancestry supplies him with the immortal or supernatural origin necessary to the hero figure.

The fact that Aragorn's immortal ancestry is played down — indeed one has to look for it in order to find it — is consonant with Tolkien's practice throughout the book of providing realistic bases for what in a true medieval narrative would be frankly supernatural, marvelous, or miraculous. His goal is the one he outlines in his essay "On Fairy-Stories," that is, "the realization . . . of imagined wonder."[4] By "realization" he means just what the word implies, *making real.* To make the wonderful as real as possible to his twentieth-century reader, Tolkien surrounds it with the ordinary. We meet Strider; he is gradually revealed as Aragorn, and his immortal ancestry is buried in supplemental records and appendixes so only after we believe him as a character are we allowed to make the heroic associations that enrich him and rank him with his predecessors in myth, epic, and romance.

Another element, almost a necessity in the medieval hero pattern, is obscurity until the right moment. Shadow provides contrast to light. Time after time we read in medieval stories of the hero whose origins are hidden, sometimes even from himself. He is buried in obscurity until the moment comes for him to step forward and announce himself by word or deed.

Often the obscurity of the hero is linked with his upbringing in a home not his own, in circumstances that train him for his future role but offer no recognition. Arthur is removed from his mother at birth by Merlin and brought up in the household of Sir Ector, ignorant, like everyone around him, of his royal lineage. The withdrawal of the sword from the anvil signals his emergence from obscurity and proclaims him as the rightful king.

Galahad, likewise, is raised in obscurity. Not until it is time for him to begin the Grail Quest is he introduced to Arthur's court. The event that announces his emergence as a hero is his withdrawal of the sword from the stone floating in the river below Camelot.

Germanic literature follows the same pattern. Sinfjotli, child of the incestuous union of Sigmund the Volsung and his sister Signy, is brought up by Sigmund in a secret woodland hideout until he is ready to avenge the slaying of his Volsung kin. Sinfjotli is fostered out to his own father, although both are ignorant of the relationship.

A hero who fits the pattern rather more loosely is Beowulf. He is not precisely raised in obscurity, but he is brought up in a home not his own, the court of his uncle Hygelac. We meet him first as a hero, and only after his killing of Grendel and Grendel's dam and his return in triumph to Hygelac's court do we learn of his unpromising beginnings.

Long was he lowly,
so that the sons of the Geats   accounted him
    not excellent
nor wished the lord of the Wederas   to give
    him title to much
on the mead-bench.   They deemed him slothful,
high-born but unbold.[5]

In accordance with the established pattern, Aragorn comes from obscurity to recognition. Strider the Ranger is looked on with suspicion by even so good-hearted a man as Butterbur, the innkeeper at Bree. His true identity is concealed from all but a few until the time comes for him to reveal himself. Humphrey Carpenter has pointed out that in the first draft of the scene in the common room of the Prancing Pony the mysterious stranger was not a man but a "queer-looking brown-faced hobbit,"[6] and his name was Trotter. I suggest that such a character could not develop into the kind of figure that Strider was eventually to become. A disguised hobbit-prince would not fit into Tolkien's world and would be utterly out of place among the middle-class Boffins, Bolgers, Tooks, Proudfoots, and even the Sackville-Bagginses. The change from hobbit to man materially alters the possibilities for the character. The change of name, too, seems to signal the development of a more serious tone to the story. "Trotter" is simply not a name that can be taken seriously. The animal associations are too strong; it smacks too much of beast fable. One thinks at best of horses, and at worst of pigs. Carpenter remarks that in writing the preliminary chapters "Tolkien was bending his tale away from the jolly style of *The Hobbit* towards something darker and grander, and closer in concept to *The Silmarillion*."[7] The alteration of the mysterious figure in the common room is certainly part of this change.

When he himself wrote of this first period of composition, Tolkien said, apropos of the scene at Bree, "I had then no more notion than [the hobbits] had of what had become of Gandalf, or who Strider was; and I had begun to despair of ever finding out."[8] This provocative statement invites comment. Paul Kocher suggests that we can find in it part of the reason why Aragorn is difficult for readers. He simply has not been prepared for. Daniel Hughes goes further and suggests that it is just here, when Tolkien discovers who Strider is and what can be done with him, that the story begins to develop its epic side.[9]

If we take Tolkien's statement at face value, we find him describing a situation not unfamiliar to writers: his narrative somehow got ahead of him. That unconscious process which often accompanies the conscious activity of the creative mind unexpectedly introduced new material. To be sure, this attitude suggests the traditional convention of authorial modesty: "I didn't write it; it wrote itself." But knowing as we do Tolkien's background in medieval literature, it seems reasonable to suppose that he did have a stockpile of literary raw material waiting to be used. We can perhaps credit his statement with a little less coyness and a little more honesty than is usual in such cases.

What seems to have happened in the creative process to translate Trotter into Strider and Strider into Aragorn is that Tolkien realized he had ready to his hand in this mysterious figure the makings of an authentic mythic hero, a medieval disguised prince. In the historical framework of Middle-earth, Aragorn is the lineal descendant of Elendil, founder of the kingdoms of Arnor and Gondor, and of Elendil's son Isildur, who took the Ring from Sauron after defeating him in the Second Age. Aragorn is therefore not only the rightful king of Gondor but the rightful owner of the Ring. True to epic convention, and also true to the circumstances of the world that Tolkien creates, his identity is concealed, with good reason. He is the son of Arathorn, a chieftain of the northern line of his house, killed when Aragorn is a child of two. Aragorn is then taken by his mother to Rivendell, where he is brought up in the House of Elrond with Elrond's two sons.

Aragorn is twenty years old before Elrond tells him his true identity and gives him the broken pieces of Elendil's sword, Narsil, to keep until they can be reforged.

The giving and receiving of the sword calls up another medieval motif — the hero and his weapon. They are inextricably linked, for the association of sword and hero is more than a medieval convention: it is a necessity in a literature which exalts heroism and deeds of arms. Beowulf may slay Grendel with his bare hands, but it takes a sword to kill Grendel's mother, a sword, moreover, of no ordinary kind — *"ealdsweord eotenisc"* — an ancient sword, made by giants.

Medieval literature is filled with swords as famous and formidable as those who wield them. Many who know no more of Arthur know of his sword, Excalibur, and those of other heroes are just as worthy of note. Beowulf's sword, Næglfar, breaks in his death struggle with the dragon. The dying Roland tries to break his sword, Durendal, so that none other shall ever use it. We have seen that for both Arthur and Galahad the withdrawing of a sword heralds the emergence of a hero.

The same motif occurs elsewhere. In the Norse *Volsungasaga* Sigmund the Volsung pulls from a tree the sword thrust into it by Odin, after others have tried and failed. He carries it for the rest of his life. It plays a curious role at the end of his adventures, when it is broken, apparently deliberately, by Odin in Sigmund's last battle. After the breaking of the sword the battle goes against Sigmund, and he is killed. The fates of sword and man are linked, and the destruction of one signals the end of the other. The fragments of Sigmund's sword are saved for his son Sigurd and reforged for the slaying of the dragon Fafnir. The reforging of the sword and the slaying of the dragon with it mark Sigurd's beginning as a hero.

Tolkien reworks this motif in fitting it to Aragorn. At the Council of Elrond, where the decision is made to take the Ring to Mordor, Aragorn stands before those assembled and makes his declaration:

He cast his sword upon the table that stood before Elrond, and the blade was in two pieces. "Here is the Sword that was Broken!" he said.

"And who are you, and what have you to do with Minas Tirith?" asked Boromir, looking in wonder at the lean face of the Ranger and his weather-stained cloak.

"He is Aragorn son of Arathorn," said Elrond; "and he is descended through many fathers from Isildur Elendil's son of Minas Ithil. He is the Chief of the Dúnedain in the North, and few are now left of that folk." (I, 259–60)

With the casting of the sword upon the table Aragorn publicly puts off Strider, assuming his rightful identity and all it implies. The sword proclaims the emergence of the hero. Arthur, Galahad, Sigmund, Sigurd all stand behind Aragorn in that moment. Tolkien is careful, however, to keep Aragorn separate from them, so that memories of the earlier heroes do not overpower his narrative. Avoiding, then, the too-familiar motif of the pulling out of the sword, Tolkien uses instead the broken sword that is to be reforged. Defined strictly, Aragorn is closer to Arthur or Sigmund than to Sigurd, since he is a king, not a dragon-slayer. The unexpected combination of king-hero with dragon-slayer's sword motif allows Aragorn to stand as a hero in his own right, in his own narrative. We remember other heroes, and other swords, but we add a new figure to the line.

What gives Aragorn his most clear-cut romance characteristics is the part of the story that treats his love for Arwen. The tradition of romantic love, which requires the knight to endure hardships and perform great deeds for the love of a lady, is necessary to the characterization of Aragorn, for all that it is subordinate to the epic side of the narrative and remains very much in the background.

As with his treatment of Aragorn's lineage, Tolkien buries much of the material relating to Aragorn and Arwen in his appendixes, where the reader, if he looks, will find the "Tale of Aragorn and Arwen." A few scattered references in the story proper relate them as romantic lovers; most of them do not even mention Arwen by name. The clearest is, perhaps, a sly remark by Bilbo at Rivendell, noting Aragorn's absence from the feast, since "the Lady Arwen was there" (I, 245).

The romance element is secondary to the epic struggle — the sweep of battle and great deeds. We know that Aragorn is grimly engaged in winning his kingdom, but we know almost nothing of his love for the half-elven princess for whom he wins it, nor do we realize until it is all over that in winning the kingdom he is also winning Arwen, and that one was a condition for the other. Nonetheless a full understanding of Aragorn as a medieval hero must encompass knowledge of his love story as well as of his epic characteristics. Aragorn's is not simply a political or national or even a personal epic trial. It is also a trial of love, and in the light of the love story, which we come to know only at the end, the struggle and the battles take on a more specific and personal meaning. The love story, too, is the perfect vehicle for the fairy-tale happy ending, almost Elizabethan in its rounding off of the story with celebrations and marriages, of which Aragorn's and Arwen's is the chief.

The romance element is manifest, too, in Aragorn's capacity to heal and to renew. It has been plain from the beginning of the story that Aragorn is a healer, for his skill and knowledge of herb lore pull Frodo through in the first hours after he is wounded at Weathertop. But at that point Aragorn is still Strider to the reader, and his ability to heal could well appear as practical knowledge of the road gained as a Ranger. Only much later, when he has healed Éowyn and Faramir and Merry, when the old wife Ioreth has told everyone who will listen that "*the hands of the king are the hands of a healer*" (III, 136), does the reader recognize that Aragorn as healer and as king is what he has always been.

The concept of the king as healer derives from the early Celtic principle of sacral kingship, whereby the health and fertility of the land are dependent on the coming of the rightful king. Where there is no king, or where the king is infirm, the land also will be barren. This idea is most explicit in the Grail legend, with its association of the Waste Land with the Maimed King whose wound, sometimes specifically located in the thighs, is a wounding of virility extending from him to his kingdom. The Maimed King in the Grail stories is counterposed to the Healing King, the Grail Knight. In Malory's Arthurian story this is Galahad, whose healing of the Maimed King restores the land to fruitfulness. Tolkien makes full use of both these figures as the wasted lands of Middle-earth are restored to fruitfulness; Aragorn's is the positive role of healer and renewer, whose presence works to restore the land. Frodo, as I will subsequently show, becomes a kind of Maimed King figure, without whose sacrifice the efforts of the Healing King would be in vain.

All of the positive, glad-hearted, youthful elements of myth, epic, and romance cluster around the man we meet as Strider, whom we come to know as Aragorn. He is the recognized, acclaimed victor in the battle against evil, the king coming into his kingdom. He is warrior, lover, healer, renewer, a hero worthy of the heroic aspects of *The Lord of the Rings*, whose presence in the story at once contributes to, and justifies, those aspects.

Frodo is quite another thing. He is no Aragorn, no obscure hero awaiting his chance to be great. He is no warrior. And far from feeling destined for greatness, he reacts to being thrust into epic events with the cry of the common man — "Why me?" He knows, or thinks he knows, his own limitations and tells Gandalf, "I am not made for perilous quests" (I, 70). He accepts an intolerable burden not from any sense that he is the proper one to bear it but simply because no one else volunteers. It is worth noting, by the way, that another "little man" — Bilbo — does volunteer, and is gently refused. The heroic figures all hang back, and the common man shoulders the burden. The point is voiced in the narrative by Elrond, who says: "Yet such is oft the course of deeds that move the wheels of the world: small hands do them because they must, while the eyes of the great are elsewhere" (I, 283). This is almost a paraphrase of something Tolkien himself once said, recorded by Carpenter: "The hobbits represent the combination of small imagination with great courage which (as Tolkien had seen in the trenches during the First World War) often led to survival against all chances. 'I've always been impressed,' he once said, 'that we are here, surviving, because of the indomitable courage of quite small people against impossible odds.'"[10]

Yet in spite of this surface appearance, Frodo like Aragorn embodies mythic and heroic elements which supply much of the strength of Tolkien's story. And there stretches behind Frodo too a long line of mythic figures. He is linked unmistakably to the dying Arthur, the dying Beowulf, the semimythical Scyld Scefing of the opening lines of *Beowulf*, and the highly symbolic figure of the Maimed King. Frodo becomes more than himself, but it is Tolkien's great gift that in enlarging Frodo he keeps him consistent with his beginnings. Frodo is changed, but he is yet the same. That which is universal and symbolic is filtered through the particular and literal. Frodo evokes the greater figures who stand behind him, but he is not engulfed by them. He remains Frodo. In putting their burdens on his shoulders Tolkien has succeeded in synthesizing the medieval and the modern, creating a character who conforms to mythic patterns and yet evokes the identification and empathy which the modern reader has come to expect from fiction.

Frodo's beginnings are plain enough. He is the only son of a middle-class hobbit couple, in no way unusual except for the manner of their death — drowning in a boating accident. But this is important, since Tolkien emphasizes the fact that hobbits are as a rule shy of boats and the water. They are inland people, hole-builders, earth-dwellers. "Most Hobbits regarded even rivers and small boats with deep misgivings, and not many of them could swim" (I, 16). The drowning of Frodo's parents is the key to one of his mythic functions, for it is thematically important that Frodo should be orphaned, and that his coming to Hobbiton be somehow associated with water.

An outstanding figure in the mythologies of the world is the child of mysterious or unknown origin who arrives, sometimes in a boat, but always associated in some way with water, and who brings with him extraordinary benefits. Perhaps the figure of this type most familiar to the Western reader is the child Moses. But to connect the mysterious child figure with Tolkien's story we need go back no further than northern European myth and literature.

The opening lines of *Beowulf* tell of Scyld Scefing, the eponymous founder of the Scyldings, Hrothgar's line, who led his people to victory in battle and brought them unparalleled prosperity. He arrived as an unknown child from the sea, and the poem describes the elaborate ship burial that sends him back over the water. Scyld is one avatar of a fertility figure ubiquitous in northern mythology who appears under various names — Scyld, Sceaf, Ing, Freyr, Frodi. They all have the same value as bringers of peace and fertility, and they are more or less connected — some remotely, some, like Scyld, specifically — with water, with death, and with ships and funeral ceremonies.

Frodo's association with the mysterious or orphan child motif is evident, and the linking of that motif with Scyld and Frodi as fertility figures suggests that Tolkien wished to invest Frodo with the mythic significance of a bringer of peace, prosperity, and fruitfulness. The name Frodo, a variant of Frodi, is surely no accident, no random choice to fit a furry-footed hobbit, but one consciously chosen to state a connection Tolkien wished to make. Carpenter's biography of Tolkien reveals that Frodo's name was originally Bingo, but Tolkien, as he wrote, grew more and more dissatisfied with that name, and with good reason. Aside from its more frivolous associations, it is phonetically too close to Bilbo. The name remained Bingo, however, until Tolkien found his story turning increasingly away from *The Hobbit* and in the direction of the older and darker subject matter of *The Silmarillion*. At that point he changed his hero's name to Frodo.

Frodo, the orphan associated with water, brings peace, prosperity, and fruitfulness to the Shire, though he himself can no longer benefit from them. In the end he is committed again to the water, and like Scyld, is sent over the waves to an unknown bourne. Frodo, like Aragorn, like Arthur, Galahad, Beowulf, is brought up in a home not his own, Bilbo's home. And here another medieval motif enters, for Frodo is Bilbo's nephew. The relationship of uncle and nephew, specifically uncle and sister's son, is prominent in medieval narrative from *Beowulf* to Malory. Jessie Weston calls it "a relationship obviously required by tradition" and cites uncle-nephew pairs in both early and late medieval epic and romance.[11] Her list includes Cuchulainn and Conchobar, Diarmid and Finn, Tristan and Mark, Roland and Charlemagne, and Gawain and Arthur. To these we might add Mordred and Arthur, Sinfjotli and Sigmund (these last two are incestuous, being son and father as well), and Beowulf and Hygelac. What all these pairs have in common is that some action initiated by the uncle is brought to its conclusion, whether for good or ill, by the nephew. In any case, the relationship is a well-established and well-recognized literary motif. We may be sure that Tolkien is giving us important information when he makes Frodo Bilbo's nephew.

The information is given obliquely, however, for, as with Aragorn, Tolkien avoids a one-to-one correlation between Frodo and earlier medieval heroes. Rather he awakens echoes of the earlier stories which will enrich his own narrative without defining it too narrowly. Thus he does not introduce Frodo into the story as a nephew but as a cousin, and he employs a comic figure — the Gaffer — to explain the relationship. "Mr. Drogo, he married poor Miss Primula Brandybuck. She was our Mr. Bilbo's first cousin on the mother's side (her mother being the youngest of the Old Took's daughter's); and Mr. Drogo was his second cousin. So Mr. Frodo is his [Bilbo's] first *and* second cousin, once removed either way, as the saying is, if you follow me" (I, 31). It is noteworthy that Frodo's mother is closest to Bilbo, being his first cousin, while Drogo is his second cousin. The female side is stressed, and the sister's son relationship is thus obliquely alluded to.

A more specific linking of Frodo with Bilbo is given in the Prologue, where Frodo is plainly called Bilbo's "favourite 'nephew'" (I, 20). What is clear, then, is that Tolkien is adding something important to his story by so carefully underlining the relationship. Action initiated earlier by Bilbo — the finding of the Ring — will be completed by Frodo, who accepts the responsibility of throwing it away. This is the thematic basis for Elrond's gentle rejection of Bilbo's offer to carry the Ring to Mordor. The task has passed from uncle to nephew. Bilbo cannot complete the action. It is Frodo in the role of nephew who must carry it to an end.

Early in the narrative Frodo joins forces with Strider, who is all that Frodo appears not to be — big, tough, experienced, a fighter and a doer, where Frodo is small, sheltered, and unaccustomed to adventure. Beneath this surface disparity, however, Tolkien links his heroes by providing each with a variant of the same epic motif. We have already noted Tolkien's restructuring of the medieval sword motif to enrich the figure of Aragorn and give him epic associations. Similar epic associations are given to Frodo as well, but they are scaled down to hobbit dimensions and pass all but unnoticed in the narrative.

As the Fellowship prepares to leave Rivendell with the Ring there is a homely farewell scene between Bilbo and Frodo:

> On the morning of the last day Frodo was alone with Bilbo, and the old hobbit pulled out from under his bed a wooden box. He lifted the lid and fumbled inside.
>
> "Here is your sword," he said. "But it was broken, you know. I took it to keep it safe but I've forgotten to ask if the smiths could mend it. No time now. So I thought, perhaps, you would care to have this, don't you know?"
>
> He took from the box a small sword in an old shabby leathern scabbard. Then he drew it, and its polished and well-tended blade glittered suddenly, cold and bright. "This is Sting," he said, and thrust it with little effort deep into a wooden beam. "Take it, if you like. I shan't want it again, I expect."
>
> Frodo accepted it gratefully. (I, 290)

More important than the sword itself is the manner of its giving. Bilbo thrusts it into a wooden beam, repeating in unobtrusive fashion Odin's thrusting of the sword into the tree for Sigmund. Frodo "accepts" it. Tolkien does not say how. But to take it he must pull it out of the beam in a repetition of Sigmund's withdrawal of his sword from the tree, Arthur's taking of the sword from the anvil, and Galahad's withdrawal of his sword from the stone floating in the river.

A mythic pattern underlies the giving and receiving of the sword, but it has been displaced and fragmented in *The Lord of the Rings*. What in the *Volsungasaga* was one sword, broken with Sigmund and reforged for Sigurd, is here two swords, and the order of events is reversed. Frodo's old sword is broken and is replaced by Sting. Sting is thrust into the beam by Bilbo and withdrawn by Frodo. The tone here is anything but epic. Instead of a supernatural event we have a quiet conversation between old friends. The speech is familiar and colloquial — "don't you know," "if you like," "I expect." The sword is small, the scabbard shabby. Bilbo fumbles in bringing it out. The gesture of thrusting it into the wooden beam is almost thrown away. The whole character of the scene is touching rather than heroic.

The surface structure of this scene makes it clear that the torch has passed. Bilbo's part in the story of the Ring is over; Ring and sword have been handed on to his nephew, who must undertake the quest. The underlying mythic pattern — the sword and the method of its transfer — aligns Frodo with his epic forebears, and with Aragorn as well.

Tolkien brings his two heroes together almost, it would seem, in order to have them part. Having established each clearly, and put them side by side, he then sends them in opposite directions — Aragorn west, expanding the scope and epic action of the story, Frodo east, intensifying our focus on the perilous nature of his quest and its effect on him. The journey into Mordor is, of course, Frodo's final test, the ultimate ordeal through which he must pass to his eventual apotheosis. For it is on the journey to Mordor and in the final moments at the Cracks of Doom that the crucial event in the medieval hero story, the confrontation and struggle with the monstrous foe, embodiment of all the forces of darkness, takes place.

To see this clearly we must first look at the thesis of Tolkien's landmark essay "*Beowulf:* The Monsters and the Critics." It is undoubtedly his best-known scholarly work. It is one of the few and certainly one of the first critical essays that value *Beowulf* as a poem rather than as a historical, or philological, or sociocultural artifact. *Beowulf,* says Tolkien, is a poem about a man fighting with monsters — a manlike monster, Grendel, who preys on men and eats them, and a dragon who guards a hoard of gold. As such, the poem reflects the northern imagination, whose vision is of "man at war with the hostile world, and his inevitable overthrow in Time." The monsters are all the forces of darkness against which men have always struggled, and by which they are always defeated. The poet's phrase "heroes under heaven" or "mighty men upon earth" evokes for Tolkien "*eormengrund,* the great earth, ringed with *garsecg,* the shoreless sea, beneath the sky's inaccessible roof; whereon, as in a little circle of light about their halls, men with courage as their stay went forward to that battle with the hostile world and the offspring of the dark which ends for all, even the kings and champions, in defeat."[12]

Clearly, for Tolkien, the monster figure is at the heart of the matter. And, important as it is, we would expect to find that he had placed such a figure at the heart of *The Lord of the Rings.* As a story in the medieval tradition, it should depend for its force as much on the monster as on the hero. And where is there a monster who confronts and battles with the hero? There are monstrous beings, to be sure, but in no case do they directly do battle with either hero. Aragorn fights orcs, but not in single combat, and only as part of a larger battle. Sam fights Shelob; Gandalf fights the Balrog. The greatest evil is Sauron, the Enemy, the Dark Lord for whom all the forces of darkness work. But he is never seen. Aragorn and Gandalf do contend with him, but at a distance and indirectly. Furthermore, while he is all evil, he is not concrete enough to fit Tolkien's criteria for monsters. For him they must be "mortal denizens of the material world, in it and of it."[13]

I suggest that Tolkien's central monster-figure is so natural a part of the material world that he goes largely unrecognized as such. He is Gollum, the twisted, broken, outcast hobbit whose manlike shape and dragonlike greed combine both the *Beowulf* kinds of monster in one figure.

To see Gollum as a manlike monster we must first accept his relationship to humanity. Tolkien makes it plain that Gollum is some kind of hobbit, "akin," says Gandalf, "to the fathers of the fathers of the Stoors." He goes on: "Even Bilbo's story suggests their kinship. There was a great deal in the background of their minds and memories that was very similar. They understood one another remarkably well, very much better than a hobbit would understand, say, a Dwarf, or an Orc, or even an Elf. Think of the riddles they both knew, for one thing." And though warped and grotesque, Gollum is not yet entirely lost to humanity:

> "There was a little corner of his mind that was still his own, and light came through it, as through a chink in the dark: light out of the past. It was actually pleasant, I think, to hear a kindly voice again, bringing up memories of wind, and trees, and sun on the grass, and such forgotten things.
>
> "But that, of course, would only make the evil part of him angrier in the end." (I, 62–64)

There we have him, of hobbit kind, murderer, outcast, maddened by reminders of joys he cannot share. He is even cannibalistic, for we learn in *The Hobbit* that he eats goblins when he can't get fish, and would have eaten hobbit if he had defeated Bilbo in the riddle game. The parallel with Grendel, the man-eating monster of *Beowulf,* is unmistakable. Grendel is outcast, a wanderer in the waste, of the race of Cain, the first murderer, and he cannot bear the sound of the harp and the song of creation.

Gollum's dragon features are not so apparent. His most obvious characteristic is greed for a treasure. Dragons are traditionally associated with hoards of gold, whereas Gollum wants only the one Ring, but the difference is quantitative, not qualitative. The most famous dragon in northern literature, Fafnir, transformed himself from man to dragon so he could guard his gold, of which the crucial portion was a ring. So Gollum, once a hobbit, has been transformed by his desire for the Ring into a creeping thing. His name, Sméagol, is related to a number of Anglo-Saxon words meaning "to creep," "to crawl," words used to describe dragons. His very word for the Ring, "precious," is an Anglo-Saxon word glossed by Klaeber in his edition of *Beowulf* as *maðum*. It is a word used in *Beowulf* for treasure, and specifically to refer to the dragon's hoard.

Gollum is a combination, then, of manlike and dragonlike monster. But a monster figure must be defined not just by what he is but by what he does. The function of the monster in medieval narrative is to oppose the hero, to body forth tangibly the evil to be overcome, to be the force against which the hero's strength and courage are tested.

It is typical of what I call Tolkien's modern medievalism that having given his story a monster in the person of Gollum, he chooses for the monster's opponent not the epic hero Aragorn but Frodo, the little man who feels he is not a hero and does not want to be one.

The battle between them is central to a reading of *The Lord of the Rings* as a modern work in the medieval tradition. For the battle is psychological, not physical, and the battleground is Frodo himself. To explicate this we must look carefully at the special relationship of Frodo and Gollum. As early as 1957 Douglass Parker called Gollum "Frodo's corrupted counterpart." Rose Zimbardo called him Frodo's "dark counterpart." George Thomson put the relationship in perspective: "It is a well-known fact of the romance tradition that because the principal characters are simple types, the complexities of human nature must be projected into the external world. The disruptive forces of darkness and inner conflict must be represented by persons or objects outside the heroic characters." Thus, Gollum as

Frodo's "double in darkness is more than a potentiality of his own nature. His double is truly his, an actual and developing darkness in his own character."[14]

Fiction abounds in dualities of this kind. Dr. Jekyll and Mr. Hyde, Victor Frankenstein and his monster, Poe's William Wilson and his double are all examples of what psychology calls the "self" and the "other," that is, the overt personality and its opposite, the light and dark sides of one's nature. Jung calls this other side of mankind the "shadow" as contrasted with the overt and recognized "ego." Often this duality is presented as two aspects of one nature, as with David Lindsay's Maskull and Nightspore, or as E. M. Forster suggests may be the case with Virginia Woolf's life-loving Mrs. Dalloway and the young suicide Septimus Smith.

Frodo and Gollum can fit the same pattern, Frodo as the self, Gollum as the other. Frodo is the overt, recognized character. Gollum is his dark side, the embodiment of his growing, overpowering desire for the Ring, the desire which at last becomes all-consuming and sweeps away (if only for a moment) the Frodo who has endured so much to destroy the Ring. Gollum represents precisely that "disruptive force of darkness and inner conflict" which Thomson says must be shown to the reader outside the heroic character. Gollum is what Frodo must fight within himself as the Ring increases its hold.

I do not mean to present Gollum as an allegorical personification. He is not simply an abstract quality or a projection of a state of mind. Any careful reader of *The Lord of the Rings* knows that Tolkien detested allegory, and to impose it on his book is to do violence to his intention. Gollum is a fully realized character in his own right, with a considerable part to play in the story. But he can suggest these other things as well.

Today's reader of a modern narrative, however medieval its spirit, may be reluctant to accept a truly medieval monster — a dragon or a fiend — but he is accustomed to accepting internal conflict, man warring with himself, for that is what much of modern fiction deals with. Frodo monster-queller might not be credible. But

Frodo tortured by growing evil in his own nature, fighting his great battle not against darkness without but against darkness within, is believable and compelling. In fighting those dark elements within himself which Gollum externalizes, Frodo fights the most insidious and powerful monster of all — and loses. Tolkien's picture of the battle, although not literal, is very much in the spirit of the northern imagination he describes in the *Beowulf* essay. It is that battle against "the offspring of the dark which ends for all, even the kings and champions, in defeat."

In the final moment, standing at the Cracks of Doom, Frodo succumbs to the darkness within him. He puts the Ring on his finger, claimed by it even as he claims it. The end is inevitable. For man always loses to the monster at last. Frodo is defeated just as surely as Beowulf is.

It is characteristic of Tolkien, however, that he does not end on this note. Frodo loses, but in losing he wins a greater victory. The climax is designed to show that just as surely as Frodo's action is inevitable, so is Gollum's. Frodo will put on the Ring, and Gollum will be driven to seize it. In so doing he saves Frodo and destroys the Ring. Frodo's dark side, externalized as Gollum, destroys the actual dark within him, and the maddened Gollum, exulting in possession, falls with the Ring into the fire. Evil destroys itself.

Although Frodo recovers from the battle, he can no longer be what he was. He is wounded by sword, sting, and tooth, and cannot find healing. He now evokes the Maimed King of the Grail legend. The loss of his finger, seen by some critics as symbolic castration, could legitimately be interpreted as a version of the archetypal fertility wound of the Maimed King. Frodo is maimed, his loss of the Ring makes possible the renewal of the land, and, as in many versions of the Grail story, he is associated with and finally committed to water. His departure from Middle-earth to be healed of his wounds unmistakably evokes yet another wounded figure, the wounded Arthur, and his departure by ship to be healed of his wounds. It rounds off the association of Frodo with the mysterious child, with Scyld Scefing, and with those fertility figures mentioned earlier, who bring prosperity and peace.

The fairy-tale hero, inconspicuous and unassuming, has been made to suffer the bitterness and loss of the medieval epic hero. Like Beowulf, like Arthur, he loses the last battle and pays a heavy price for his struggle. Such an end is dreadfully inappropriate. If he is not given half the kingdom and the princess's hand in marriage he ought at least to be able to live happily ever after. He should get some recognition, some recompense. It is not fair.

And that, of course, is just Tolkien's point. It is not meant to be fair. We are beyond the epic now, beyond romance and beyond the fairy-tale ending. In the real world things seldom turn out as we would like them to, and the little man is as subject to tragedy as the great one. For Beowulf to die, for Arthur to lose Camelot, these are, in their way, great endings to great lives. They come at the end of brave days and brave deeds. Their stories end not happily but fittingly, and that is as it should be. To take the epic ending and give it to the fairy-tale hero is to reveal new values in the old pattern. The sacrifice is all the greater for being made by one so small.

But the story must have Aragorn to give it point. Without the two heroes much of the impact would be lost. Frodo is the passing of the old, Aragorn the emergence of the new. Both happen at the same time, and each because of the other.

Tolkien read *Beowulf* as a poem of balance, the opposition of ends and beginnings. He says of it: "In its simplest terms it is a contrasted description of two moments in a great life, rising and setting; an elaboration of the ancient and intensely moving contrast between youth and age, first achievement and final death."[15] He has built these same values, this same balance and opposition, into *The Lord of the Rings* in a synchronous rather than sequential pattern. By giving us both Aragorn and Frodo he has used the contrast between them to widen and deepen the meaning of his story.

PAUL KOCHER

Middle-earth:
An Imaginary World?

*In this essay Kocher discusses the means by which Tolkien makes the
fantasy world of* The Lord of the Rings *credible and thereby able to
command the "Secondary Belief" of the reader. Among the many devices the author uses is the common fiction of the writer's posing as a
modern scholar, translating, compiling, and editing a manuscript from
the ancient past. To lend weight to the fictional "records," Tolkien creates
elaborate histories and mythological pasts for the inhabitants of Middle-
earth as well as for their languages. He invents a geography that relates
Middle-earth to England as it might have been eons ago, and provides
maps further to delineate it. The locales of Middle-earth often bear close
resemblance to places in ancient Celtic and Norse mythologies. The
Lands of the Guardian Valar, for instance, are quite similar to the
Blessed Lands Saint Brendan encountered in his voyages. Kocher clearly
shows that the appendixes to* The Lord of the Rings *are by no means
vestigial but rather so orient their topics as to become facets of the cultural histories of all the races in the book. Middle-earth, then, is our own
earth as it was in the minds of dreamers long ago in the deep abyss of
time.*

In 1938 when Tolkien was first beginning to write *The Lord of the
Rings* he also delivered a lecture at the University of Saint Andrews in

which he offered his views on the types of world that it is the office of fantasy, including his own epic, to "sub-create," as he calls it. Unlike our primary world of daily fact, fantasy's "Secondary Worlds" of the imagination must possess, he said, not only "internal consistency" but also "strangeness and wonder" arising from their "freedom from the domination of observed fact."[1] If this were all, the secondary worlds of faërie would often be connected only very tenuously with the primary world. But Tolkien knew, none better, that no audience can long feel sympathy or interest for persons or things in which they cannot recognize a good deal of themselves and the world of their everyday experience. He therefore added that a secondary world must be "credible, commanding Secondary Belief." And he manifestly expected that secondary worlds would combine the ordinary with the extraordinary, the fictitious with the actual: "Faërie contains many things besides elves and fays, and besides dwarfs, witches, trolls, giants or dragons: it holds the seas, the sun, the moon, the sky; and the earth and all things that are in it: tree and bird, water and stone, wine and bread, and ourselves, mortal men, when we are enchanted."[2]

Tolkien followed his own prescription in composing *The Lord of the Rings*, or perhaps he formulated the prescription to justify what he was already intending to write. In either case the answer to the question posed by the title of this chapter is "Yes, but —." Yes, Middle-earth is a place of many marvels. But they are all carefully fitted into a framework of climate and geography, familiar skies by night, familiar shrubs and trees, beasts and birds on earth by day, men and manlike creatures with societies not too different from our own. Consequently the reader walks through any Middle-earth landscape with a security of recognition that woos him on to believe in everything that happens. Familiar but not too familiar, strange but not too strange. This is the master rubric that Tolkien bears always in mind when inventing the world of his epic. In applying the formula in just the right proportions in the right situations consists much of his preeminence as a writer of fantasy.

Fundamental to Tolkien's method in *The Lord of the Rings* is a standard literary pose which he assumes in the prologue and never thereafter relinquishes even in the appendixes: that he did not himself invent the subject matter of the epic but is only a modern scholar who is compiling, editing, and eventually translating copies of very ancient records of Middle-earth which have come into his hands, he does not say how. To make this claim sound plausible he constructs an elaborate family tree for these records, tracing some back to personal narratives by the four hobbit heroes of the War of the Ring, others to manuscripts found in libraries at Rivendell and Minas Tirith, still others to oral tradition (I, 23–24). Then, in order to help give an air of credibility to his account of the war, Tolkien endorses it as true and calls it history, that is, an authentic narrative of events as they actually happened in the Third Age. This accolade of history and historical records he bestows frequently in both prologue and appendixes. With the Shire Calendar in the year 1601 of the Third Age, states the prologue, "legend among the Hobbits first becomes history with a reckoning of years" (I, 13). A few pages farther on, Bilbo's 111th birthday is said to have occurred in Shire year 1401: "At this point this History begins" (I, 23). And in appendix F Tolkien declares editorially, "The language represented in this history by English was the *Westron* or 'Common Speech' of the West-lands of Middle-earth in the Third Age."[3]

Many writers of fantasy would have stopped at this point. But Tolkien has a constitutional aversion to leaving Middle-earth afloat too insubstantially in empty time and place, or perhaps his literary instincts warn him that it needs a local habitation and a name. Consequently he takes the further crucial step of identifying it as our own green and solid Earth at some quite remote epoch in the past. He is able to accomplish this end most handily in the prologue and appendixes, where he can sometimes step out of the role of mere editor and translator into the broader character of commentator on the peoples and events in the manuscripts he is handling. And he does it usually by comparing conditions in the Third Age with what they have since become in our present.

About the hobbits, for instance, the prologue informs the reader that they are "relations of ours," closer than elves or dwarves, though the exact nature of this blood kinship is lost in the mists of time. We and they have somehow become "estranged" since the Third Age, and they have dwindled in physical size since then. Most striking, however, is the news that "those days, the Third Age of Middle-earth, are now long past, and the shape of all lands has been changed; but the regions in which Hobbits then lived were doubtless the same as those in which they still linger: the North-West of the Old World, east of the Sea" (I, 11).

There is much to digest here. The Middle-earth on which the hobbits lived is our Earth as it was long ago. Moreover, they are still here, and though they hide from us in their silent way, some of us have sometimes seen them and passed them on under other names into our folklore. Furthermore, the hobbits still live in the region they call the Shire, which turns out to be "the North-West of the Old World, east of the Sea." This description can only mean northwestern Europe, however much changed in topography by eons of wind and wave.

Of course, the maps of Europe in the Third Age drawn by Tolkien to illustrate his epic show a continent very different from that of today in its coastline, mountains, rivers, and other major geographical features. In explanation he points to the forces of erosion, which wear down mountains, and to advances and recessions of the sea that have inundated some lands and uncovered others. Singing of his ancestor Durin, Gimli voices dwarf tradition of a time when the earth was newly formed and fair, "the mountains tall" as yet unweathered, and the face of the moon as yet unstained by marks now visible on it (I, 329–30). Gandalf objects to casting the One Ring into the ocean because "there are many things in the deep waters; and seas and lands may change" (I, 280). Treebeard can remember his youth when he wandered over the countries of Tasarinan, Ossiriand, Neldoreth, and Dorthonion, "and now all those lands lie under the wave" (II, 72). At their parting Galadriel guesses at some far distant future when "the lands that lie under the wave are lifted up again," and she and Tree-beard may meet once more on the meadows of Tasarinan (III, 259). Bombadil recalls a distant past, "before the seas were bent" (I, 142). By many such references Tolkien achieves for Middle-earth long per-spectives backward and forward in geological time.

One episode in particular, the reign of Morgoth from his strong-hold of Thangorodrim somewhere north of the Shire for the three thousand years of the First Age, produces great changes in Middle-earth geography. To bring about his overthrow the Guardian Valar re-lease titanic natural forces, which cause the ocean to drown not only his fortress but a vast area around it, including the elf kingdoms of Beleriand, Nargothrond, Gondolin, Nogrod, and Belagost. Of that stretch of the northwestern coast only Lindon remains above the waves to appear on Tolkien's Third Age maps. The flooding of rebel-lious Númenor by the One at the end of the Second Age is a catastro-phe of equal magnitude. But Tolkien gives the realm of Morgoth an extra level of allusiveness by describing it as so bitterly cold that after its destruction "those colds linger still in that region, though they lie hardly more than a hundred leagues north of the Shire" (III, 321). He goes on to describe the Forodwaith people living there as "Man of far-off days," who have snow houses, like igloos, and sleds and skis much like those of Eskimos. Add the fact that the Witch-king of Angmar (hereafter called simply Angmar), Morgoth's henchman, has powers that wane in summer and wax in winter and it becomes hard not to associate Morgoth in some way with a glacial epoch, as various commentators have already done. In his essay "On Fairy-Stories" Tolkien refuses to interpret the Norse god Thorr as a mere person-ification of thunder.[4] Along the same lines, it is not his intention, I think, to portray Morgoth as a personification of an ice age. However, it would seem compatible with his meaning to consider Morgoth a spirit of evil whose powers have engendered the frozen destructiveness of such an age.

The possibility thus raised of fixing the three Ages of Middle-earth in some interglacial lull in the Pleistocene is tempting and may be legitimate, provided that we do not start looking about for exact data to establish precise chronologies.[5] The data are not there, and Tolkien has no intention whatever of supplying them. The art of fantasy flourishes on reticence. To the question how far in Earth's past the Ages of Middle-earth lie, Tolkien gives essentially the storyteller's answer: Once upon a time — and never ask what time. Choose some interglacial period if you must, he seems to say, but do not expect me to bind myself by an admission that you are right. Better for you not to be too sure.

Tolkien's technique of purposeful ambivalence is well shown too in the Mûmak of Harad, which Sam sees fighting on the side of the Southrons against Faramir's men in Ithilien: "indeed a beast of vast bulk, and the like of him does not now walk in Middle-earth; his kin that live still in the latter days are but memories of his girth and majesty" (II, 269). As compared with its "kin," the elephant of today, the ancestral Mûmak was far more massive.[6] Is Tolkien hinting that it is a mammoth? Perhaps, but it is not shaggy, it is coming up from the warm south, and it is totally unknown to the hobbits farther north, where that sort of creature might be expected to abound. Tolkien is equally evasive about Angmar's huge winged steed, featherless and leathery: "A creature of an older world maybe it was, whose kind, lingering in forgotten mountains cold beneath the Moon, outstayed their day" (II, 115). A pterodactyl? It certainly sounds like one, but Tolkien avoids naming it, and casts all in doubt with a "maybe." If it is a pterodactyl, or a close relative, then the Age of Reptiles in which those species throve is "older" than the Third Age, apparently much older. Gwaihir is an eagle of prodigious size whose ancestor "built his eyries in the inaccessible peaks of the Encircling Mountains when Middle-earth was young" (III, 226). All these half-mythical creatures of Middle-earth are meant to subsist partly in our world, partly in another in which the imagination can make of them what it will.

Tolkien's lifelong interest in astronomy tempts him into observations which have a bearing on the distance of Middle-earth back in Earth's prehistory. In appendix D, opening a discussion of the calendars devised by its various peoples, he remarks, "The Calendar in the Shire differed in several features from ours. The year no doubt was of the same length, for long ago as those times are now reckoned in years and lives of men, they were not very remote according to the memory of the Earth" (III, 385). A footnote on the same page gives "365 days, 5 hours, 48 minutes, 46 seconds" as the period of Earth's annual revolution around the sun according to our best modern measurements. The year length for Middle-earth of the Third Age was the same, Tolkien says. In other words, Earth's orbit around the sun (or vice versa) was the same then as it is now. This bit of information is not as informative as it looks. In the absence of modern technology nobody before today could possibly have calculated the orbit with sufficient accuracy to tell at what epoch it began being different. But the implication is that at least the Third Age was not many millions of years ago. Tolkien wants for Middle-earth distance, not invisibility.

To strengthen visibility, and also to counterbalance the alien topography of Middle-earth's Europe, Tolkien lights its night skies with the planets and constellations we know, however different their names. Orion is seen by hobbits and elves meeting in the Shire woods: "There leaned up, as he climbed over the rim of the world, the Swordsman of the Sky, Menelvagor with his shining belt" (I, 91). Unmistakably Orion. Looking out the window of the inn at Bree, "Frodo saw that the night was still clear. The Sickle was swinging bright above the shoulders of Bree-hill" (I, 187). Tolkien takes the trouble to add a footnote on that page, that "the Sickle" is "the Hobbits' name for the Plough or Great Bear." Glowing like a jewel of fire, "Red Borgil" would seem to be Mars. Eärendil's star is surely Venus, because Bilbo describes it as shining just after the setting sun ("behind the Sun and light of Moon") and just before the rising sun ("a distant flame before the Sun, / a wonder ere the waking dawn") (I, 249).

The heavens of Middle-earth and Earth being not noticeably dissimilar, the lapse of time between the two epochs is short by planetary standards ("the memory of the Earth"), however long it may seem "in years and lives of men." Middle-earth has the same seasons we have in the same length of year, which means that it tilts its northern and southern hemispheres alternately toward and away from the sun as does Earth today. And apparently its days and nights are of the usual duration, which means that Middle-earth rotates on its axis in our twenty-four-hour period. All these are comfortable touches designed not only to show that Middle-earth could not possibly be another planet but also to reassure the reader that fundamentally he is on home territory. I have described the phenomena above in modern heliocentric terms, but they are equally valid for a geocentric view, which there is reason to think the peoples of the Third Age believed in, as will be discussed in a moment.

Strange but not too strange. Further to offset the alienness of the large-scale topography of Third-Age Europe, Tolkien makes sure that on the small scale its local terrain, climate, and dominant flora and fauna are much as we know them today. We feel at ease with them at once. Spring in the Shire brings warm sun, a wind from the south, new green "shimmering in the fields," and Sam clipping the grass borders of Frodo's lawn. Tobacco grows in the more sheltered bottomland. The fox that sees the hobbits sleeping out overnight as they leave the Shire sniffs and marvels aloud in intelligent speech, but it is a fox, not a Jabberwock. The travelers are later spied upon by birds, but they are crows, ordinary in everything except a heightened consciousness. When the Fellowship depart from Lórien they hear "the high distant song of larks" (I, 388). Fangorn Forest may be dire and mysterious, but its trees are the same oaks, chestnuts, beeches, and rowans that make up our woods. As for the day-by-day scenery and climate through which his travelers move on their many journeys, no writer was ever more constantly aware than Tolkien of all the details of mountain, grassland, wood, and swamp, of variations in temperature, wind or calm, rain or cloud, the quality of sunlight and starlight, the hues of each particular sunset. He keeps our senses wide awake. Picking out at random almost any one day during Frodo's tramp to Rivendell or Aragorn's pursuit of the orcs, a reader is likelier than not to be told exactly what the weather was and what their camping spot for the night looked like. Given this unbroken running account of familiar homely things, he is buoyed by a psychological reassurance that never fails him, and that allows him to absorb very large doses of the marvelous without disbelieving it. This is one of the hallmarks of Tolkien's personal style in fantasy.

As summarized in appendixes A and B, the formal history of Middle-earth begins with the temptation and fall of the great elf leader Fëanor in Valinor and extends for about ten thousand years into the start of the Fourth Age. But into *The Lord of the Rings* Tolkien introduces the two oldest living beings on earth, Bombadil and Treebeard, whose memories stretch much farther back, to the first beginnings of life on the planet. Through them he is able to give his story full chronological depth by opening up the longest possible vistas into the past of its various races. Bombadil lived in unimaginable times before there was any vegetation, before even the rains began to fall. He saw the coming of men, "the Big People," and hobbits, "the little People." Before that the elves, earliest of intelligent peoples, passed him on their way westward from some unknown birthplace to the continent's edge, and thence across the sea to Valinor. All this "before the seas were bent" or Morgoth came to Middle-earth from "Outside" to breed his loathsome orcs.

For his part, Treebeard also antedated the elves, but ents did not know how to speak until the first wandering elves taught them. Treebeard has seen the day when the separate patches of forest surviving into the Third Age were joined in one unending woodland that covered the face of primeval Europe. And, along with the other ents, he has suffered the loss of the entwives, the females of his species, who in some prehistoric time left the woods to practice agriculture in the open fields and there taught their arts to primitive men. This is almost a parable of how Earth's originally nomadic tribes settled down in one place when they learned to till the soil.

All these are glimpses into Middle-earth's prehistoric past. At the end of his epic Tolkien inserts also some forebodings of its future which will make Earth what it is today. Apart from gigantic geological upheavals still to come, he shows the initial steps in a long process of retreat or disappearance by all other intelligent species, which will leave man effectually alone on Earth. The greater elves are already going home to Eldamar, from which they will not return, while the lesser ones who remain sink into oblivion. Orcs shut themselves into their caverns under the mountains. After an estrangement from mankind . . . hobbits will retire from all communication with us, reduced in size, numbers, and importance. The slow reproductive rate of the dwarves foreshadows their gradual extinction, leaving behind them imperishable monuments of stone. Ents may still be there in our forests, but what forests have we left? The process of extermination is already well under way in the Third Age, and in works outside the epic Tolkien bitterly deplores its climax today. The hunger men still feel to converse with birds and animals is a residual trace of the free intercourse between the species prevailing on Middle-earth, and since lost.[7]

Tolkien is sure that modern man's belief that he is the only intelligent species on Earth has not been good for him. Cut off from nature and its multitudes of living beings, mankind has developed a hard, artificial industrialism stifling to that side of him which is sympathetic, imaginative, free. One symptom of our loss is the trivializing in contemporary folklore and fairy tales of the lordly elves and formidable dwarves traditional to them. In appendix F of his epic Tolkien condemns with angry sadness the "fancies either pretty or silly" (III, 415) which now dishonor those and other great races of Middle-earth. "Smith of Wootton Major," written later, is a short story dealing in part with the scorn of our skeptics for a charming world of fancy that their imaginations are no longer flexible enough to enter. According to the essay "On Fairy-Stories," creative fantasy has the power to heal this blindness by "Recovery" of fresh knowledge of ourselves and the world about us, and of the kindly insight we once had into other species, other minds.

But to return to Middle-earth. One region of it is so far outside our experience that Tolkien can only ask us to take it completely on faith. This region contains the Undying Lands situated far out in the ocean west of the continental land mass, home of the Guardian Valar and their pupils, the immortal elves. Eldamar of the elves is definitely an island, but nearby Valinor seems to be attached to a "mighty Mountain Wall" encircling the whole of Middle-earth. Both places are therefore at World's End, the Uttermost West, beyond which living beings cannot go. Early in the First Age and before, access to the Undying Lands was by an arduous though otherwise ordinary sea voyage, but elves were the only race permitted to make it. After their rebellion and self-exile in that age, Elbereth Star-kindler, Queen of the Valar, cast a deep belt of shadow across its ocean approaches, through which the exiles could return only when forgiven, as most of them were after Morgoth's defeat at the end of the age.[8] When this barrier proved insufficient in the Second Age to keep out the armadas of Númenor sailing in to seize immortality by force, the One made the Undying Lands forever inaccessible to men.

Because of the integral place these lands have in the geography and spiritual history of Middle-earth they are not strictly an otherworld. Their closest counterpart in literature is in those early medieval Celtic tales known as *imrama*, about voyages made by Irish explorers to the western Atlantic in search of the Land of Promise. That Tolkien knew these tales is clear, for he wrote a poem which he entitled "Imram" narrating such a voyage by Saint Brendan, which takes him after seven years of adventure to an island of refuge set aside by God for his saints. In the Latin prose version of the Brendan search, almost certainly read and used by Tolkien for his poem,[9] the Land of Promise has many elements in common with the Undying Lands of *The Lord of the Rings,* raising the possibility that it also provided Tolkien with ideas for his epic.

For instance, Brendan's Land of Promise is screened by a miraculous circle of darkness through which all comers must pass, as the Undying Lands are walled off by Elbereth's belt of shadow. The saint and his monks are allowed to walk only to a river where an angel in the form of a shining man forbids them to advance farther and sends them back to Ireland. Similarly, the Valar are demiurgic spirits in human or elven form, radiant in appearance, and they not only exile the elves at one time but also impose the Ban against all mankind which precipitates so much tragedy in the epic. The angel tells Brendan that the Land of Promise is being reserved by God for a refuge at a future time when Christians will be persecuted. Likewise, the Valar have occupied the Undying Lands "because of their love and desire for the Children of God (*Erusen*) for whom they were to prepare the 'realm'" against the day when elves and men shall have attained "their future forms."[10] Most important for our present purposes, both lands are at the extreme western limit of the physical world but still a geographical part of it.

If the navigable sea has any such boundaries, Middle-earth cannot be a rounded sphere as we now conceive Earth. In the *imrama* tales this point posed no difficulty to the wonder-oriented Celtic mind of the Dark Ages, which popularly accepted the world as bounded and flat anyway, or, when it did not, was quite willing to forget roundness under the spell of a good story. But is such a prescientific cosmology intended by Tolkien for Middle-earth? He never discusses the question explicitly one way or the other. He leaves us to survey the text of the epic and its appendixes for ourselves. Quite possibly he considers the question to be of no real importance to the story, and so is indifferent whether it is raised or not. Those who wish to raise it will find, I think, that none of the astronomical passages are incompatible with a geocentric view of a flat, saucerlike Middle-earth. Since such a view is implicit in the conception of Valinor as being at World's End, consistency would require its acceptance as representing the beliefs of the inhabitants of Middle-earth.

But does the divine act of the One in removing the Undying Lands "forever from the circles of the world" at the end of the Second Age signal a change to a more advanced astronomy? Possibly so, if that cryptic phrase means that they were taken out of the physical continuum of Middle-earth, which then becomes free to be spherical. One difficulty is that the encircling mountains may still be there (the text is silent). Also, Tolkien continues to allow the elves still on Middle-earth during the Third Age to act as if the Undying Lands are visible and reachable. In the *palantír* at the Grey Havens Gildor and his company still can see Valinor, where the white figure of Elbereth stands gazing out and listening to their prayers. And, returning home when the Fourth Age begins, the great elves have only to take ships from the Havens, though these have been specially built by Círdan for the journey, to be sure. On the whole it seems wise not to inquire too curiously into a question that Tolkien himself chooses to ignore.

The appendixes are not mere barnacles on the epic as some critical opinion would have them. For example, appendix D on the calendars of Middle-earth and appendixes E and F on its languages so orient their specialized topics as to become facets of the cultural history of all the major races. By this method the basic traits of each are revealed. Elvish empathy for the gradations of growth and dormancy in vegetation is reflected in their division of the year into six, rather than four, seasons, and these of unequal length. The Númenóreans' insensitivity to such gradations and preoccupation rather with practical affairs lead to their abandonment of those divisions and substitution of twelve mathematically equal months. The hobbit love of holidays and feasting multiplies Lithedays in the summer and Yuledays in the winter, all given over to parties. That the elves are indeed "People of the Stars" and worshipers of the Valar could be known, if from no other source, from the objects and persons determining the names they give to the six days of their week: Stars, Sun, Moon, the Two Trees (of Valinor), the Heavens, and the Valar. They also have many special names for the hours of star-opening and star-fading. The experience of Númenóreans exclusively with the White Tree causes them to substitute its name for that of Two Trees, and, being great mariners, they insert a Sea-day after Heavens' Day. Conservative by nature, the hobbits take over the Númenórean week but soon forget its meaning.

Nothing tells more about a people than the language it speaks and writes. This is bound to be a product of its psychological peculiarities, its traditions, its institutions, its whole outlook on life. Well aware of this truth, Tolkien as a professional philologist makes of his appendixes E and F on the languages he has invented for the several races of Middle-earth not only a tour de force of philological analytic imagination but also one more revelation of the races themselves from a new direction. These appendixes have the added interest of being the adult equivalent of Tolkien's boyhood games with invented tongues. Aimed first at demonstrating the alphabets, pronunciation, and to some extent the grammar of the two inflected, superbly melodious Elvish dialects, Quenya and Sindarin, their material evidently comes straight out of that "history of Elvish tongues" which Tolkien prepared in the 1930s before he came to write *The Lord of the Rings.* When this history proved unpublishable he set it aside in order to proceed with a narrative about the races who spoke these languages. So the epic was born.

Nobody knows better than Tolkien that languages are not static but change continually. Hence part of the function of appendix E is to trace some of the developments of the original Elvish spoken and written speech into Númenórean, and thence into Westron, the "Common Speech" of the West. Inevitably, I suppose, the laws of linguistic evolution which Tolkien sees at work on Middle-earth are the same as those discovered by modern philology to have governed the development of the Indo-European tongues in recent millennia on Earth. In this way another parallel is drawn, this time in the realm of philology, between events on ancient Middle-earth and those known to have taken place among us in our own era.

The linguistic history of Middle-earth corroborates and fleshes out other aspects of its history, with a corresponding gain in the credibility of all. In language, as in much else, the Noldor elves who have crossed the sea to Valinor are the fountainhead of culture. They carry back with them to Middle-earth the noble Quenya speech and the first written alphabet, invented by their most brilliant genius, Fëanor, who also made the *Silmarilli*. Cultural contact with the Sindar elves, who have remained behind on the continent, enriches both groups, modifies their speech and writing, and spreads their influence eastward among the Edain of the north and the dwarves of Moria to the south. Even the orcs are affected. When given the island of Númenor, the Edain, too, abandon their former linguistic patterns in favor of the Elvish. It is a sign of the arrogance and rebellion to come that gradually they cast off all things Elvish and revert to a version of their former tongue. Out of this, in later years after their destruction, there emerges in the Gondor lands they have settled the lingua franca of the west known as Westron, bearing the mark of influences of the more primitive human tribes already there as well as others from commerce with remaining colonies of elves. The rivalry between Westron and Sauron's Black Speech, spoken by all his servants, typifies the enmity of the two cultures, if Sauron's tyranny can be called a culture. This bald summary can give but a paltry idea of the profusion of detail poured in by Tolkien to show how the languages of Middle-earth both shape and reflect the destinies of those who use them.

[There] are many instances [in] Tolkien's art [that gain] credence for his history of Middle-earth by introducing episodes of various sorts that tease us with their resemblance to episodes that we

know have actually occurred in our not-too-distant past. A few . . .
parallels, which designedly are never quite parallel, deserve mention
too because they skirt the edges of large events in the history of Western civilization.[11] Just as Earth has seen wave after wave of tribal mi-
grations into Europe from east and north, so on Middle-earth the
elves, the Edain, the Rohirrim, and the hobbits have drifted west
at various periods from the same directions. Also, our Europe has
warred from early times against Arabs from the south and Persians,
Mongols, and Turks from the Near or Far East. Similarly Gondor re-
sists Easterlings and Southrons, who have pressed against its borders for millennia and have become natural allies of Sauron. The
Haradrim of the south even recall Saracens in their swarthy hue,
weapons, and armor, and suggest other non-European armies in their
use of elephant ancestors, while the Wainriders from the east come in
wagons rather like those of the Tartar hordes. The men of Gondor
live and fight in a kind of legendary Arthurian, protomedieval mode,
and the Rohirrim differ from early Anglo-Saxons mainly in living by
the horse, like Cossacks.

The Tolkien style in creating secondary worlds did not spring
full-blown but developed out of his experience in writing *The Hobbit*,
his first attempt at narrative. In that story Bilbo travels from Shire to
Rivendell, as Frodo does, and meets Gandalf, Elrond, Gollum, and
other characters who appear also in the epic. But the world of *The
Hobbit* is not called Middle-earth, its vegetation and creatures are not
visualized in patient detail, and it has no larger geographical or historical context whatever. Nor are the characters the same, although
they bear the same names. Gandalf is merely a funny old wizard, for
instance. And in a mistaken attempt to please an audience of children, Tolkien trivializes and ridicules his elves and dwarves in precisely the manner he later comes to deplore. To call *The Lord of the
Rings* a sequel to this childhood tale, as Tolkien does for the sake of
continuity in the Ring plot, is to disguise the immense progress in
technique evident in his epic fantasy.

Having once found his characteristic combination of the familiar with the unfamiliar, Tolkien never departed from it in any of the short verse and prose fiction he wrote after finishing the epic.[12] "The Homecoming of Beorthnoth" is an imagined sequel to the battle of Maldon between Vikings and Saxons in Essex in A.D. 991. *Farmer Giles of Ham* is set in the valley of the Thames in pre-Arthurian Britain. "Smith of Wootton Major" takes place in an essentially medieval English village, slightly hobbitized, which is a point of departure and return for excursions into a country called Faëry. "Imram" tells of Saint Brendan's sea voyage into the west in the sixth century. It starts and ends in Ireland. "The Lay of Aotrou and Itroun" is a Breton lay centering on the south coast of Britain in the chivalric age. "Leaf by Niggle" shows us a modern English village complete with neighbors, bicycles, housing regulations, a town council, and the rest, before taking off into a rather minutely pictured landscape where the soul after death goes through purgation.

In his unfinished *The Silmarillion* Tolkien faces the same problem in naturalizing the potentially fabulous happenings of Middle-earth's First Age.

PATRICK GRANT

Tolkien: Archetype and Word

*Starting with the premise that the principles of Christian epic, while
they are never explicit in Tolkien's epic, are experienced as embodied
themes, a map of values, Grant employs twin Jungian theories, those of
the archetype and the inner journey toward individuation, to explore*
The Lord of the Rings. *Like medieval commentators on epic, Grant sees
the deep structure of Tolkien's work as a "journey to wisdom" and uses a
modern philosopher-psychologist to plot its course. Grant argues that
the main action of the book charts Frodo's movement through a process
equivalent to Jung's individuation. The characters Frodo encounters
are Jungian archetypes. For example, Gollum is Frodo's "shadow" and
Galadriel his "anima," a bridge to deeper elements of the psyche, while
Gandalf is the Jungian "Wise Old Man." Each archetype is also double-
sided so that while Galadriel is the good anima, Shelob is the destructive
anima, who poisons to kill. The good aspect of each of the archetypes
leads the hero's inner journey toward understanding and fellowship, the
evil toward isolation and death. With the union of complementary
types, Jungian "syzygy," or psychic wholeness, is achieved. Grant is careful to say, however, that* The Lord of the Rings *is not merely an inner
psychodrama, for its magic participates in Christian consciousness in
the Primary World, in apprehension of the Incarnate Word.*

*   *   *

The Lord of the Rings embodies an inherent morality, which derives largely from the traditions of Christian and epic poetry. Yet the trilogy is not explicitly religious and is neither allegorical nor doctrinal. Tolkien well knows that the Dantesque form of Christian epic, wherein history effortlessly assumes the framework of dogma, cannot be successfully imitated in post-Romantic times. In Milton's *Paradise Lost* the sacramentalism fundamental to Dante's vision is already transformed. For Milton, subjective experience, not a doctrinal formula of words, is the key to faith, and medieval "realism," which assumes the participation of words in the extramental reality they signify, is not part of the consciousness that produced *Paradise Lost*.

What remain in Milton are, in generalized form, the great themes of the Christian epic: first, and most important, that true heroism is spiritual; also, that love is obedience and involves freedom; that faith and hope are based on charity; that Providence directs the affairs of the world. The reader is repeatedly challenged to establish an attitude to these issues, and the vast shifts of time and space — heavenly, infernal, past, future, prelapsarian, postlapsarian — are means of pressing the challenge upon his attention. In no other Christian poem does the real (inner) meaning so energetically parody the canonical orthodoxies of the external form.

By the time of Blake (who, significantly, saw Milton as a noble spirit except for his doctrine) the "paradise within" has found expression in language even further removed from canonical orthodoxy than Milton's. The Romantics primarily inherit Blake's vision, and so, basically, does Tolkien, essentially a post-Romantic like his friends C. S. Lewis, Owen Barfield, and Charles Williams. One consequence is that the principles of Christian epic are experienced in Tolkien not explicitly but as embodied themes, a map of values as in *Paradise Lost,* and without the traditional dogmatic theology that Milton's great poem is already in process of casting off. The trilogy is, significantly, set in the essentially inner realm of faërie, close to the world of dream and myth, where, Tolkien tells us, "primordial human desires" are met and interpreted.[1]

The archetypal flavor of Tolkien's description of faërie, together with his dreamlike settings in Middle-earth, have readily evoked among critics the language and thought of Jung, and, in a historical context, Jung is certainly a prime explicator in the twentieth century of the "interiorization" of spiritual experience so characteristic of post-Romantic religion. In this respect the psychoanalyst complements the writer of fairy stories. *The Lord of the Rings* can be read with surprising consistency as an interior journey through the psyche as Jung describes it, and archetypal structures in the trilogy will be a central concern of this essay. Yet I wish to establish from the outset that a purely Jungian approach has limitations, for Tolkien at all times evaluates the archetypes, however implicitly, in light of the literary conventions of Christian epic. The Word, in a Christian sense, is a primary archetype which both spiritualizes and revalidates for man the extramental world of history and material extension. Only in carefully observed physical reality can the sub-creation of faërie achieve its real enchantment and open into the truth which Tolkien describes, in the old language, as Eucharistic.[2] The great pains taken with the historical background to Middle-earth are not without point. They save the book from becoming allegory, or a thin fantasy of "interior space," and in his "Eucharistic" view of history and of the Word, Tolkien addresses again the key problems of the Christian epic in modern times: the possibilities of sacramentalism, and the relation of the archetypes of inner vision to Christian ordinances and heroic themes.

The group of friends to whom Tolkien first read *The Lord of the Rings,* the Inklings, found Jung temperamentally attractive, though they regarded him also with a certain suspicion. C. S. Lewis avows that he is "enchanted" by Jung and has, on occasion, "slipped into" a Jungian manner of criticism.[3] He admits that Maud Bodkin, the pioneer critic of Jungian archetypal patterns in literature, exerted considerable influence on him. Owen Barfield praises Jung for understanding the spiritual nature of consciousness and its evolution: the Jungian "collective unconscious" and appeal to myth are much-needed antidotes to twentieth-century materialism which threatens to make an object of man himself.[4] On the negative side, Lewis thinks that Jung's explanation of "primordial images" itself awakens a primordial image of the first water, while Barfield feels that in Jung the "Spiritual Hierarchies" have withdrawn from the world and exist, interiorized, within the individual will and too much cut off from the extramental world.[5]

It is important not to put the words of Lewis and Barfield into Tolkien's mouth (he was as difficult to influence as a bandersnatch, according to Lewis),[6] yet Tolkien at least shared the interests and temperament of his friends. Certainly the reader of his essay on fairy stories cannot easily avoid the Jungian flavor of several of Tolkien's key theories. He describes faërie in relation to dream, stating that in both "strange powers of the mind may be unlocked" (p. 13). He talks of the encounter in fairy stories with "certain primordial human desires" (p. 13), and claims the stories are "plainly not primarily concerned with possibility but with desirability" (p. 40). He talks of a "Cauldron of Story" which waits "for the great figures of Myth and History" (p. 29). These are added like fresh pieces to a stock which has been simmering from the beginnings of story-telling — that is, from the beginnings of the human mind itself. In the essay on *Beowulf,* Tolkien especially appreciates the balance and "opposition of ends and beginnings," the progress from youth to old age in the hero, and the satisfaction that comes from perceiving the "rising and setting" of a life.[7]

We can easily enough feel here the typical Jungian insistence on dream and fantasy, the theory of a collective unconscious which (like Tolkien's cauldron) contains archetypes stirred into activity by the artist, and the theory of transformation in the individual psyche, whereby beginnings and ends are balanced in a successful human life. But more important, Tolkien's theory finds full embodiment in *The Lord of the Rings.* The trilogy is set in faërie, in this case the imaginary world of Middle-earth, at a time near the beginnings of man's ascendance in the history of the world. Middle-earth is often dreamlike: a world of shifting contours and of magic, of nightmarish fear and exquisite ethereal beauty. Helpful and treacherous creatures work for the powers of good and evil, and landscapes become sentient embodiments of human fears and desires. It is a short step to the appearance of nature spirits, like Tom Bombadil, or to the magic of the elves, and, as we move closer to those who possess more than human wisdom and power, the contours of time and space themselves begin to blur. Although controlled by the narrative art and by basic structural oppositions such as those between light and dark, good and evil, the story moves basically in a world where forms and images blend and flow and interpenetrate, and where the eye of the beholder determines fear and terror, beauty and glory. All this has the very quality of that "interior space" that Barfield names as Jung's special province.[8]

For Jung, certainly, fairy stories and dreams are characteristically inhabited by helpful and treacherous animals and monsters, and landscapes, especially when they involve woods and mountains, are favorite representations of the unconscious.[9] Jung also talks of a common figure, the "vegetation numen," king of the forest, who is associated with wood and water in a manner that recalls Tom Bombadil. Magic too is important, and Jung explains that "the concentration and tension of psychic forces have something about them which always looks like magic." He stresses also a "contamination" of images, by which he means a tendency to overflow contours — "a melting down of images."[10] This, says Jung, may look like distortion and can be terrifying, but it can also be a process of assimilation and a source of great beauty and inspiration. His perception applies precisely to the viewpoint technique of *The Lord of the Rings*. Jung also points to certain characteristic formal elements in dreams and fairy stories, such as "duality," "the opposition of light and dark," and "rotation (circle, sphere)" but insists that they should not be considered apart from the complex flowing energy of the psyche.[11] Moral choices are not simply a matter of black or white. Jung stresses "the bewildering play of antinomies" which contribute to higher awareness.[12] Good may be produced by evil and possibly lead to it. This process, which Jung calls "enantidromia,"[13] is of central importance in the art of Tolkien: a broad opposition of light and dark, and of good and evil, becomes confused in the trilogy as we enter the minds of individuals in process of finding their way on the quest. Though Gollum hates light and loves shade, Frodo's relation to Gollum is extremely complex, and throughout the trilogy the minds of the men in particular are continually ambivalent.

That Jung and Tolkien isolate such similar motifs from fairy stories, dreams, fantasy, and myth is hardly surprising, but in *The Lord of the Rings* the inner drama corresponds also with particular fidelity to the details of the psychic process Jung calls "individuation." This is, basically, the "realization of the whole man" achieved in a balanced and fulfilled life when consciousness and the unconscious are linked together in a living relation. The process involves a journey to the self, which Jung describes as not only the center of a person's psyche but also the circumference that embraces both conscious and unconscious.[14] Characteristically, the self is represented in dreams and mythology as a mandala — a square within a circle, or circle within a square, or in figures that are spherical, representing wholeness.

Jung insists that individuation, or selfhood, is not mere ego-consciousness. As the shortsighted ego responds to the demands of inner growth, the way to the self is indicated by representations of archetypes, those primordial and recurring images in human experience which express the basic structures of the psyche and which become increasingly numinous, impressive, and dangerous as they emerge from the deeper levels of the unconscious. First and nearest to the surface, so that we can become aware of it by reflection, is the shadow. The shadow is the *"personal unconscious,"* and among the archetypes, is the "easiest to experience."[15] It represents the elements a person represses as incompatible with his chosen ideal — "for instance, inferior traits of character and other incompatible tendencies."[16] The shadow is ambiguous — it contains morally reprehensible tendencies but can also display good qualities, such as normal instincts that have been repressed but are necessary to consciousness. In dreams it is represented as a figure of the same sex as the dreamer and, in accord with its ambiguous status, may be either a threat that follows him or a guide.

Further from consciousness is the anima/animus archetype. This is a representation of the feminine side of a man's unconscious, or the masculine side of a woman's. The anima (the more important for Tolkien) is, like the shadow, ambivalent. She is both the nourishing and the destructive mother. On the one hand, she is Dante's Beatrice, the Virgin Mary, the Muses who inspire man to create, the dream girl of popular fantasy and song. On the other hand, she is a witch, poisonous and malevolent, or a Siren who, however beautiful, lures a man to his death and destruction. For Jung, "the animus and the anima should function as a bridge, or a door, leading to the images of the collective unconscious."[17]

More profound, and often presented with the anima as friend or protector, is the archetype of the hero. He is often represented in a dangerous situation or on a difficult quest, the anticipation of the individuation process, an approach to wholeness. The hero often has an aura of the supernatural, which offsets his vulnerability, another essential trait, for he is both semidivine and a child. "This paradox . . . runs through his whole destiny like a red thread. He can cope with the greatest perils, yet, in the end, something quite insignificant is his undoing."[18] The hero archetype is often accompanied by the strange and numinous "dragons, helpful animals, and demons; also the Wise Old Man . . . all things which in no way touch the boundaries of everyday. The reason for this is that they have to do with the realization of a part of the personality which has not yet come into existence but is still in the process of becoming."[19]

The deepest archetype on the journey towards the self is the figure of the Wise Old Man, a helpful figure who, when the hero is in a hopeless situation, can extricate him. He is magician, guru, a personification of wisdom. He seems not to be bound by time, and he is strongly endowed with numinous power — for instance, magic. Also, "apart from his cleverness, wisdom, and insight," the Wise Old Man is "notable for his moral qualities."[20] But along with the other archetypes he is also an ambivalent figure, like Merlin, in whom the enantiodromia of good and evil can appear most paradoxically.

In *The Lord of the Rings* the theme of a quest involving a ring, symbol of binding and wholeness, which must be preserved from the powers of darkness and evil by the powers of light and goodness, suggests the beginnings of a typical journey towards individuation: the promise of a "true conjunctio" which involves the threat of dissolution, or "false conjunctio." Frodo, at the beginning, is childlike and must endure the terrors of monsters, dragons, and the underworld. Aragorn, his companion, who likewise undergoes such trials, is of strange and royal origins, protector of a noble lineage, and a semidivine figure with the magic power of healing. Frodo and Aragorn represent different aspects of the hero — Frodo his childlike quality, Aragorn his nobility and power; and each must support and learn from the other. The hobbit, for good reason as we shall see, receives foremost attention, and the story is in a special sense his. As it proceeds, Frodo more and more puts off the childlike ways of the Shire and assumes the lineaments of heroism, acquiring, at the end, a truly numinous quality. Moreover, as his understanding deepens, Frodo moves through a process equivalent to Jung's individuation, which is charted by the main action of the book. He encounters the shadow (Gollum), anima (Galadriel), and Wise Old Man (Gandalf). Each archetype has a good and bad side, the good leading to understanding and fellowship, the bad to death, isolation, and the loss of identity or self. So Galadriel is contrasted with Shelob, the heroes with the Ringwraiths, and Gandalf with the evil magician Saruman. Gollum is, by nature, ambivalent. He is the shadow, or personal unconscious, and we will deal with him first.

At the beginning Frodo does not realize his shadow personality;

he does not know that he is being pursued by Gollum. He knows only a vaguely uncomfortable feeling that increases as the story develops. As the fellowship sets out for Lothlórien, Frodo "had heard something or thought he had. As soon as the shadows had fallen about them and the road behind was dim, he had heard again the quick patter of feet" (I, 351). The others do not notice. Soon after, Frodo is startled by "a shadowy figure," which "slipped round the trunk of the tree and vanished" (I, 360). Again, he alone sees Gollum, who has been pursuing the Ring, moving in the dark because he fears light.

Significantly, Gollum is of the same race and sex as Frodo, as is appropriate for a shadow figure. He is a hobbit, fallen into the power of the Ring and debased to a froglike, emaciated, underground creature of primitive cunning and instinct. He is clearly a threat which Frodo must learn to acknowledge as a potentiality in his own being. To ignore the shadow, as Jung indicates, is to risk inflation of the ego.[21] The relationship between Frodo and the repulsive Gollum therefore must become one of mutual acknowledgment. Sam, to his own consternation, sees the peculiar link between the two: they "were in some way akin and not alien: they could reach one another's minds" (II, 225). So Frodo insists on unbinding Gollum and trusting his promise, and the shadow, ever ambivalent, becomes a guide without ceasing to be dangerous. Gollum leads Frodo to Shelob's lair, but he also saves him at the last moment from a fatal inflation of pride which would constitute the failure of the quest: "But for him, Sam, I could not have destroyed the Ring. . . . So let us forgive him!" (III, 225).

Frodo has confronted Gollum before the party arrives at Lothlórien, but only after the encounter with Galadriel can he bind and release the shadow. The meeting with Galadriel is an overwhelming experience for the entire company, not just for Frodo. Although she deals more with him than with the others, she is not bound to Frodo in the particular way that Gollum is. Her significance has less to do with the personal unconscious than with the collective unconscious.

She is a striking representative of the anima, a figure which, Jung says, is often "fairy like" or "Elfin,"[22] and Galadriel is, indeed, an elf. She is also a bridge to the deeper elements of the psyche and can reveal hidden elements in the souls of the company. "None save Legolas and Aragorn could long endure her glance" (I, 372), and she shows to each one the dangers of the quest and the personal weakness he brings to it. In her mirror she shows Frodo the larger history in which he is involved, and he responds with awe and terror. The numinous power characteristic of the anima almost overwhelms him, so that he even offers her the Ring. Galadriel replies in words that clearly indicate the dangers of fixation on anima and warn of her destructive aspect: "You will give me the Ring freely! In place of the Dark Lord you will set up a Queen. And I shall not be dark, but beautiful and terrible as the Morning and the Night! . . . All shall love me and despair!" (I, 381). Frodo instead must use Galadriel's knowledge and wisdom to further the quest: she is a bridge to the darkness of Mordor, to which the hero must journey. So Frodo carries with him the influence of Galadriel's fairylike, timeless, and magically radiant beauty, and it serves to protect him. Symbolically, she gives him a phial of light to bear to the darkness. The light not only shows Frodo the way but helps him against the Ringwraiths, and, most important, enables him to face Shelob.

If Galadriel is the anima in its beneficent aspect, Shelob the spider-woman is the destructive anima who poisons to kill. Gollum talks of a mysterious "she" who will help him win back the Ring, and he means Shelob — "all living things were her food, and her vomit darkness" (II, 332). As Frodo meets her, he holds up the light: "'Galadriel,' he called, and gathering his courage he lifted up the Phial once more" (II, 330). Galadriel's light and Shelob's darkness, the principles of life and death, of nourishment and destruction, contend for Frodo, who must meet them both — the anima in both aspects, beneficent and malevolent.

Other anima figures throughout *The Lord of the Rings* present an appeal much like Galadriel's. Mainly we think of Arwen, another elf, whose "loveliness in living thing Frodo had never seen before nor imagined in his mind" (I, 239). She is destined to marry Aragorn, and their union represents the "syzygy," the ideal union of anima and animus. The self is often represented by the marriage of such a "divine, royal, or otherwise distinguished couple."[23] Less fortunate than Arwen, however, is Éowyn, whose love for Aragorn cannot be reciprocated, with the result that she becomes the victim of her own animus. When Aragorn leaves her, as he must, Éowyn assumes the disguise of the warrior, Dernhelm, who "desired to have nothing, unless a brave death in battle" (III, 242). Éowyn, in Jungian terms, is possessed by the negative animus (often represented as a death-demon), which in this case drives towards suicide. Such a possession often results, says Jung, in "a transformation of personality" which "gives prominence to those traits which are characteristic of the opposite sex."[24] Only through the love of Faramir does Éowyn change — "or else at last she understood it. And suddenly her winter passed, and the sun shone on her" (III, 243).

The heroic figures of *The Lord of the Rings* are, as we have said, Aragorn and Frodo. Aragorn is a king in exile, preserver of a noble lineage, who passes through the Paths of the Dead, fights a crucial turn in the epic battle, and proclaims a new dispensation. The hero, as Jung says, is a "greater man . . . semi-divine by nature," who meets "dangerous adventures and ordeals" and encounters the Wise Old Man.[25] Significantly, the numinous quality of the semidivine hero is not immediately obvious in Aragorn, who appears first as the Ranger Strider, suspected by the party and by us. Only when we pass more deeply into the quest do we learn of his noble lineage, of his destiny and his power of healing. He grows in our minds in stature as he looks into the magic *palantír*, passes through the Paths of the Dead, and is received, finally, as king. Aragorn is very much the traditional quest hero, but we observe him primarily from the outside.

Frodo, though his birth is peculiar among hobbits, is not a born hero like Aragorn, and we observe him from within, often sharing his point of view. As the story opens, we find in Frodo the vulnerability of the child which, according to Jung, often accompanies the hero's powers. But Frodo gradually develops away from his early naïveté, from the diffident hobbit, wondering why he was chosen and thinking to destroy the Ring with a hammer (I, 70). Growth into higher consciousness is painful; yet as Frodo carries the burden, his power increases, and as he passes through the dark experiences that lead to the Council of Elrond, the numinous aura and magic of the heroic archetype increasingly adhere to him. He finds he can see more clearly in the dark. In Galadriel's mirror he sees the depths of the history in which he is involved, and he becomes the bearer of magic light into the perilous realms. Slowly he acquires wisdom and a nobility comparable to that of Aragorn, so that, as we accompany Frodo's development and participate in it, we come to understand Aragorn himself more fully. As the tale ends, Frodo has achieved a heroic sanctity verging on the otherworldly.

The heroes throughout *The Lord of the Rings* are opposed by the Ringwraiths. As each archetype has a negative aspect, so the hero, says Jung, is especially threatened by dissolution "under the impact of the collective forces of the psyche." The characteristic challenge is from "the old, evil power of darkness," which threatens to overwhelm the hero and the self-identity he is striving to bring about.[26] The power of Sauron the Dark Lord is exactly such an old and evil force, and in *The Lord of the Rings* his representatives, the negative counterparts of the heroes, are the Black Riders. The menace they present balances perfectly the power that emanates from the heroic Aragorn, while their dissolution in Sauron's old and evil darkness, representing the loss of self, is indicated by the fact that the Black Riders have no faces.

The heroes must resist such loss of self and grow towards wisdom, a spiritual quality represented by the profound archetype of the Wise Old Man. More mysterious than the heroes, Gandalf's part in the quest is often beyond the reach of the story, and his knowledge remains unfathomable. When we first meet him, he seems more an old clown than a powerful magician. The interpretation of wisdom as foolishness is a traditional error of fools. In this case, it reflects the naïveté of the comfortable hobbits: Gandalf's "fame in the Shire was due mainly to his skill with fires, smokes, and lights. . . . To them he was just one of the 'attractions' at the Party" (I, 33). But Gandalf, like Aragorn, grows in stature as we, with Frodo, learn more about him. He is continually ahead of the quest, exercising a strange, almost Providential control. He reproves Frodo for many mistakes and seems to know the whole story in detail, even though it happened in his absence. "You seem to know a great deal already" (I, 231), says Frodo. We do not question Gandalf's knowledge but believe simply that its source is beyond our ken.

Gandalf also has a knack for appearing when he is needed. At the ford he sends a flood in the nick of time as Frodo's will fades. His wisdom leads the armies to Mordor and circumvents the trap set by the enemy who possesses Frodo's clothes. His eagles rescue Frodo and Sam at the last moment, and in the final episode of the story he makes sure (though we do not know how he knows) that Merry and Pippin will accompany Sam on his ride home, after Frodo departs for the Havens: "'For it will be better to ride back three together than one alone'" (III, 310). Here Gandalf provides, as he does throughout, for the deeper need, and there is a touch of magic in his actions.

For Jung, the Wise Old Man, as we have seen, appears especially when the hero is in trouble — "in a situation where insight, understanding, good advice, determination, planning, etc., are needed but cannot be mustered on one's own resources." He often, moreover, adopts the guise of a magician and is, essentially, a spirit archetype. Thus, the Wise Old Man is sometimes a "real" spirit, namely, the ghost of one dead. Tolkien, interestingly, has described Gandalf as "an angel," and we are to believe that he really died in the struggle with the Balrog, reappearing as Gandalf the White, an embodied spirit and a figure of great numinous power. Also, the Wise Old Man gives the necessary magical talisman, which, in Gandalf's case, is the Ring it-self.[27]

The Old Man, however, has a wicked aspect, too. Just as Galad-riel has her Shelob, and the heroes their Ringwraiths, so Gandalf has his antitype, the magician Saruman. They meet on equal ground, and between them the great struggle for self or dissolution of self is once again fought: "Like, and yet unlike" (II, 183), says Gimli pointedly, as he observes the two at Isengard. Their contest is based on a symbol-ism of light: Saruman is at first white, and Gandalf, a lesser magician, is grey. But Gandalf becomes white as Saruman falls to the powers of darkness and his robes become multicolored, "woven of all colours, and if he moved they shimmered and changed hue so that the eye was bewildered" (I, 272). Saruman's multicolor, like the facelessness of the riders, indicates a dissolution of identity. White is whole; fragmented, it is also dissipated.

The final and most elusive archetype is that of the self. Perhaps Tolkien's trilogy as a work of art which is more than the sum of its parts is the most satisfactory representation of this archetype, for the whole meaning is activated within the reader, who alone can experi-ence its completeness. But the most effective mediator between the ordinary reader and the "whole" world of Middle-earth, the character who in the end is closest to ourselves and who also must return to or-dinary life, is Sam Gamgee. Sam has become, in the process of the story, Samwise, but he is less removed from ourselves than Frodo or the other characters. As he leaves, Frodo says to Sam: "You will have to be one and whole, for many years. You have so much to enjoy and to be, and to do" (III, 309). The commendation of Sam's wholeness, and the directive to return to the ordinary world bearing that whole-ness with him, are a directive to the reader: ripeness is all. But such wisdom as Sam achieves is not easily come by, as the entire book indi-cates, and there is no case for critical denunciation of Tolkien on the grounds that his hobbits are simplistic or escapist. The Shire is not a haven, and the burden of the tale is that there are no havens in a world where evil is a reality. If you think you live in one, you are probably naïve like the early Frodo, and certainly vulnerable.

The archetypal patterns we have examined indicate the extent to which the trilogy can be read as a contemporary exploration of "interior space" analyzed in such novel terms in this century by Jung. Like Barfield and Lewis, however, Tolkien assumes a firmer stance before the archetypes than Jung. Lewis's criticism that Jung offers a myth to explain a myth can be met only by the assertion: there is a myth that is true, and fundamental. Following such a line of thought, Tolkien insists that successful fairy stories give a glimpse of truth which he describes as Eucharistic. The typical "eucatastrophe," the "turn" at the end of a good fairy story, has the sudden effect of a miraculous grace and gives a fleeting glimpse of "Joy," a momentary participation in the state that man most desires.[28] This joy, says Tolkien, is "a sudden glimpse of the underlying reality of truth" (p. 71). In this sense, the Christian story has "entered History and the primary world," and in it the "desire and aspiration of sub-creation has been raised to the fulfillment of Creation. The Birth of Christ is the eucatastrophe of Man's history. The Resurrection is the eucatastrophe of the story of the Incarnation" (pp. 71–72). In Western culture, the Christian story has thus contributed, and also transformed, the "Cauldron of Story" which Tolkien has discussed earlier in his essay. The basic Christian ingredient substantially alters the flavor of the entire simmering stock.

There are two significant implications in Tolkien's theory. First, the Christian influence on great poetry is profound, particularly on the epic, which addresses itself especially to the values by which men should live. Tolkien's essay on *Beowulf* indicates his appreciation of this fact. Second, the insistence on an ideal Eucharistic participation of the fantasy in the real world leads to a view of art analogous to the Christian Incarnation of the Word. In the greatest story, history and archetype interpenetrate. So in the fairy story, which typically activates the archetypes, historical verisimilitude is of the utmost importance. We must accept that the land of faërie is "true" before it can fully affect us.

The Lord of the Rings, therefore, as a fairy story based on these premises, is more than the inner psychodrama that a purely Jungian interpretation suggests, in which outer object is offset by inner, and in which a fairy tale typically depicts, as Jung says, "the unconscious processes that compensate the Christian, conscious situation."[29] For Tolkien, if it is good, the fairy tale participates in the Christian, conscious situation, and in the primary archetype of the Word made Incarnate from which that Christian consciousness derives. Tolkien faces, therefore, the crucial problem for the Christian writer — the problem faced first by Milton — of formulating a vision in which Christian assertion, history, and imagination can coinhere. For Tolkien, the "paradise within" must, ideally, be raised to fulfillment in the primary world of history, and this implies a sacramental, if nondoctrinal, view of reality. But it does not imply any simple reversion to medievalism: Tolkien does not write allegory, which assumes a corporate acceptance of dogmatic formulas based on a "realist" epistemology. The morality of his story is, as we have seen, implicit. His theory does, however, help to explain the inordinate pains spent on the appendixes, the background history, the landscape, names, traditions, annals, and the entire sense of a "real world" of Middle-earth. History and the "Primary World" are more fully rendered in Tolkien than in Milton, and, essentially, they mark the difference between a Eucharistic and a nonsacramental view of the world. Yet the great themes of the Christian epic remain implicit as a map of values in much the same form in *The Lord of the Rings* as in *Paradise Lost*. First, and most important, is the concept of Christian heroism, a spiritual quality that depends on obedience rather than prowess or personal power. Second, heroism is basic to the meaning of love. Third, charity, or love, is the foundation of faith and hope. And last, Providence directs the affairs of the world.

Tolkien first broaches the question of Christian heroism in the essay on *Beowulf* and in the "ofermod" appendix to "The Homecoming of Beorthnoth Beorhthelm's Son." Echoing a tradition of Christian thought as old as Augustine's *De Doctrina,* Tolkien points out that Beowulf's fame is "the noble pagan's desire for the merited praise of the noble." Consequently, his "real trust was *in his own might,*"[30] and Beowulf does not understand heaven or true "fame" in the eyes of God. This attitude leads only to excess and drives Beowulf towards chivalry by which, when he dies, he hopes to be remembered. The possible ill consequences of such chivalry are also evident in Beorthnoth, "hero" of "The Battle of Maldon." In allowing the invading Northmen to cross the ford for a fair fight when they were in fact trapped, Beorthnoth "was chivalrous rather than strictly heroic." The most grievous consequence of his action was that he sacrificed "all the men most dear to him" in his own desire for glory. The truly heroic situation, says Tolkien, is that of Beorthnoth's soldiers. "In their situation heroism was superb. Their duty was unimpaired by the error of their master." Consequently, "it is the heroism of obedience and love not of pride or willfulness that is the most heroic and the most moving."[31]

The Christian distinction between true and false heroism is thus already at work in *Beowulf* and "The Battle of Maldon," and certainly in *Paradise Lost* true Christian heroism based on obedience is at odds with mere glory won in deeds of arms. The feats of war in *Paradise Lost,* especially the War in Heaven, are best read as a parody of the futility of epic battles. The true heroism depends not on the acclaim of men but on the love of God, as Adam must discover. The theme is central also in *The Lord of the Rings,* and it helps to explain why we are closer to Frodo and Sam than to Aragorn. The hobbits are more purely heroic in that there is nothing chivalrous about them, and their heroism of obedience burns brightest because it is often without any hope of yielding renown or good name among men. Aragorn, true, is heroic, but he is chivalrous as well, and his fame is significantly reinforced by the acclaim of men. In total contrast is Sam

Gamgee, whose part is least publicly acclaimed of all, but who, in the sense in which we are now using the word, is especially heroic. His unfailing devotion to Frodo is exemplary, and here again Sam is a key link in bringing the meaning of the book to the reader, the everyman who admires great deeds but wonders what his own part might be in important events which seem well enough wrought without him.

The spiritual interpretation of heroism is the most significant Christian modification of the epic tradition and contains in essence the other motifs we have named. Their presence in *The Lord of the Rings* will therefore be indicated more briefly. First, if Tolkien is careful to show his most moving moments of heroism in the context of obedience to transcendent principles, he is also careful to point out that the most binding love derives directly from such obedience. The marriages at the end of the trilogy are clearly possible because the quest has been faithfully completed. Also, among the company, the strongest fellowship develops from a shared dedication to the quest and obedience to directives from higher sources of knowledge. The ensuing fellowship is strong enough to break even the age-old enmities between dwarves and elves, as is shown, for instance, by the intense loyalty the dwarf Gimli feels to the elf Galadriel. The fellowship breaks only when the bond of obedience is also broken, as it is by Boromir, whose pride and lust for personal power are evidence of false heroism.

The love of Sam for Frodo is the most consistent, and the most heroic, of all such relationships in the trilogy, and in it the ancillary theme that love subsumes faith and hope becomes plain. Though Frodo does not waver in faith until the very last moment at the Cracks of Doom, he loses hope as he and Sam face the plain of Gorgoroth: "I am tired, weary, I haven't a hope left" (III, 195). Soon he states, even more defeated: "I never hoped to get across. I can't see any hope of it now" (III, 201). Finally, Frodo's hope dissolves entirely, and he tells Sam: "Lead me! As long as you've got any hope left. Mine is gone" (III, 206). Gradually Frodo's physical power is affected, and

Sam carries him on his back. The story is, at this point, almost allegorical, as Sam's charity sustains his master's hope and faith. And there is no doubt about the contribution of Sam's heroic love to the success of the quest.

In the last resort, heroic obedience based on love of God and one's fellows must also involve faith in God's Providence, so that events that may appear undeserved or random can be accepted as part of a greater design. The wiser a man is, the more deeply he can see into that design. So Gandalf, for example, knows that Frodo and Gollum may meet. He also guesses that Aragorn has used the *palantír*, and his knowledge depends less on coincidence than on his perception of the design in events. On the other hand, those characters who are less wise are more at the mercy of unexplained events. Merry and Pippin, for example, do not suspect that their "chance" meeting with the ents is to cause the offensive that overwhelms Isengard. Early in the story we are directed to the importance of the complex relations of chance and Providence by Frodo's question to Tom Bombadil: "Was it just chance that brought you at that moment?" Tom replies, enigmatically: "Just chance brought me then, if chance you call it. It was no plan of mine, though I was waiting for you" (I, 137). Examples could be multiplied, but Tolkien plainly enough indicates throughout *The Lord of the Rings* that on some profound level a traditional Providence is at work in the unfolding of events. And in a world where men must die, where there are no havens, where the tragedy of exile is an enduring truth, the sense, never full, always intermittent, of a providential design, is also a glimpse of joy.

This essay has been centrally concerned with the analogy between Tolkien and Jung, but it is not simply an "archetypal" assessment of *The Lord of the Rings*. That the trilogy seems to correspond so closely to Jungian classifications certainly redounds to the mutual credit of Tolkien the teller of tales, that he should intuit the structure of the psyche so well, and to Jung the analyst, that he should classify so accurately the elusive images of the poets. For both, man participates in the spiritual traditions of his culture, and in a period such as the present the Christian expression of such a participation must be an especially private and "inner" one. Tolkien, in his theory, is aware of this, and an explication of the trilogy in terms of Jung provides some insights about the structure and dynamics of Tolkien's epic of "interior space." Yet Tolkien believes that his "inner" world partakes of spiritual truth that has found a special embodiment in history: the Word, as Archetype, was made flesh. Consequently, Tolkien insists on the "real" truth of faërie, and his Eucharistic understanding of literature causes him, in *The Lord of the Rings,* to expend great pains on the historical and linguistic background of Middle-earth. We must believe that it is true, and its truth must involve history as well as the great themes deriving, in literature, from the fundamentally important Christian story which is basic as both archetype and history. We find the morality of the story not in doctrinal formulations, which are the staples of allegory, but in the traditional and implicit motifs of Christian heroism, obedience, charity, and providence. Just as, historically, the simmering stock in the cauldron of story is substantially flavored by the Christian ingredient, so are the archetypes in *The Lord of the Rings.*

LIONEL BASNEY

Myth, History, and Time
in *The Lord of the Rings*

In this essay, Basney shows that The Lord of the Rings *presents us with a "secondary world" that is wholly coherent and consistent within itself. Its vision is obedient to certain basic structures and movements on all levels, the most comprehensive of them being "myth" and "history." The world of Middle-earth has a history that extends before and after the events upon which the central narrative, Frodo's quest, is focused. The quest, as well as all the actions subordinate to and surrounding it, comprise only a brief, if crucially important, incident within the greater history of this imagined world. It is in the interplay between history and myth, or lore, that the core meaning of the work lies. The distinction between action and lore, the existential and the literal, is the central component of the story. For example, characters caught in the exigencies of their immediate actions recall the greater visions of wholeness that impel them, as Aragorn carries with him the vision of Lórien, and Sam, struggling through the desolation of Mordor, calls to mind his beloved Shire. Lore not only underlies every action but is realized in it. Legend is fulfilled as a character suddenly recognizes that some reality he has known only in legend stands before him in actuality. This movement from legendary to real, Basney says, extends into a conception of time, and time, of course, is the governing idea in* The Lord of the Rings: *where each of us stands in it, the choice each makes either to attempt to*

183

arrest it or to yield to its passage, and the growth of each, and of the world itself, to fullness.

The Lord of the Rings is the story of a quest, and of a world in which the quest takes place, a world in which it can be meaningful. All fiction, in a sense, creates its own world, in that it is thoroughly intentional; all the details of the fictional world are chosen. But few stories create worlds so different from our own as Tolkien's. Few bother with nonhuman races, extinct languages, magical powers. Not all fiction, in other words, is fantasy.

Not all fantasy, moreover, is so successful as Tolkien's at creating a world that seems to possess solidity, orderliness, and integrity as well as vivacity and color. The reader's sensation in *The Lord of the Rings* is that he can trust the vision presented — not, of course, to be more than a vision, but to be wholly coherent and consistent within itself. Once he enters the "Secondary World," as Tolkien would say, he may trust the laws of that world to govern all appearances and events.[1] The narrative unfolds the world to us. But it also validates it; new characters, events, and topography fulfill, rather than violate, the expectations that have been raised in our minds.

The central characteristic of Tolkien's work — thus the one the critic must explain first and most carefully — is this structural and tonal integrity. It is not mere thematic unity. Indeed Tolkien tended to reject most efforts to define the "themes" of his work. Nor is this integrity simply a matter of the suspense generated by a well-told story. Though a function of the story, integrity is not a property of the story alone but of the entire project. Tolkien's success depends rather on his project's obedience to certain basic structures and movements on all its levels: plot, fantasy-world, the literary form of the work as a whole. The most comprehensive of these structures are "myth" and "history"; the most general movement, the growth of one into the other. Before substantiating this claim, however, we must develop a series of parallel contrasts that stand behind the dualism of myth and history in the text of *The Lord of the Rings*.

The first of these contrasts affects the work's format as a book. It opposes the "world" Tolkien has invented to the main events narrated by his story. The world, "Middle-earth," exists before and after these events; it is ordered, hierarchical, historical, all but static. The specific occurrence Tolkien narrates — not the whole history of Middle-earth but a brief, intense incident from that history — is Frodo's quest, a journey, full of chance, disconnected experience, frequent shifts in rhythm, the gradual maturation, under stress, of given qualities good and bad. This second structure is essentially dynamic, motive. From the perspective of Middle-earth as a world, the events of Frodo's journey are seen sub specie aeternitatis (in a fictional sense), as a pattern of historical events rescued from time by having been recorded, fitted into the larger pattern of the world's history. For the journey, Middle-earth as a world provides its inalienable conditions, determining, in the most general sense, what can and cannot happen. It also contains the past: the roots of present conflict and the repository of ideals.

Some readers have expressed a critical preference for one of these structures over another. William Ready, for instance, gives his attention to the quest, wishing that Tolkien had not included the appendixes which summarize Middle-earth's genealogical and philological history.[2] But the opposing structures are both necessary. The quest reveals and illuminates the world; the world provides the determining conditions of the quest.

According to Tolkien, moreover, the mock scholarly apparatus which contains Middle-earth's lineaments as a world was conceived before the quest (I, 5). *The Lord of the Rings* developed from Tolkien's children's story, *The Hobbit* (1937), but not directly. What intervened was an effort to set in order the pre-*Hobbit* past of Middle-earth by providing philological histories of its ancient tongues (especially Elvish). In this there was little narrative invention. Tolkien was only recalled to narrative by his friends' curiosity about the "present-day" story, the matter of the Ring; then, over a period of a decade and a half, he composed the six narrative books we now have. By distinguishing between "ancient history," with its mock philology and imaginary genealogies, and the *story* of the Ring, Tolkien shows that the opposition of cosmos and journey has its counterpart in the work's format. In a sense, *The Lord of the Rings* may be regarded as a descendant of *A Tale of a Tub* and *Sartor Resartus*, with its combination of narrative and "scholarly" material — introduction, appendixes, index, maps, and the pretense of translation from older literatures. Tolkien and Swift are different largely in mood. Swift was intent on multiple satire. Tolkien's "scholarship" validates and supports his story, giving it a context, the "Secondary World," to inhabit.

Two further contrasts between the static and the dynamic are to be found in the narrative itself. The first works as a fundamental organizing device of Tolkien's plot: movement versus tableau. The flight to Rivendell versus the enclosed, comfortable scenes of Bree and the Shire; Rivendell itself versus the journey to Moria; Lothlórien, the still center of Middle-earth with its memory of the Elder Days, versus the turmoil of war in Rohan and Gondor. Dominating the story's climax is the tableau of the serene White Tower versus the nightmarish creeping trek of Sam and Frodo through Mordor. Tolkien varies this device as a way of emphasizing distance and loneliness: Pippin in Gondor thinks of Sam and Frodo. The device is further, but logically, extended to include a contrast between a character's immediate effort and his ultimate vision. In the absence from Middle-earth of explicitly noumenal values, this vision must usually be phenomenal and spatial: Aragorn carries with him the vision of Lórien. Struggling in Mordor's desolation, Sam thinks of the Shire, which means to him all the things he is ready to sacrifice himself for: home, comfort, the earth's fruitfulness, the hobbits' secure bourgeois contentment.

The second plot distinction leads us near our larger dualism. Tolkien makes a distinction between action and lore, between the existential and the literal, and the distinction is an essential component of the story. Part of the effort against Sauron, a part that is almost exclusively Gandalf's responsibility, is the identification of the One

Ring. To assemble its history, to link it with "Isildur's Bane" and the Gladden Fields, Gandalf exercises what is essentially historical research; this carries him from hearsay and legend to the formal archives of Minas Tirith. Without this coherent lore, the Ring, unrecognized, would have been calamitously easy for Sauron to recover.

The importance of "lore" in Middle-earth is not only utilitarian. It is valued for itself. Further, we find it undergoing a definite evolution. During the time covered by Tolkien's narrative, the fundamentally oral-mythical traditions of Rohan and Rivendell are in the process of being written down, of assuming specifically literary form. This process derives from an impulse belonging primarily to hobbits, whose tidy minds demand comfortable, transparent orders and accurate records. (It is significant that hobbits are the only race in Middle-earth to construct museums. This indicates the relatively low-key, companionable though precise reminiscence which fills the same demand in the Shire that epic song fills in Rohan.)

But the immediate stimulus of the process is the War of the Ring, which brings the hobbits out of xenophobic isolation and makes them the historians of the reestablished Kingdom. The ancient legend which gets written down is that most closely associated with the War. Bilbo, for instance, composes creditable poetry about the Elder Days. This is appreciated, in the Rivendell manner, through communal recitation. But he also works at setting in order the written account of his travels, which later becomes, with Frodo's crucial additions, the core of the Ring's official history. This history is finally completed by the hobbits, though it is glossed and edited as well in Gondor (I, 23–25).

A different stage in the progression from legend to history appears in Rohan. Midway between the hobbits' bourgeois democracy and the aboriginal state of the "wild men," the Rohirrim live in a heroic honor-culture where manhood means military prowess and knowledge, the "ancient lay." Their relatively primitive historical consciousness is at root identical with their limited insight in the scope of Middle-earth. Of Lórien they know only nursery tales about Galadriel, whom they think a sorceress. Ignorant of Sauron or magic seeing-stones, Rohan sees Saruman and Gondor simply as military enemy and ally. Though they regard themselves as ancient, the Rohirrim are in fact perilously young and naïve; their limited awareness defines, and is defined by, their lack of comprehensive "lore," their estrangement from the mythical springs of ancient history at Rivendell and Lórien.

The hobbits' transformation of oral-mythical legend into formal history is the most literary example of the story's "realization" of myth. But it is not the only example. The plot also "realizes" the cultural myths of its races by matching events with their mythical equivalents, allowing the legend to be fulfilled by actual enactment in the plot. Because of their relative ignorance, the Rohirrim are the prototype of a people seeing its legends and nursery rhymes come to actual life. But others have the same experience. Frodo's quest is a birth into knowledge for the hobbits who accompany him. Moreover, the races who encounter the hobbits find their appearance a challenge to credulity and scepticism. The hobbits seem literally a myth come to life, to living fact.

The general pattern of this repeated incarnation is as follows: an individual character, often on his home ground and thus confident of his ability to judge rightly, suddenly recognizes that some reality of which he had known only in legend now faces him in broad daylight, or is attested to by authority he cannot gainsay. The character's response is normally a blend of surprise, assent, and wonder. For the reality he confronts does not thereby lose its mythical fascination. Rather the myth merges with experience, or into experience, its wonder intact, but having gained empirical solidity.

This experience of recognition occurs in pure form at least fifteen times in the trilogy. It is worth specifying these, to indicate their variety, and also to suggest their importance to the larger pattern of events. First are the three instances of characters encountering hobbits: Haldir, an elf (I, 357); Éothain in Rohan (II, 37); Beregond in Minas Tirith (III, 33). The hobbits encounter two specifically legendary beings: Pippin comes across the trolls of Bilbo's tale (I, 218); Sam sees an oliphaunt (II, 255, 270). Boromir learns from Elrond about the Ring's fate, about which Gondor's tales have only hinted (I, 256); he also hears from Celeborn about ents (I, 390). With him in this are Aragorn and Legolas, who hear more particulars from Gandalf (II, 102). Gandalf also tells Gimli of the Endless Stair, which he has visited (II, 105). Several encounters are closely related to the War itself. Éomer meets Aragorn and his identifying sword, and hears from the three companions about the reality of Galadriel (II, 35–36). Like his brother, Faramir encounters the Ring (II, 289), and later tells Denethor of the halflings "that I have seen walking out of northern legends" (III, 84). The men of Lossarnach and Rohan march to battle in Mordor, which had been only a legend to them (III, 162). Finally, Imrahil's family story about elf ancestry is confirmed by Legolas, who can see it in him (III, 148). In each case some intimation of hobbits, ents, and so on, had been given by a familiar story: the story, once ignored or disbelieved, turns out to be a version of sober fact.

"Dreams and legends," says Éomer, "spring to life out of the grass" (II, 36). C. S. Lewis commented that Éomer's distinction between legend and reality was "rash."[3] But if this distinction were less clear to the peoples of Middle-earth, their shock and wonder would also be less. The experience of myth-realization is to Éomer the harbinger of a new and special era, a time in which ultimate battles must be fought. Nor does the experience take place indiscriminately. It generally opens to certain characters the existence of others of whom we have already been aware; and, in any case, it must obey the ontological limits of Middle-earth as a world. Plainly, many legends remain legends; and Tolkien is selective on principle. It is through the transformation of certain myths into experience that the free peoples recognize each other, and their common destiny and enemy. Their common knowledge becomes an active bond among them. It is as if their alliance had been latent in cultural and racial myth, awaiting the special events which actualize it and bring it into dynamic focus.

It should be plain where our initially structural dualism is leading us. The movement from legend to experience, from "imaginary" to "real" (though even the real is fictive), extends inevitably to a conception of time, one of the two which jointly govern Middle-earth. These two conceptions spring from opposing *ethoi.* The less important is pagan, "northern," its paradigm *Beowulf;* its corresponding time pattern is cyclical and deterministic, seeing human civilization as an effort to buy time from forces of evil which always rise after defeat to be met again.[4] We glimpse this *ethos* in Gandalf's counsel that Frodo should concern himself with the affairs of his time, and that the shadow of which Sauron is only a manifestation can never be fully destroyed (I, 60).

To this pagan pattern the unfolding, evolving movement which realizes legend is clearly opposed. The *ethos* here is Judeo-Christian; its corresponding notion is the "fullness of time," the progressive blossoming of mysterious intent that produces a necessary answer at the instant it is needed. There is, indeed, little messianism in Tolkien's plan. It seems to Frodo that he is singled out by chance. But the time pattern of messianic promise is essential: the gradual unfolding of mythical possibilities, or of possibilities grasped only by myth, into plain reality. This revelation obeys the tempo of its time. We see Middle-earth in a state of crisis. Each day summons its myth "out of the grass." But, as Gandalf's painful research into the Ring's course from Isildur to Frodo makes plain, the progress of time toward its realizing moment has never stopped; it has only been ignored, or preserved in the amber of legend.

Thus the main characters of *The Lord of the Rings* sense that they are living in a time of prophecy-fulfillment. These are the days when "it has come to pass, which was spoken of." Tolkien calls them the "Great Years" at the close of the Third Age (III, 372). The Fourth Age opens with the passing of Elrond Halfelven across the sea and the final disappearance from Middle-earth of all who had had direct dealings with the Ring (III, 363, 378). This period is also the transition from the "Elder Days" to the age of men (i.e., our age). Though in the prologue to *The Lord of the Rings* (I, 10) Tolkien suggests that hobbits still inhabit the world, the passing of the Elder Days effectively closes the day of fantasy, and we find ourselves at the dawn of man's hegemony. The unfolding of Tolkien's time scheme brings him inevitably from the world of myth to that of human history. The nonhuman "speaking peoples" pass to the West, die, or retreat into silence, and the story ends when all the "faërie" potentials of Tolkien's plan have been, or are about to be, exhausted.

At the trilogy's end, therefore, we are in some sense in the present-day world. We are, at least, out of the world of faërie. Tolkien makes no effort to merge the Fourth Age with any recognizable epoch of human record. But the *sine qua non* of faërie has been lost: the opportunity for contact between man and the other beings and traditions.[5] It is thus perfectly logical that after completing *The Lord of the Rings* Tolkien returned to his earlier preoccupation, the history of former ages. *The Silmarillion,* on which he worked sporadically in the years before his death, was to carry us back to the Elder times, the ages which are merely legend even to Aragorn. It is clear that Tolkien had no more to say of the Fourth Age. The proper evolution of its fantasy time carries Middle-earth from the far past to which memory can penetrate only by means of imagination, of myth, to the virtual present, after the possibility of the fantasy experience has disappeared along with the faërie races.

The agency of this evolution is never defined. The elves' desire to pass to the West obeys a sort of paradisal nostalgia that is their racial possession and, in a sense, their identity. But it is consequently confined to them. Nor are the historical "ages" in any way causal. They end, generally, with a defeat of the Shadow and a new lease on life for Middle-earth's population. But what determines the makeup of this population, or the ways in which it seems unavoidably to change,

Tolkien does not specify. The "West" holds both purpose and power; it is, however, up to the races of Middle-earth to attend to their own business. Gandalf tells Frodo that he was *"meant"* to receive and own the Ring (I, 65) — in which case some of the events in the ensuing narrative were also "meant." But the agency can be no clearer.

This causal vagueness is essential, I think, because it inhibits our critical impulse to read some abstract dogma into Tolkien's story. Tolkien himself insisted that he was not writing allegory (I, 7); and the conflicting *ethoi* in Middle-earth's time patterns should warn us off. The movement from past to present obeys a definite, ingrained teleology, but this is the urge of Tolkien's fictional mode and not of a dictating creed. It is a movement from myth to history, from the mythical world communicated by imagination to the historical record embodied in Tolkien's charts, tables, and glosses.

Tolkien's enigmatic insistence that in *The Lord of the Rings* he was writing "history" (I, 7) becomes clearer in the light of this overall movement. For the essential development of Tolkien's narrative is the conversion of myth or legend into history, that is, into the real and calculable: from the vague prophecies of communal tradition, to the halflings "walking out of legend" into broad daylight, to the meticulous records of the hobbit historians. The culminating step of this process is Tolkien's own act of composition. Middle-earth's Fourth Age has no discernible connection with human history, as we have said; on the contrary, Middle-earth's "present" is in Tolkien's writing, his pretense of translation from recovered old-language histories, his careful setting in order of the ancient evidence. This is what the nature of his world demands. One of Middle-earth's governing cosmic conditions is the growth of legend into history. And Tolkien's work is the final reduction of the Elder Days into present-day form. As long as the hobbits were, so to speak, elaborating their history, Middle-earth's story (and nature) remained fluid. But with Tolkien's act of composition, this potential is actualized, fixed, final, entire. In *The Lord of the Rings*, Tolkien at once imagines and fulfills the historical development of his world.

For his work, therefore, history is the mode of fixed and completed reality, existence rescued from time and adumbrated in logic. Tolkien could not have written the history of the Ring until the characters and events associated with it — until its world — had become "historical," that is, irredeemably past. The way fantasy is exhausted at the close of the Third Age makes Tolkien's history possible. No further development of the seminal myth could be expected. On the other hand, the Ring's affairs may be said to comprise history only in the act of Tolkien's writing. Only in the fixed, intentional record which is his narrative is his fantasy fixed, specified, made real. By telling his story, Tolkien has realized his myth, and also the myths his mythical characters possess and create.

The link between the "past" of Middle-earth and Tolkien's work is his pretense of scholarship. The imagined transcription and translation of materials from hobbit manuscripts — the very tables and charts which some readers find tiresome — make the integrity of Tolkien's work possible. Because he treats his work not as deliberate fiction — allegory, which depends for validity on something truer than itself — but as history, his invented world can itself claim historical solidity and independence. It determines and fulfills its own historical conditions. One of these conditions, moreover, is our central dualism, which can be seen on all levels of the work: the dualism of myth (or story) and history (or fact), along with the realization of the first in the second.

The crucial difference between the realization of myth within Tolkien's narrative and outside it should also be clear. For Middle-earth's inhabitants, myth becomes history by way of experience. For us, myth becomes experience only by way of Tolkien's history. The culturally juvenile impulse to treat Middle-earth as having other than literary existence — other than a *feigned* history — stems from the failure to remember that Middle-earth exists only in words, in the chosen details of Tolkien's narrative, to which nothing can be added. By inventing Middle-earth, Tolkien also fixed it beyond change. The dynamism of myth and history is only an inner dynamism, which nevertheless explains some of the story's narrative interest. It also explains part of the "integrity" of Middle-earth: our sense that Tolkien's manner of presenting his invention is wholly at one with its nature.

Tolkien liked to talk of fantasy as an unfolding of the potentials of God's creation, an addition to the actual cosmos.[6] Middle-earth too is a kind of cosmos; but we can make no additions to it. It unfolds no further than the text. We are not mistaken, however, if we feel that Middle-earth does "unfold" within its own boundaries. Its very nature as a world is to develop and grow, particularly to develop realities out of apparent fiction. Like those of the real world, Middle-earth's values and structure are revealed dynamically, in the course of a process of development which is also a growth of perception. As readers we observe this process affecting the lives and destinies of Tolkien's characters. But it affects as well the very form of the work we are reading and, thus, the kind of reading we do. We too experience the gradual realization of imagined beings and events. We too, after our fashion, meet halflings "walking out of legend."

JANE CHANCE

The Lord of the Rings:
Tolkien's Epic

*Using as her starting point the conflict between two contributory
streams in English epic, the Christian and the Germanic, Chance examines the conjunction of the ideals of each and the moral systems that
grow out of them in Tolkien's epic. The ideal heroes fostered by each of
the epic traditions are the Germanic Earl and the Christian Elf-king.
The former rules by oath and discipline, while the latter is intent upon
sacrificing himself for the good of others. In a close and fascinating reading, Chance takes us, book by book, on an exploration of the conflicting
moral poles of ultimate good and evil that arise from Tolkien's amal-
gamation of the heroic types. The highest moral good for the Middle
Ages is* caritas, *a chain of love that binds together all creatures on earth
as well as the spheres in heaven. Its obverse,* cupiditas, *is diseased self-
love that values nothing outside of the self which cannot be put to the use
of self, and which ends in ruin. Chance traces the growth of these two
concepts in the unfolding action of the novel.*

The epic form has proved useful in reflecting the clash of value
systems during periods of transition in literary history. In the Old
English *Beowulf*, Germanic heroism conflicts with Christianity: the
chivalric pride of the hero can become the excessive *superbia* con-
demned in Hrothgar's moralistic sermon. Similar conflicts occur in

195

other epics or romance-epics: between the chivalric and the Christian in the twelfth-century German *Nibelungenlied* and in Sir Thomas Malory's fifteenth-century *Morte Darthur;* between the classical and the Christian in the sixteenth-century *Faërie Queene* of Sir Edmund Spenser; and between chivalric idealism and modern realism in the late-sixteenth-century Spanish epic novel of Cervantes, *Don Quixote.* Tolkien's *Lord of the Rings* delineates a clash of values during the passage from the Third Age of Middle-earth, dominated by the Elves, to the Fourth Age, dominated by Men. Such values mask very medieval tensions between Germanic heroism and Christianity evidenced earlier by Tolkien in his *Beowulf* article.

In this sense *The Lord of the Rings* resembles *The Hobbit,* which . . . must acknowledge a great thematic and narrative debt to the Old English epic, even though *The Hobbit*'s happy ending renders it closer to fantasy in Tolkien's definition than to the elegy with its tragic ending. The difference between them stems from form: Randel Helms notes that the children's story narrated by the patronizing adult in *The Hobbit* has "grown up" sufficiently to require no fictionalized narrator in the text itself and to inhabit a more expansive and flexible genre like the epic:

> [W]e have in *The Hobbit* and its sequel what is in fact the same story, told first very simply, and then again, very intricately. Both works have the same theme, a quest on which a most unheroic hobbit achieves heroic stature; they have the same structure, the "there and back again" of the quest romance, and both extend the quest through the cycle of one year, *The Hobbit* from spring to spring, the *Rings* from fall to fall.[1]

Although Helms does not mention their relationship with medieval ideas or even with the *Beowulf* article, still, given this reworking of a theme used earlier in *The Hobbit,* I would speculate that *The Lord of the Rings* must also duplicate many medieval ideas from *The Hobbit* and elsewhere in Tolkien.

As an epic novel *The Lord of the Rings* constitutes, then, a *summa* of Tolkien's full development of themes originally enunciated in the *Beowulf* article and fictionalized later in other works. It was, after all, begun in 1937 — the same year *The Hobbit* was published and a year later than the *Beowulf* article — and completed in 1949, prior to the publication of many of the fairy-stories (1945–67) and the medieval parodies (1945–62). Its medial position in Tolkien's career indicates how he articulated his major ideas generally and comprehensively in this mammoth work before delving into their more specialized aspects in the later fairy-stories and parodies.

As a synthesis, then, of Tolkienian ideas, both Germanic heroic or medieval and Christian, *The Lord of the Rings* reconciles value systems over which its critics have debated incessantly and single-mindedly. Some critics have explored its major medieval literary sources, influences, and parallels, particularly in relation to northern saga and Old and Middle English literature, language, and culture, chiefly *Beowulf* and *Sir Gawain and the Green Knight*.[2] Other critics have explored its direct and indirect religious, moral, or Christian (Roman Catholic) aspects.[3] No one seems to have understood fully how the dual levels of the *Beowulf* article might apply to *The Lord of the Rings,* although Patricia Meyer Spacks suggests provocatively that at least one level does apply: Tolkien's view of the "naked will and courage" necessary to combat chaos and death in the context of northern mythology (as opposed to Christianity) resembles the similar epic weapons of the Hobbit-heroes of his trilogy.[4] In addition, no critic has seemed to notice that even in genre and form this work combines an explicitly medieval bias (as epic, romance, or *chanson de geste*) with an implicitly Christian one (as fantasy or fairy-story).[5] The most interesting and most discussed genre has been that of medieval romance, with its tales of knights and lords battling with various adversaries.[6]

Its title, "The Lord of the Rings," introduces the ambiguous role of the ruler as leader ("The Lord") with power over but also responsibility for others ("the Rings"). Elsewhere in Tolkien's critical and creative works the lord has been depicted as an excessively proud Germanic warrior bent on the sacrifice of his men for his own ends . . . or as a humble Elf-king modeled on Christ, intent on sacrificing himself for the sake of his followers. . . . So in this epic Sauron typifies the Germanic lord in his monstrous use of his slaves as Gandalf typifies the Elf-king or Christ figure in his self-sacrifice during the battle with the Balrog. But there are hierarchies of both monstrous and heroic lords in this epic, whose plenitude has frustrated critical attempts to discern *the* hero as either Aragorn, Frodo, or Sam.[7] Aragorn may represent the Christian hero as Frodo and Sam represent the more Germanic hero — that is, the subordinate warrior — yet all three remain epic heroes. The complexity of Tolkien's system of heroism and monstrous "lords" in the trilogy becomes clearer through an examination of its structural unity.

In defining the parameters of the work's structure,[8] Tolkien declares that "[t]he only units of any structural significance are the books. These originally had each its title."[9] This original plan was followed in the publication in 1999 of the "Millennium Edition," with its seven slim volumes, one for each renamed book and the appendices: book 1 is "The Ring Sets Out"; book 2, "The Ring Goes South"; book 3, "The Treason of Isengard"; book 4, "The Ring Goes East"; book 5, "The War of the Ring"; book 6, "The End of the Third Age"; and book 7, "Appendices." Apparently Tolkien had initially substituted titles for each of the three parts at the instigation of his publisher, although he preferred to regard [the whole] as a "three-decker novel" instead of as a "trilogy" in order to establish it as a single, unified work, not three separate works.[10] But in either case, with six books or with three parts, the title of each thematically and symbolically supports the crowning title, "The Lord of the Rings," by revealing some aspect of the adversary or the hero through a related but subordinate title that fixes on the Ring's movements and the ambiguity of its "owner" or "bearer," and each of the three parts is itself supported thematically and symbolically by its two-book division.

In *The Fellowship of the Ring* the focus falls upon the lord as both a hero and a monster, a divided self. . . . Frodo as the "lord" or keeper of the Ring in the first part mistakes the chief threat to the Hobbit Fellowship (a symbol of community) as physical and external (for example, the Black Riders) but matures enough to learn by the end of the second book that the chief threat exists in a more dangerous spiritual and internal form, whether within him as microcosm (the hero as monster) or within the Fellowship as macrocosm (his friend Boromir). *The Fellowship* as bildungsroman echoes the development of the hero Bilbo in *The Hobbit.* . . .

The Two Towers shifts attention from the divided self of the hero as monster to the more specifically Germanic but also Christian monster seen in Saruman (representing intellectual sin in book 3) and Shelob (representing physical sin in book 4), who occupy or guard the two towers of the title. This part duplicates material in *The Hobbit* outlining monstrosity in terms of the *Beowulf* article and the *Ancrene Wisse.* . . .

The evil Germanic lord often has a good warrior to serve him; the figure of the good servant merges with the Christian king healer (Aragorn) who dominates *The Return of the King* in opposition to the Germanic destroyer (Denethor) in book 5, the consequences of whose reign lead to a "Return" or regeneration in the macrocosm in book 6. . . . The structure of the epic then reveals a hierarchy of heroes and monsters implied by its title but also summoned from Tolkien's other critical and creative works.

I. THE FELLOWSHIP OF THE RING: THE HERO AS MONSTER

Because the title of *The Fellowship of the Ring* links the wandering "Fellowship" with the "Ring," . . . a subtitle for the first part of the epic might be "All that is gold does not glitter, / Not all those who wander are lost." Thematically, the title and its "subtitle" suggest that appearance does not equal reality: the Ring appears valuable because it glit-

ters; the wandering Fellowship appears lost. But in reality the gold
Ring may not be as valuable as it appears, and the Fellowship may not
be lost; further, the wanderer to whom the lines refer, despite his
swarthy exterior and wandering behavior as Strider the Ranger, may
be real gold and definitely not lost. As the king of light opposed to
the Dark Lord, Strider returns as king after the Ring has been finally
returned to Mount Doom, ending the aspirations of the Lord of
the Rings. "The Fellowship of the Ring" as a title stresses the heroic
mission of Aragorn's "followers" to advance the cause of the good
king. The band of gold represents by synecdoche the power of the evil
Lord of the Rings, to be countered by the "band" of the Fellowship,
whether the four hobbits in book 1 or the larger Fellowship of hobbits, wizard, Elf, Dwarf, and man in book 2.

Because the Fellowship is burdened with the responsibility of
bearing the Ring and because its presence attracts evil, the greatest
threat to the Fellowship and its mission comes not from without but
within. The hero must realize that he can become a monster. The two
books of the *Fellowship* trace the process of this realization: the first
book centers on the presentation of evil as external and physical, requiring physical heroism to combat it; and the second book centers
on the presentation of evil as internal and spiritual, requiring a spiritual heroism to combat it. The hero matures by coming to understand the character of good and evil — specifically, by descending
into an underworld and then ascending into an overworld, a natural
one in the first book and a supernatural one in the second. The second book, then, functions as a mirror image of the first. These two
levels correspond to the two levels — Germanic and Christian — of
Beowulf and *The Hobbit*. For Frodo, as for Beowulf and Bilbo, the ultimate enemy is himself.

Tolkien immediately defines "the hero as monster" by introducing the divided self of Gollum-Sméagol and, then, to ensure the
reader's understanding of the hero as monster, Bilbo-as-Gollum. The
Cain-like Sméagol rationalizes the murder of his cousin Déagol for

the gold Ring he holds because it is his birthday (I, 84). Sméagol deserves a gift, something "precious" like the Ring, because the occasion celebrates the fact of his birth, his special being. The parable of Sméagol's fall illustrates the nature of evil as *cupiditas,* or avarice, in the classical and literal sense. But as the root of all evil (in the words of Chaucer's Pardoner, alluding to St. Paul's letter to Timothy) *cupiditas* more generally and medievally represents that Augustinian selfishness usually personified as strong desire in the figure of Cupid (=cupidity, concupiscence or desire). The two names, Gollum and Sméagol, dramatize the fragmenting and divisive consequences of his fall into vice, the "Gollum" the bestial sound of his swallowing as an expression of his gluttony and greed, the "Sméagol," in its homonymic similarity to "Déagol," linking him to a group of others like him (the Stoors, as a third family-type of hobbit) to establish his common hobbitness — and heroism.[11] That is, Gollum's psychological resemblance to the hobbits is revealed when good overpowers the evil in him and, as he witnesses his master Frodo asleep in Sam's lap, he reaches out a hand to touch his knee in a caress. At that moment he seems "an old weary hobbit, shrunken by the years that had carried him far beyond his time, beyond friends and kin, and the fields and streams of youth, an old starved pitiable thing" (II, 411).

But also, Tolkien takes care to present the good Hobbit and heroic Bilbo as a divided self, "stretched thin" into a Gollum-like being because of his years carrying the Ring. The scene opens after all with Bilbo's birthday party, to re-enact the original fall of Gollum, on his birthday. The role of Déagol is played by Bilbo's nephew Frodo: on Bilbo's birthday, instead of receiving a gift, Bilbo, like Gollum, must give away a gift — to the other hobbit relatives and friends and to Frodo, recipient of the Ring. But at the moment of bequest Bilbo retreats into a Gollum-like personality as illustrated by similar speech patterns: "It is mine, I tell you. My own. My precious. Yes, my precious" (I, 59). Bilbo refuses to give away the Ring because he feels himself to be more deserving and Frodo less deserving of carrying it.

Later the feeling is described as a realization of the Other as monstrous (presumably with the concomitant belief in the self as good). In the parallel scene at the beginning of book 2, Bilbo wishes to see the Ring, and so he reaches out a hand for Frodo to give it to him; Frodo reacts violently because "a shadow seemed to have fallen between them, and through it he found himself eyeing *a little wrinkled creature with a hungry face and bony groping hands*. He felt a desire to strike him" (I, 306; my italics). The Ring, then, a sign of imperial or ecclesiastical power in medieval contexts and a sign of the conjugal bond in personal and familial contexts, appropriately symbolizes here the slavish obeisance of Sméagol to Gollum and a wedding of self to self, in lieu of a wedding of self to Other.

That is, wedding the self to Other implies a giving up of selfishness out of love and concern for another being. An expression of such *caritas* is hinted at in Gollum's momentary return to Hobbitness, when he seems to show love for his master, Frodo, and is symbolized by the "band" of the Fellowship to which each member belongs — another "Ring." Such *caritas* opposes the view of the Other as monstrous. Even Frodo at first sees monstrous Gollum as despicable: "What a pity that Bilbo did not stab that vile creature, when he had a chance!" (I, 92). But just as the hero can become monstrous, so can the monster become heroic: it is Gollum who helps Frodo and Sam across the Dead Marshes and, more important, who inadvertently saves Frodo from himself; Gollum also saves Middle-earth by biting the Ring off Frodo's finger as they stand on the precipice of Mount Doom in the third part. Therefore, Gandalf cautions Frodo to feel toward the despicable Gollum not wrath or hatred but love as pity, such as Bilbo has manifested toward Gollum: "Pity? It was Pity that stayed his hand. Pity, and Mercy: not to strike without need" (I, 92). Gandalf explains:

> "Many that live deserve death. And some that die deserve life.
> Can you give it to them? Then do not be too eager to deal out

death in judgment. For even the very wise cannot see all ends. I have not much hope that Gollum can be cured before he dies, but there is a chance of it. And he is bound up with the fate of the Ring. My heart tells me that he has some part to play yet, for good or ill, before the end; and when that comes, the pity of Bilbo may rule the fate of many — yours not least." (I, 93)

This pity as charity, or love binding one individual to another, cements together the "fellowship" of the hobbits in book 1 and later, in book 2, the differing species who form the enlarged Fellowship. The "chain of love" such fellowship creates contrasts with the chains of enslavement represented by Sauron's One Ring. Described as "fair" in the Middle Ages, the chain of love supposedly bound one individual to another and as well bound together the macrocosm of the heavens: Boethius in *The Consolation of Philosophy* terms it a "common bond of love by which all things seek to be held to the goal of good."[12] After Boethius explains that "love binds together people joined by a sacred bond; love binds sacred marriages by chaste affections; love makes the laws which join true friends," he wistfully declares, "O how happy the human race would be, if that love which rules the heavens rules also your souls!" (book 2, poem 8, p. 41).

The chain of enslavement, in contrast, involves a hierarchy of power, beginning with the

One Ring to rule them all, One Ring to find them,
One Ring to bring them all and in the darkness bind them
        (I, vii),

and encompassing the seven Dwarf-rings (could they be found) and the nine rings of the "Mortal Men doomed to die," the Ringwraiths.[13] If love binds together the heavens and the hierarchy of species known in the Middle Ages as the Great Chain of Being — which includes angels, humankind, beasts, birds, fish, plants, and stones — then hate and envy and pride and avarice bind together the hierarchy of species under the aegis of the One Ring of Sauron the fallen Vala. Only the "Three Rings for the Elven-kings under the sky" — the loftiest and most noble species — were never made by Sauron because, says Elrond, the Elves "did not desire strength or domination or hoarded wealth, but understanding, making, and healing, to preserve all things unstained" (I, 352).

Tolkien intentionally contrasts the hierarchy of good characters, linked by the symbolic value of fellowship into an invisible band or chain of love, with the hierarchy of evil characters and fallen characters linked by the literal rings of enslavement — a chain of sin.[14] It is for this reason that the miniature Fellowship of Hobbits in the first book draws together in love different representatives from the Hobbit "species" or families — Baggins, Took, Brandybuck, Gamgee — as the larger Fellowship in the second book draws together representatives from different species — the four Hobbit representatives, Gimli the Dwarf, Strider and Boromir the men, Legolas the Elf, and Gandalf the Wizard. In both cases, however, these representatives are young — the heirs of the equivalents of the "old men" who must revitalize and renew Middle-earth because it too has become "old" and decrepit, governed by the spiritually old and corrupt influence of Sauron. Symbolically, then, these "heirs," as the young, represent vitality, life, newness: Frodo is Bilbo's nephew and heir, Gimli is Glóin's, Legolas is Thranduil's, Strider is Isildur's, Boromir is Denethor's, and the remaining hobbits are the still-youthful heirs of their aged fathers. Only Gandalf as the good counterpart to Sauron is "old." In part Gandalf constitutes a spiritual guide for Frodo, especially in book 2, as Aragorn-Strider constitutes a physical (literally powerful) guide in book 1.

The necessity for the young figure to become the savior hero (like the *novus homo*) of the old is introduced by Tolkien in the first pages of *The Fellowship*. Note the spiritual oldness of the fathers of the miniature "Fellowship" of Hobbits; the old Hobbits view those who are different, or "queer," as alien, evil, monstrous, or dangerous because the fathers themselves lack charity, pity, and understanding. They condemn the Brandybucks of Buckland as a "queer breed" for engaging in unnatural (at least for hobbits) activities on water (I, 45). Yet these old hobbits are not evil, merely "old." Even the Gaffer vindicates Bag End and its "queer folk" by admitting, "There's some not far away that wouldn't offer a pint of beer to a friend, if they lived in a hole with golden walls. But they do things proper at Bag End" (I, 47). Gaffer's literalness — his oldness — is characteristic of the Old Law of justice ("proper") rather than the New Law of mercy. Such old Hobbits also lack imagination, an awareness of the spirit rather than the letter. Sam's father expresses a literalism and earthiness similar to Sauron's: "*'Elves and Dragons!' I says to him. 'Cabbages and potatoes are better for me and you'*" (I, 47). This "Old Man" Tolkien casts in the role of what might be termed the "Old Adam," for whom Christ as the New Adam will function as a replacement and redeemer. A gardener like Adam at Bag End, Gaffer condemns that of which he cannot conceive and accepts that of which he can — cabbages and potatoes — and presents his condemnation in the appropriately named inn, the Ivy Bush. Although his son Sam is different and will become in effect the New Adam of the Shire by the trilogy's end, generally, however, earth-bound Hobbits (inhabiting holes underground) display a similar lack of imagination, symbolized by their delight in the pyrotechnic dragon created by Gandalf. They may not be able to imagine Elves and dragons, but they love what they can *see,* a "terribly lifelike" dragon leaving nothing to the imagination (I, 52). This dragon, however, unlike that in *Beowulf,* poses no threat to their lives. In fact, it represents the "signal for supper."

The "New Man" represented by the Hobbits Frodo, Sam, Merry, and Pippin then must overcome a natural inclination toward "oldness," toward the life of the senses inherent in the Hobbit love of food, comfort, warm shelter, entertainment, and good tobacco. All of the Hobbits do so by the trilogy's end, but Frodo as Ring-bearer changes the most dramatically and centrally by the end of *The Fellowship.* His education, both oral lessons from guides and moral and life-threatening experiences, begins with the gift of the Ring after Bilbo's birthday party.

Designated as Bilbo's heir and recipient of the Ring at the birthday party (chapters 1–5) in the first book, Frodo is also designated as the official Ring-bearer after the Council of Elrond (chapters 1–3) in the second book, to which it is parallel. In the first book Gandalf relates the history of Gollum's discovery of the Ring and Bilbo's winning of it, and he explains its nature and properties. In the second book, at this similar gathering, the history of the Ring, from its creation by Sauron to the present, and the involvement therein of various species are related. The birthday party that allows Bilbo to "disappear" as if by magic from the Shire is like the council that allows Frodo and other members of the Fellowship to "disappear" as if by magic from Middle-earth — and from the searching Eye of Sauron, for the Dark Lord will never imagine them carrying the Ring *back* to Mordor. Further, the distribution of gifts to friends and relatives after the party resembles the council's decision to give back the "gift" of the Ring to its "relative," the mother lode of Mount Doom. The gifts in each episode make explicit the flaws of the recipient: Adelard Took, for example, receives an umbrella because she has stolen so many from Bilbo. In a sense Sauron too will indirectly receive exactly what he has always wanted and has continually tried to usurp or steal — the Ring. The point of these parallels should be clear: the concept of the divided self or the hero as monster was revealed in the symbolic birthday party through the figures of Gollum-Sméagol, Bilbo-Gollum, Frodo-Gollum — the hero as monster suggested by the notion of the "birthday." For the reader, Tolkien warns that the most dangerous evil really springs from inside, not from outside.

This message introduced at the beginning of *The Fellowship of the Ring* is what Frodo must learn by its end. The Council of Elrond, its very title suggesting egalitarian debate among members of a community rather than group celebration of an individual, symbolically poses the converse message, that the most beneficial good similarly springs from the inside but must be directed to the community rather than to oneself. The humble member of the council — the insignificant Hobbit Frodo — is ultimately chosen to pursue the mission of the Ring because he *is* insignificant.[15] Frodo's insignificance in the community there contrasts with Bilbo's significance as a member of the Shire community. However, as the chapter . . . "A Long-Expected Party" (or what might be called "The Birthday Party") had dramatized the presence of evil among inheritance-seeking relatives (specifically the greedy and self-aggrandizing Sackville-Bagginses) so "The Council of Elrond" indicates the potential of evil threatening the Fellowship from within through the greed and self-aggrandizement of some of its members — Men like Boromir.

In the first book Frodo comes to understand evil as external and physical through the descent into the Old Forest, a parallel underworld to the supernatural underworld of Moria[16] in the second book. Both Old Man Willow and the barrow-wights represent the natural process of death caused, in Christian terms, by the Fall of Man.[17] Originally the Old Forest consisted of the "fathers of the fathers of trees" whose "countless years had filled them with pride and rooted wisdom, and with malice" (I, 181), as if they had sprung from the one Tree of Knowledge of Good and Evil in Eden. The ensuing history of human civilization after the Fall of Adam and Eve resulted in similar falls and deaths: "There was victory and defeat; and towers fell, fortresses were burned, and flames went up into the sky. Gold was piled on the biers of dead kings and queens; and mounds covered them and the stone doors were shut; and the grass grew over all" (I, 181). As Old Man Willow and his malice represent the living embodiment of the parent Tree of Death, so the barrow-wights represent the ghostly embodiment of the dead parent civilizations of men: "Barrow-wights walked in the hollow places with a clink of rings on cold fingers, and gold chains in the wind" (I, 181). The Hobbits' first clue to the character of the *Old* Forest (note again Tolkien's emphasis on oldness) resides in the falling of the hobbits' spirits — a "dying" of merriment — when they first enter. Their fear, depression, and gloom are followed by the deathlike sleep (again, a result of the Fall) as the chief weapon of Old Man Willow (I, 165). All growth in nature is abetted by sleep and ends in death, usually after oldness (again, the Old Man Willow figure). The barrow-wights who attack the Hobbits later in the Old Forest are also linked to the earth, like the roots of Old Man Willow, but here through the barrow, a Man-made grave which they inhabit as ghosts. The song of the barrow-wights invokes coldness and death, literally the "bed" of the human grave, where "Cold be hand and heart and bone, / and cold be sleep under stone" (I, 195).

The attacks of . . . Old Man Willow and the barrow-wights on the Hobbits are stopped by Tom Bombadil and his mate, Goldberry, who personify their complementary and positive counterparts in Nature.[18] The principle of growth and revivification of all living things balances the process of mutability and death: what Goldberry lauds as "spring-time and summer-time, and spring again after!" (I, 173), omitting autumn and winter as antithetical seasons. Tom Bombadil as master of trees, grasses, and the living things of the land (I, 174) complements the "fair river-daughter" dressed in a gown "green as young reeds, shot with silver like beads of dew," her feet surrounded by water lilies (I, 172). Because their role in nature involves the maintenance of the existing order, their songs often praise the Middle-earth equivalent of the medieval Chain of Being:

> Let us sing together
> Of sun, stars, moon and mist, rain and cloudy weather,
> Light on the budding leaf, dew on the feather,
> Wind on the open hill, bells on the heather,
> Reeds by the shady pool, lilies on the water:
> Old Tom Bombadil and the River-daughter! (I, 171)

As the Old Forest depresses the Hobbits, Tom Bombadil cheers them up so much that, by the time they reach his house, "half their weariness and all their fears had fallen from them" (I, 171). It is no accident that Tom Bombadil always seems to be laughing and singing joyously.

Frodo learns from the descent into this underworld of the Old Forest that the presence of mutability, change, and death in the world is natural and continually repaired by growth and new life. In the second book he learns through a parallel descent into the Mines of Moria that the spiritual form of death represented by sin stems from within the individual but is redeemed by the "new life" of wisdom and virtue counseled by Galadriel, the supernatural equivalent of Tom Bombadil, who resides in the paradisal Lothlórien. The descent also involves a return to the tragic past of the Dwarves, who fell because of the "oldness" of their kings, their avarice; the ascent involves an encounter with the eternal present of Lothlórien, where all remains new and young, and filled with the healing spirit of Elven mercy and *caritas*.

The Dwarves led by both Durin and later Balin fell because of their greed for the jewels mined in Moria[19] — its depths a metaphorical equivalent of Old Man Willow's buried roots and the deep barrows inhabited by the wights. But unlike the sense of material death pervading the Old Forest, the death associated with the mines is voluntary because it is spiritual in nature and one chooses it or at least fails to resist its temptation: this spiritual death exists in the form of avarice. Gandalf declares that "even as *mithril* was the foundation of their wealth, so also it was their destruction: they delved too greedily and too deep, and disturbed that from which they fled, Durin's Bane" (I, 413). Durin's Bane, the Balrog, monstrously projects the Dwarves' internal vice, which resurfaces later to overpower other Dwarves, including Balin. It is no accident that Balin dies at Mirrormere, a very dark mirror in which he is blind to himself. His mistaken goal of *mithril* and jewels contrasts with that of the Elves of Lórien, whose Galadriel possesses a clear mirror of wisdom.

Lórien of the Blossom boasts an Eternal Spring where "ever bloom the winter flowers in the unfading grass" (I, 454), a "vanished world" where the shapes and colors are pristine and new, for "no blemish or sickness or deformity could be seen in anything that grew upon the earth. On the land of Lórien there was no stain" (I, 454–55).[20] In this paradise of restoration . . . time almost ceases to pass and seems even to reverse, so that "the grim years were removed from the face of Aragorn, and he seemed clothed in white, a young lord tall and fair" (I, 456). Evil does not exist in this land nor in Galadriel unless brought in from the outside (I, 464). The physical and spiritual regeneration or "life" characteristic of these Elves is embodied in their *lembas,* a food that restores spirits and lasts exceedingly long — a type of communion offered to the weary travelers. Other gifts of the Lady Galadriel — the rope, magic cloaks, golden hairs, phial of light, seeds of *elanor* — later aid them either physically or spiritually at times of crisis in their quest, almost as a type of Christian grace in material form.[21] Like Adam and Eve forced to leave Paradise for the wilderness, although taking with them its memory as a "paradise within, happier far," in Miltonic terms, the travelers leave Lórien knowing "the danger of light and joy" (I, 490). Legolas reminds Gimli the Dwarf that "the least reward that you shall have is that the memory of Lothlórien shall remain ever clear and unstained in your heart, and shall neither fade nor grow stale" (I, 490). Gimli's dwarvish and earth-bound nature compels him to deny the therapeutic value of memory: "Memory is not what the heart desires. That is only a mirror, be it clear as Kheled-zâram" (I, 490). The mirror to which he refers in Westron is called "Mirrormere" and, instead of reflecting back the faces of gazers, portrays only the reflection of a crown of stars representing Durin's own destructive desire. In contrast, the Mirror of Galadriel with its vision of the Eternal Present, connoting supernatural wisdom, invites the gazer to "see" or understand himself, however unpleasant. Gimli is wrong; memory *is* a mirror and reflects back the consolation of truth, at least for those wise and steadfast beings like the Elves, whose "memory is more like to the waking world than to a dream. Not so for Dwarves" (I, 490).

This lesson in natural and supernatural evil and good also functions as a mirror for Frodo to see himself. He must learn there is both Dwarf and Elf in his heart, a Mines of Moria and Lothlórien buried in his psyche. Having learned, he must then exercise free will in choosing either good or evil, usually experienced in terms of putting on or taking off the Ring at times of external or internal danger. While his initial exercises are fraught with mistakes in judgment, the inability to distinguish impulse from deliberation or an external summons from an internal decision, eventually he does learn to control his own desires and resist the will of others. Told by Gandalf to fling the Ring into the fire after just receiving it, "with an effort of will he made a movement, as if to cast it away — but he found that he had put it back in his pocket" (I, 94). As Frodo practices he grows more adept but still slips; at the Inn of the Prancing Pony, his attempt at singing and dancing to divert the attention of Pippin's audience from the tale of Bilbo's birthday party allows him to become so "pleased with himself" that he puts on the Ring by mistake and becomes embarrassingly invisible. The physical dangers Frodo faces in these encounters culminate in the attack of the Black Riders one night and later at the Ford. The Ring in the first instance so controls his will that "his terror was swallowed up in a sudden temptation to put on the Ring. The desire to do this laid hold of him, and he could think of nothing else. . . . [A]t last he slowly drew out the chain, and slipped the Ring on the forefinger of his left hand" (I, 262–63). As a consequence, Frodo can see the Ringwraiths as they really are, but unfortunately, so can they see him, enough to wound him in the shoulder. The worst test in the first book involves the encounter at the Ford. Counseled first by Gandalf to "Ride!" from the Black Rider attacking them, Frodo is then counseled silently by the Riders to wait. When his strength to refuse diminishes, he is saved first by Glorfindel, who addresses his horse in Elvish to flee, and again by Gandalf, who drowns the horses of the Black Riders when they prevent Frodo's horse from crossing the Ford.

While Frodo fails these major tests in the first book and must rely on various manifestations of a deus ex machina to save himself, his established valor and courage represent the first steps to attaining the higher form of heroism expressed by wisdom and self-control in the second book, a heroism very like that Germanic form exhibited by Beowulf in the epic of the same name.[22] Frodo's physical heroism evolves in the combat with physical dangers in book 1: his cry for help when Merry is caught by Old Man Willow; his stabbing of the barrow-wight's hand as it nears the bound Sam; his dancing and singing to protect Pippin and their mission from discovery; his stabbing the foot of one Rider during the night attack; and his valor (brandishing his sword) and courage (refusing to put on the Ring, telling the Riders to return to Mordor) at the edge of the Ford. But this last incident reveals his spiritual naïveté: he believes physical gestures of heroism will ward off the Black Riders.

Only after Frodo's education in the second book, which details supernatural death and regeneration instead of its more natural and physical forms, does he begin to understand the necessity of *sapientia*, in addition to that heroism expressed by the concept of *fortitudo*. In the last chapter, "The Breaking of the Fellowship," he faces a threat from the proud and avaricious Boromir *within* the macrocosm of the Fellowship. Fleeing from him, Frodo puts on the Ring to render himself invisible and safe. But this unwise move allows him to see clearly (too clearly) as he sits, symbolically, upon Amon Hen (Hill of the Eye), built by the kings of Gondor, the searching of Sauron's own Eye.[23] What results is a second internal danger — the threat from *within* Frodo, the microcosm. A battle is staged within his psyche, and he is pulled first one way, then another, until, as a fully developed moral hero, he exercises the faculty of free will with complete self-control:

> He heard himself crying out: *Never, never!* Or was it: *Verily I come, I come to you?* He could not tell. Then as a flash from some other point of power there came to his mind another thought: *Take it off! Take it off! Fool, take it off! Take off the Ring!*

He feels the struggle of the "two powers" within him:

> For a moment, perfectly balanced between their piercing points,
> he writhed, tormented. Suddenly he was aware of himself again.
> Frodo, neither the Voice nor the Eye: free to choose, and with one
> remaining instant in which to do so. He took the Ring off his
> finger. (I, 519)

In this incident, parallel to the encounter of the Riders at the Ford in
the last chapter of the first book, Frodo here rescues *himself* instead of
being rescued by Glorfindel or Gandalf. Further, in proving his moral
education by the realization that he must wage his own quest alone to
protect both their mission and the other members of the Fellowship,
he displays *fortitudo et sapientia* (fortitude and wisdom) and *caritas*
(charity) — hence, he acts as that savior of the Fellowship earlier witnessed in the figures of Tom Bombadil and Strider in the first book
and Gandalf and Galadriel in the second. His education complete,
Frodo can now function as a hero for he understands he may, at any
time, become a "monster."

The turning point in the narrative allows a shift in Tolkien's
theme and the beginning of the second part of the epic novel in *The
Two Towers.* The remaining members of the Fellowship are divided
into two separate groups in this next book, a division symbolizing
thematically not only the nature of conflict in battle in the macrocosm but also the psychic fragmentation resulting from evil. It is
no mistake that the title is "The Two Towers" — the double, again,
symptomatic of the divided self. There are not only two towers but
two monsters.

II. *THE TWO TOWERS:* THE GERMANIC KING

The two towers of the title belong to Saruman and in a sense to
Shelob because the quest of the remainder of the Fellowship in book
3 culminates in an attack on Orthanc and because the quest of Frodo

and Sam in book 4 leads to their "attack" on Cirith Ungol, the sentry tower at the border of Mordor guarded by the giant spider.[24] Both Orthanc and Cirith Ungol copy the greatest tower of all, the Dark Tower of Sauron described as a "fortress, armory, prison, furnace . . . secure in its pride and its immeasurable strength" (II, 204). Through these two monsters represented by their towers, this second part of *The Lord of the Rings* defines the nature of evil in greater detail than in the first part. Thus, it also introduces the notion of the Christian deadly sins embodied in the monsters (found in the *Ancrene Wisse*), which must be combated by very Germanic heroes.[25]

The tower image is informed by the Tower of Babel in Genesis 11. In this biblical passage, at first, "[t]hroughout the earth men spoke the same language, with the same vocabulary," but then the sons of Noah built a town and "a tower with its top reaching heaven." They decided, "Let us make a name for ourselves, so that we may not be scattered about the whole earth."[26] Their desire to reach heaven and "make a name" for themselves represents the same desire of Adam and Eve for godhead. Because they believe "[t]here will be nothing too hard for them to do" (11:6–7), the Lord frustrates their desire by "confusing" their language and scattering them over the earth. Their overweening ambition and self-aggrandizement result in division of and chaos within the nation.

Selfishness, or *cupiditas,* symbolized by the Tower of Babel, shows how a preoccupation with self at the expense of the Other or of God can lead to confusion, alienation, division. The recurring symbolism of *The Two Towers* in Tolkien's work helps to break down this idea of *cupiditas* as perversion of self. The tower of Saruman, or Orthanc, means "Mount Fang" in Elvish but "Cunning Mind" in the language of the Mark, to suggest perversion of the mind; the tower of Shelob, or Cirith Ungol, means "Pass of the Spider," to suggest perversion of the body. While the creation of the Tower of Babel results in differing languages to divide the peoples, the two towers in Tolkien express division in a more microcosmic sense, in terms of the separation and perversion of the two parts of the self. Saruman's intellectual perversion has shaped his tower (formerly inhabited by the wardens of Gondor) to "his shifting purposes, and made it better, as he thought, being deceived — for all those arts and subtle devices, for which he forsook his former wisdom, and which fondly he imagined were his own, came but from Mordor" (II, 204). Specifically, the pride and envy of Sauron impel him to achieve ever more power as his avarice impels him to seek the Ring and conquer more lands and forests through wrathful wars. Like Saruman, Shelob "served none but herself" but in a very different, more bestial way, by "drinking the blood of Elves and Men, bloated and grown fat with endless brooding on her feasts, weaving webs of shadow; for all living things were her food, and her vomit darkness" (II, 422). Her gluttony is revealed in her insatiable appetite, her sloth in her demands that others bring her food, and her lechery in her many bastards (perhaps appropriately and symbolically quelled by Sam's penetration of her belly with his sword). Never can Shelob achieve the higher forms of perversion manifested by Saruman: "Little she knew of or cared for towers, or rings, or anything devised by mind or hand, who only desired death for all others, mind and body, and for herself a glut of life, alone, swollen till the mountains could no longer hold her up" (II, 423). Guarding the gateway to Mordor at Cirith Ungol, Shelob suggests another guardian — of the gateway to hell. In Milton's *Paradise Lost*, Satan's daughter, Sin, mated with her father to beget Death, [who] pursued her lecherous charms relentlessly and incessantly.[27] In this case, Shelob is depicted not as Satan's daughter but as Sauron's cat (II, 424).

Tolkien shows the analogy between the two monsters and their towers by structuring their books similarly. The perversion of mind embodied in Saruman is expressed by the difficulty in communication through, or understanding, words or gestures in book 3, and the perversion of body personified in Shelob is expressed by the difficulty in finding food and shelter, or hospitality, in book 4. Specifically

Wormtongue, Grishnákh, and Saruman all display aspects of the higher sins of pride, avarice, envy, and wrath through their incomprehension or manipulation of language. Gollum and Shelob both illustrate the lower sins of gluttony, sloth, and lechery. Each book centers on the adventures of only part of the Fellowship, the nobler members in book 3 (Legolas, Gimli, Aragorn, and Merry and Pippin) and the more humble members in book 4 (Sam and Frodo). In each book, too, the adventures progressively become more dangerous, the enemies encountered more vicious.

The Uruk-hai in book 3 illustrate the disorder and contention caused by the literal failure to understand languages. When Pippin first awakens after being captured, he can understand only some of the Orcs' language: "Apparently the members of two or three quite different tribes were present, and they could not understand one another's orc-speech. There was an angry debate concerning what they were to do now: which way they were to take and what should be done with the prisoners"(II, 60); debate advances to quarrel and then to murder when Saruman's Uglúk of the Uruk-hai kills two of Sauron's Orcs led by Grishnákh. The parable suggests that the tongues of different species or peoples create misunderstanding and hence conflict, disorder, and death, because of the inability to transcend selfish interests. Because they do not adhere to a common purpose their enmity allows the hobbits [to escape] when Grishnákh's desire for the Ring overcomes his judgment and he unties the hobbits just before his death.

This literal failure to communicate is followed in book 3 by a description of a deliberate manipulation of language so that misunderstanding will occur. Worm*tongue*'s ill counsel renders the king impotent and his people leaderless. As a good counselor, Gandalf begs Théoden to "come out before your doors and look abroad. Too long have you sat in shadows and trusted to twisted tales and crooked promptings" (II, 151). When Théoden spurns the "forked tongue" of the "witless worm" (the satanic parallels are surely intentional) in exchange for wise counsel, the king of Rohan leaves the darkness; he stands erect and drops his staff to act as "one new-awakened." Unlike Wormtongue, who has manipulated others by means of belittling words into death and despair, Gandalf wisely counsels life and hope. Such good words unite the Rohirrim and the Fellowship in a common purpose — fighting Saruman — [as opposed to language that] divides, like that of the quarrelsome Uruk-hai and Orcs.

If Gandalf awakens Théoden from a sleep caused by evil counsel, then Merry and Pippin awaken Treebeard from no counsel at all, given his sleepy neglect of his charge as Shepherd of the Trees.[28] While Treebeard has been used as a source of information by Saruman, the latter has not reciprocated, even evilly: "His face, as I remember it . . . became like windows in a stone wall: windows with shutters inside" (II, 96). But Treebeard must realize the threat to Fangorn posed by Saruman, who "has a mind of metal and wheels; and he does not care for growing things, except as far as they serve him for the moment" (II, 96). Saruman has abused Nature's growing things by destroying the trees and twisted human nature by creating mutants and enslaving the will of Men like Théoden to obtain his own will. In the Entmoot, an orderly civilized debate in contrast to the quarrels of the Orcs and the one-sided insinuation of Wormtongue, language serves properly to unite the Ents by awakening them to Saruman's threat. These talking trees — signifying the principle of reason and order inherent in Nature as the higher complement to the principle of life and growth signified by Tom Bombadil — join with the Men of Rohan (. . . Riders complementary to the Rangers we met in the figure of Strider in the first book) to combat the evil represented by "Cunning Mind."

These episodes that delineate the problem of language and communication in the attempt to join with or separate from the Other culminate in the most important episode of all in the chapter entitled "The Voice of Saruman." Here, in the final debate between the fallen and the reborn Wizards, Saruman fails to use language cunningly enough to obtain his end and hence he loses, literally and symboli-cally, that chief weapon of the "cunning mind," the *palantír* (far-seer). Unctuous Saruman almost convinces the group that he is a gentle Man much put upon who only desires to meet the mighty Théoden. But Gimli wisely perceives that "the words of this wizard stand on their heads. . . . In the language of Orthanc help means ruin, and sav-ing means slaying, that is plain" (II, 235). In addition Éomer and Théoden resist the temptation to believe the wily ex-Wizard, so that his truly corrupt nature[29] is then revealed through the demeaning im-precations he directs toward the House of Eorl.

The emphasis upon language in this book shows that human speech can reflect man's highest and lowest aspirations: good words can express the love for another as cunning words can seek to subvert another for the speaker's own selfish ends. The archetypal Word is Christ as the Incarnation of God's love;[30] but words or speech in gen-eral, according to St. Thomas Aquinas in his essay "On Kingship," naturally distinguish human from the beast because they express his rational nature. However, the misuse of reason to acquire knowledge forbidden by God leads to human spiritual degeneration and the de-humanization of the Other. On the one hand, such behavior marks Saruman as a perverted Wizard accompanied by his equally per-verted servant, Wormtongue — their perversion makes them mon-strous. On the other hand, to underscore the extent of Saruman's per-version this book is filled with examples of the heroes' difficulty in communicating with others and understanding the signs and signals of another's language.

Thus, for example, when Aragorn, Legolas, and Gimli find the Hobbits missing [and] their whereabouts unknown, they face an "evil choice" because of this lack of communication, just as Merry and Pippin, once captured, almost succumb to despair because they do not know where they are or where they are going (II, 59). In the at-tempt to pursue the Hobbits, the remainder of the Fellowship must learn to "read" a puzzling sign language: the letter *S* emblazoned on a dead Orc's shield (killed in Boromir's defense of the Hobbits); the footprints of Sam leading *into* the water but not back again (II, 25); the heap of dead Orcs without any clue to the Hobbit presence (II, 53); the appearance of a strange old man bearing away their horses (II, 116); the mystery of the bound hobbits' apparent escape (II, 116). All of these signs or riddles can be explained, and indeed, as Aragorn suggests, "we must guess the riddles, if we are to choose our course rightly" (II, 21). Man's quest symbolically depends on his correct use of his reason; the temptation is to know more than one should by consulting a magical device like the *palantír*.

If book 3 demonstrates the intellectual nature of sin, then book 4 demonstrates its physical, or material, nature. Although the structure of Shelob's tower of Cirith Ungol ends this book as Orthanc ends the third, the tower is never described in this part. Instead, another tower — Minas Morgul — introduces the weary group to the land they approach at the book's end. In appearance Minas Morgul resembles a human corpse:

> Paler indeed than the moon ailing in some slow eclipse was the light of it now, wavering and blowing like a noisome exhalation of decay, a *corpse-light*, a light that illuminated nothing. In the walls and tower windows showed, like countless black holes *looking inward* into emptiness; but the topmost course of the tower revolved slowly, first one way and then another, *a huge ghostly head* leering into the night. (II, 396–97; my italics)

The holes might be a skull's. As a type of corpse it focuses attention on the human body, whose perverse desires preoccupy Tolkien in this book.

. . . Gollum's obsession with fish and dark things of the earth disgusts Frodo and Sam: his name as the sound of swallowing aptly characterizes his monstrously gluttonous nature. Again, when Gollum guides the Hobbits across the Dead Marshes, it is dead bodies from the battle between Sauron and the Alliance in the Third Age, or at least their appearance, that float beneath the surface and tempt Gollum's appetite (II, 297). But the Hobbits' appetites result in trouble too: they are captured by Faramir when the smoke of the fire for the rabbit stew cooked by Sam and generously intended for Frodo is detected. Faramir's chief gift to the weary Hobbits is a most welcome hospitality, including food and shelter, as a respite from the barren wasteland they traverse. Finally, the Hobbits are themselves intended as food by Gollum for the insatiable spider, Shelob. Truly the monster (whether Gollum or Shelob) is depicted as a glutton just as the hero — past, present, or future (the corpse, the Hobbits, Faramir) — is depicted as food or life throughout this book. Physical life can end without food to sustain the body; it can also end, as the previous book indicated, because of an inaccurate interpretation of language to guide rational judgment.

These monsters representing sin are opposed by heroes constructed as Germanic lords and warriors. As we have seen, Théoden, the weak leader of Rohan, is transformed by Gandalf's encouragement into a very heroic Germanic king in book 3. . . . In book 4 the Germanic warrior or subordinate (chiefly Sam) vows to lend his aid to his master out of love and loyalty. . . . The bond between the king as head of a nation and reason as "lord" of the individual corresponds to that between the subordinate warrior as servant of the king and the subordinate body.

To enhance these Germanic correspondences Tolkien describes Rohan as an Old English warrior nation complete with appropriate names[31] and including a suspicious hall guardian named Hama, very similar to one in *Beowulf,* and an *ubi sunt* poem modeled on a passage from the Old English "Wanderer":

> Where now the horse and rider? Where is the horn that was
>   blowing?
> Where is the helm and the hauberk, and the bright hair
>   flowing? (II, 142)

Where went the horse, where went the man? Where went the
treasure-giver?
Where went the seats of banquets? Where are the hall-joys?[32]

. . . Throughout book 3 Tolkien stresses the physical heroism of the
Rohirrim and the Fellowship in the battle at Helm's Deep, which resembles those described in "The Battle of Maldon," "Brunanburh,"
and "The Fight at Finnsburg."

But in book 4 the heroism of the "warrior" depends more on
love and loyalty than on expressions of valor in battle. Four major
subordinates emerge: Gollum, Sam, Frodo, and Faramir. Each offers a
very Germanic oath of allegiance to his master or lord: Gollum, in
pledging not to run away if he is untied, swears by the Ring, "I will
serve the master of the Precious" (II, 285). So Frodo becomes a lord,
"a tall stern shadow, a mighty lord who hid his brightness in grey
cloud, and at his feet a whining dog" (II, 285). Gollum must also
swear an oath to Faramir never to return to the Forbidden Pool or
lead others there (II, 379). Sam similarly serves his master Frodo but,
like Gollum, betrays him, not to Shelob but [unconsciously] to Faramir, by cooking the rabbit stew. Likewise, Frodo the master seems to
betray his servant Gollum by capturing him at the Forbidden Pool
even though Gollum has actually saved him from death at the hands
of Faramir's men — "betray" because the "servant has a claim on the
master for service, even service in fear" (II, 375). Finally, because
Faramir has granted Frodo his protection, Frodo offers him his service while simultaneously requesting a similar protection for his servant, Gollum: "take this creature, this Sméagol, under your protection" (II, 380). Ultimately even Faramir has vowed to serve his father
and lord, Denethor, by protecting this isolated post. In the next part
of the epic Denethor will view Faramir's service as incomplete, a betrayal. Because Faramir has not died instead of his brother, Boromir,
he will seem to [have] fail[ed], just as the warriors lying in the Dead
Marshes have apparently succeeded only too well, given the fact of

their death in battle. While the exchange of valor or service for protection by a lord duplicates the Germanic contract between warrior and king, the exchange in *The Two Towers* seems fraught with difficulty either because of the apparent laxity of the lord or the apparent disloyalty of the subordinate.

The enemy, interestingly enough, functions primarily as a version of Christian rather than Germanic values, but still there is some correspondence between the *ofermod* of the Germanic lord and the *superbia* of the Christian, both leading to other, lesser sins. The Germanic emphasis in this volume does continue in the next part of the epic but ultimately merges with a more Christian definition of both servant and king.

III. *The Return of the King*: The Christian King

This part of *The Lord of the Rings* sees the climax of the struggle between good and evil through battle between the Satan-like Dark Lord and the Christlike true king, Aragorn. Because Aragorn "returns" to his people to accept the mantle of responsibility, the volume is entitled "The Return of the King," with emphasis upon "kingship" in book 5 and "return" in book 6. Dramatic foils for the Christian king as the good steward are provided in book 5 by the good and bad Germanic lords Théoden and Denethor, whose names [are almost] anagrams of [each other]. . . . The good Germanic subordinates Pippin and Merry, whose notion of service echoes that of the good Christian, similarly act as foils for the archetypal Christian servant Sam, whose exemplary love for his master, Frodo, transcends all normal bounds in book 6. Finally, the concept of renewal attendant upon the return of the king pervades the latter part of the sixth book as a fitting coda to the story of the triumph of the true king over the false one.

The contrast between the two Germanic lords is highlighted early in book 5 by the offers of service presented respectively by Pippin to Denethor in chapter 1 and by Merry to Théoden in chapter 2. As the Old Man, the Germanic king more interested in glory and honor than in his men's welfare, Denethor belittles Pippin because he assumes smallness of size equals smallness of service. This literalistic mistake has been made earlier by other "Old Men," especially *Beowulf* critics, the narrator of *The Hobbit,* and Nokes in "Smith of Wootton Major." Why, Denethor muses, did the "halfling" escape the Orcs when his much larger son, Boromir, did not? In return for the loss of Denethor's son, Pippin feels moved — by pride — to offer in exchange himself, but as an eye-for-an-eye, justly rendered payment of a debt: "Then Pippin looked the old man in the eye, for pride stirred strangely within him, still stung by the scorn and suspicion in that cold voice. 'Little service, no doubt, will so great a lord of Men think to find in a hobbit, a halfling from the northern Shire; yet such as it is, I will offer it, in payment of my debt'" (III, 30). Pippin's offer is legalized by a contractual vow binding him both to Gondor and the steward of the realm either until death takes him or his lord releases him. The specific details of the contract invoke the usual terms of the bond between lord and warrior: according to the Germanic *comitatus* ethic, Denethor must not "fail to reward that which is given: fealty with love, valour with honor, oath-breaking with vengeance" (III, 31).

Merry's vow to Théoden, in contrast, expresses a voluntary love for, rather than involuntary duty to, his king, characteristic of the ideal Germanic subordinate in Tolkien's "Ofermod" commentary. And Théoden, unlike Denethor, represents the ideal Germanic lord who truly loves [rather than uses] his men. Viewing Merry as an equal, he invites him to eat, drink, talk, and ride with him, later suggesting that as his esquire he ride on a hill-pony especially found for him. Merry responds to this loving gesture with one equally loving and spontaneous: "Filled suddenly with love for this old man, he knelt on one knee, and took his hand and kissed it. 'May I lay the sword of Meriadoc of the Shire on your lap, Théoden King?' he cried. 'Receive my service, if you will!'" (III, 59). In lieu of the legal contract between the lord Denethor and the servant Pippin there is Merry's oral promise of familial love: "'As a father you shall be to me,' said Merry" (III, 59).

These private vows of individual service to the governors of Gondor and Rohan are followed in chapters 2 and 3 by more public demonstrations of national or racial service. In the first incident the previous oathbreakers of the past — that is, the Dead of the Gray Company — redeem their past negligence by bringing aid to Aragorn in response to his summons. This contractual obligation fulfilled according to the letter of prophecy, Théoden and his Rohirrim can fulfill their enthusiastic and loving pledge of aid by journeying to Gondor. They themselves are accompanied by the Wild Men in chapter 5 as a symbolic corollary to their spontaneity, love, and enthusiasm — the new law of the spirit.

In addition, two oath*makers* of Rohan — Éowyn and Merry — in contrast to the oathbreakers mentioned above, literally appear to violate their private vows of individual service but actually render far greater service than any outlined in a verbal contract. When Éowyn relinquishes her duty to her uncle and king, Théoden, to take charge of the people until his return, by disguising herself as the warrior Dernhelm so that she may fight in battle, she also allows Merry to break his vow to Théoden when he secretly rides behind her into battle. But when Théoden is felled by the Nazgûl Lord, it is she who avenges him — Dernhelm "wept, for he had loved his lord as a father" (III, 141), as does Merry: "'King's man! King's man!' his heart cried within him. 'You must stay by him. As a father you shall be to me, you said'"(III, 141). Dernhelm slays the winged creature ridden by the Lord of the Nazgûl; Merry helps her slay its rider. The service they render, a vengeance impelled by pity and love for their lord, is directed not only to the dead king and father Théoden, or to Rohan and Gondor, but to all of Middle-earth. Interestingly, Éowyn's bravery in battle arouses Merry's: "Pity filled his heart and great wonder, and suddenly the slow-kindled courage of his race awoke. He clenched his hand. She should not die, so fair, so desperate! At least she should not die alone, unaided" (III, 142). Simple love for another results in Merry's most charitable and heroic act. These subordinates have completely fulfilled the spirit, if not the letter, of their pledges of allegiance to their lords.

Tolkien also compares and contrasts the lords of book 5. The evil Germanic lord Denethor is matched by the good Germanic lord Théoden; both contrast with the Christian lord Aragorn. Denethor fails as a father, a master, a steward, and a man (if the characteristic of Man is rationality). In "The Siege of Gondor" (chapter 4) and later in "The Pyre of Denethor" (chapter 7), Denethor reveals his inability to love his son Faramir, when, Lear-like, he measures the quality and quantity of his worth. The Gondor steward to the king prefers the dead Boromir to Faramir because of the former's great courage and loyalty to him: "Boromir was loyal to me and no wizard's pupil. He would have remembered his father's need, and would not have squandered what fortune gave. He would have brought me a mighty gift" (III, 104). So he chastises Faramir for his betrayal: "Have I not seen your eye fixed on Mithrandir, seeking whether you said well or too much? He has long had your heart in his keeping" (III, 103). Even in the early chapters Denethor has revealed his failure as a master: he has assumed that the service of a small individual like Pippin must be domestic and menial in character, involving waiting on Denethor, running errands, and entertaining him (III, 96). As a steward of Gondor Denethor fails most egregiously by usurping the role of lord in his misguided zeal for power and glory and by using his men to further his own ends. He views this act in monetary terms: the Dark Lord "uses others as his weapons. So do all great lords, if they are wise, Master Halfling. Or why should I sit here in my tower and think, and watch, and wait, spending even my sons?" (III, 111). Unlike Théoden, who heads his troops on the battlefield, Denethor remains secure in his tower while his warriors die in the siege of Gondor. Most significantly, he fails to exhibit that rational self-control often described in the Middle Ages through the metaphor of kingship. Such unnatural behavior results in despair and irrationality, and he loses his head. When he nurses his madness to suicide and adds even his son Faramir to the pyre he is termed by Gandalf a "heathen," among those kings dominated by the Dark Power, "slaying themselves in pride and despair, murdering their kin to ease their own death" (III, 157). As Denethor succumbs to his pride he refuses to "be the dotard chamberlain of an upstart. . . . I will not bow to such a one, last of a ragged house long bereft of lordship and dignity" (III, 158). Symbolically, the enemy hurls back the heads of dead soldiers branded with the "token of the Lidless Eye" to signal the loss of reason and hope — the loss of the "head" — and the assault of despair on this city and its steward (III, 117).

In contrast, Théoden and Aragorn epitomize the good king. As a Germanic king Théoden serves . . . heroically after [he has driven out] Wormtongue, giving leadership in battle and loving and paternal treatment of his warriors outside it, as . . . with Merry. So he rides at the head of his troop of warriors as they near the city and provides a noble and inspiring example for them to follow:

> Arise, arise . . .
> Fell deeds awake: fire and slaughter!
> spear shall be shaken, shield be splintered,
> a sword-day, a red day, ere the sun rises!
> Ride now, ride now! Ride to Gondor! (III, 137)

The alliterative verse echoes the Old English heroic lines of "The Battle of Maldon" both in form and content.

Aragorn differs from Théoden in his role as Christian king because of his moral heroism as a healer rather than his valor as a destroyer.[33] Ioreth, Gondor's wise woman, declares, *"The hands of the king are the hands of a healer, and so shall the rightful king be known"* (III, 169). In "The Houses of Healing" (chapter 8) Aragorn carries the herb kingsfoil to the wounded Faramir, Éowyn, and Merry to revive and awaken each of them in highly symbolic acts. Also known as *athelas,* kingsfoil brings "Life to the dying": its restorative powers, of course, transcend the merely physical. It represents life itself juxtaposed with death. . . . Indeed, when Aragorn places the leaves in hot water, "all hearts were lightened. For the fragrance that came to each was like a memory of dewy mornings of unshadowed sun in some land of which the fair world in Spring is itself but a fleeting memory" (III, 173). In awakening Faramir, Aragorn awakens as well knowledge and love so that the new steward to the king responds in words that might be spoken by a Christian disciple: "My lord, you called me. I come. What does the king command?" (III, 173). In contrast, instead of responding rationally to the king, Éowyn awakens from her deathlike sleep to enjoy her brother's presence and to mourn her father's death. Merry awakens hungry for supper. The revival of self witnessed in these three incidents symbolizes what might be called the renewal of the three human faculties: rational, appetitive, and sensitive.

Structurally, Tolkien supports his thematic contrasts and parallels. The House of Healing . . . in chapter 8 occurs back-to-back with chapter 7's house of the dead, [wherein] Denethor commits fiery suicide. More than physical, Denethor's death is chiefly spiritual. Both a spiritual and [a] physical rebirth follow Aragorn's laying on of kingsfoil in the House of Healing. This ritualistic and epiphanic act also readies the narrative for the final symbolic Christian gesture of all the free peoples in the last two chapters of book 5. In "The Last Debate" (chapter 9) they decide to sacrifice themselves, if necessary, out of love for their world in hope that their action will distract Sauron long enough for Sam and Frodo to reach Mount Doom. As a whole community of "servants," they each alone act as freely, spontaneously, and charitably as Merry or Éowyn did toward Théoden earlier. Aragorn declares, "As I have begun, so I will go on. . . . Nonetheless I do not yet claim to command any man. Let others choose as they will" (III, 192). Even the title of "The Last Debate" portrays the egalitarian spirit of the group.

In contrast, in the last chapter (10), "The Black Gate Opens," only one view — that of the Dark Lord, voiced by his "Mouth," the Lieutenant — predominates. Sauron demands not voluntary service but servitude: the Lieutenant "would be their tyrant and they his slaves" (III, 205). Finally, the arrogance of Sauron's "steward" functions antithetically to the humility and love of the good "servants" and stewards. Mocking and demeaning them, Sauron's Lieutenant asks if "any one in this rout" has the "authority to treat with me? . . . Or indeed with wit to understand me?" (III, 202). The Lieutenant's stentorian voice grows louder and more defensive when met with the silence of Aragorn, whom he has described as brigandlike.

Although this "attack" of the free peoples on the Black Gate of Mordor seems to parallel that of Sauron's Orcs on the Gate of Gondor in chapter 4, it differs in that this attack on the Black Gate, from Tolkien's point of view, is not so much a physical attack as a spiritual defense by Gondor. In this present instance, when the peoples realize that the Lieutenant holds Sam's short sword, the gray cloak with its Elven brooch, and Frodo's *mithril*-mail, they almost succumb to despair — Sauron's greatest weapon, as in the siege of Gondor. But Gandalf's steely self-discipline and wisdom so steady their nerves that they are buoyed by his refusal to submit to the Mouth's insolent terms. He refuses even as Sauron surrounds them on all sides, betraying his embassy of peace. They are saved from physical destruction by the eagles as deus ex machina and from spiritual destruction by Frodo, Sam, and Gollum as they near Mount Doom in book 6.

The Ring finally reaches its origin in the first three chapters of book 6. Initiating the romance idea of "Return,"[34] this event introduces tripartite division of the book in narrative and theme. In chapters 4 to 7 Aragorn returns as king of his people and for marriage to Arwen. Their union and that of Faramir to Éowyn constitute and symbolize the renewal of society in the conjunction of species (Elf and Man) and cultures (Rohan and Gondor). A later marriage will represent a more natural form of rejuvenation, when Sam the gardener marries an appropriately named Rosie Cotton, as if to illustrate further the fertility that will emblazon the reborn Shire in their conception of Elanor, whose Elven name sums up the equivalent of grace. Finally, in the third part (chapter 8), Frodo and his hobbits return to the Shire, where the false "mayor," Sharkey, is ousted and a new one, Sam, elected. In the last chapter Tolkien hints at more supernatural forms of return and rebirth. On one level those chosen few "return" to the Grey Havens, where they seem to acquire immortality. . . . But on another level, others of a less spiritual cast must return to the duties of the natural world. So Sam returns at the very end, a "king" who must continue to serve his "people," his family, and his "kingdom," the Shire, by remaining in this world: "'Well, I'm back,' he said" (III, 385).

Throughout the first part of book 6 before the Ring has been returned and Sauron similarly "returns" to a grey smoke (in contrast to the Grey Havens reached by Frodo and Gandalf), Sam exemplifies the ideal Christian servant to his master, Frodo, in continuation of the Christian-king-as-servant theme enunciated in the last part. Physically Sam provides food for Frodo as he weakens, offers him his share of the remaining water, carries him bodily over rough terrain, and lifts his spirits. But spiritually Sam serves Frodo through the moral character that reveals him to be, as the most insignificant Hobbit and character in the epic, the most heroic.[35] Sam will become an artist by the work's end, but even during the trek across Mordor his sensitivity to spiritual reality is expressed by his understanding of the beauty beneath the appearance of waste, of light beyond darkness, of hope beyond despair.

This insight is triggered by the appearance of a star, an instance of divine grace that illumines understanding and bolsters hope: "The beauty of it smote his heart, as he looked up out of the forsaken land, and hope returned to him. For like a shaft, clear and cold, the thought pierced him that in the end the Shadow was only a small and passing thing: there was light and high beauty for ever beyond its reach. . . . Now, for a moment, his own fate, and even his master's ceased to trouble him" (III, 244). Strangely, Sam remains the only character who has worn the Ring but who is never tempted to keep it. Yet like Frodo earlier, Sam refuses to kill the detested Gollum when an opportunity arises because of his empathy for this "thing lying in the dust, forlorn, ruinous, utterly wretched" (III, 273). Having borne the Ring himself, Sam finally understands the reason for Gollum's wretchedness. This charitable refusal permits Gollum as a foil for the good servant to serve his master and Middle-earth in the most ironic way imaginable. When Frodo betrays himself enough to keep the Ring at the last moment, Gollum bites off both Ring and finger only to fall into the furnace of Mount Doom. The most ignominious "servant" finally achieves the coveted role of "Lord of the Rings." The least dangerous adversary finally fells the most dangerous — Sauron.

In the last two parts, the reunion of the entire Fellowship and all the species, the coronation of the king, and the double weddings mark the restoration of harmony and peace to Middle-earth. Symbolically the Eldest of Trees blooms again to replace the barren and withered Tree in the Court of the Fountain (III, 308–9). A new age — the age of men, the Fourth Age — begins. Even in the Shire rejuvenation occurs: note the domestic and quotidian image implied by the title of chapter 8, "The *Scouring* of the Shire" (my emphasis).

In a social sense the Shire must be washed and purified of the reptilian monsters occupying it. Once Sharkey and Worm have disappeared, Sam, the new mayor as gardener, can replenish its natural stores as well. After he plants the seed given him by Galadriel, new trees burst into bloom in the spring, including a mallorn with silver bark and gold flowers. The lush growth introduces a season of rebirth in Shire year 1420 . . . ,

> an air of richness and growth, and a gleam of beauty beyond that of mortal summers that flicker and pass upon this Middle-earth. All the children born or begotten in that year, and there were many, were fair to see and strong, and most of them had a rich

golden hair that had before been rare among hobbits. The fruit was so plentiful that young hobbits very nearly bathed in strawberries and cream. . . . And no one was ill, and everyone was pleased, except those who had to mow the grass. (III, 375)

Sam as gardener becomes a natural artist. . . .

The ending of this epic may seem optimistic. But as the Second Age has passed into the Third, so now the Third passes into the Fourth, a lesser one because dominated by Man, a lesser species than the Elf. Also, as Sauron replaced Morgoth, perhaps an even darker lord will replace Sauron in the future. Yet Tolkien's major interest does not lie in predicting the future or in encouraging Man to hope for good fortune. He wishes to illustrate how best to conduct one's life, both privately and publicly, by being a good servant and a good king, despite the vagaries of fortune, the corruption of others, and the threat of natural and supernatural death.

So this epic constitutes a sampler of Tolkienian concepts and forms realized in other works. The critic as monster depicted in the *Beowulf* article reappears as Tolkien the critic in the prologue to *The Lord of the Rings,* a "grown-up" version of Tolkien the narrator in *The Hobbit.* The hero as monster finds expression, as it has earlier in Bilbo, in Frodo, who discovers the landscape of the self to be harsher terrain than that of Mordor. The series of monsters typifying the deadly sins — Saruman, Shelob — ultimately converge with the evil Germanic king of the trilogy — Denethor — combining ideas of the "King under the Mountain" in *The Hobbit* with the idea of the Germanic lord presented in "The Homecoming" and other medieval parodies. The good Germanic lord, hero-as-subordinate, too, from *The Hobbit* and the medieval parodies, converges with the Christian concept of the king-as-servant from the fairy stories, in the last two volumes of the trilogy.

In addition the genres and formal constructs that Tolkien most loves reappear here. The preface, lecture, or prose nonfiction essay is transformed into the prologue; the "children's story" for adults is expanded into the adult story of the epic . . . ; the parody of medieval literature recurs not only in the epic or romance form used here but also in the presentation of the communities of Rohan and Gondor; the fairy story with its secondary world of Faërie governed by a very Christian Elf-king is translated into Elven form here.

Thus all of Tolkien's work manifests a unity, with understanding of its double and triple levels, in this respect like the distinct dual levels, Germanic and Christian, of *Beowulf* first perceived in Tolkien's own *Beowulf* article. So the Tolkien reader, like Bilbo in *The Hobbit* and Sam in *The Lord of the Rings,* must return to the beginning — not to the Shire, but to the origin of the artist Tolkien — in "*Beowulf:* The Monsters and the Critics."

TOM SHIPPEY

Another Road to Middle-earth: Jackson's Movie Trilogy

Most page-to-screen analyses are superficial encomia; not so this brilliant essay by Tom Shippey, author of two essential critical works on Tolkien: The Road to Middle-earth *and* J.R.R. Tolkien: Author of the Century. *That is because Shippey thoroughly understands the nature of the two media — narrative prose and cinema — their strengths and weaknesses, and, as in the case of Peter Jackson's movies, the ways in which one can transform the other and yet retain its deeper meanings. One basic difference between the two forms of artistic representation is that while the novel can provide entrance for the reader to another world, the movie can go further, taking us into the interior of the minds of characters and making us see that world through a character's eyes and experience his feelings. Shippey closely examines the ways in which Jackson's movies bridge universal truth and personal application, as Tolkien so skillfully does in his novel. He takes us on a journey in understanding that allows us to examine the techniques by means of which Jackson's scenes emphasize Tolkien's thematic and moral intentions without having to reproduce Tolkien's scenes themselves. He shows us the ways in which the movies can clarify the action of the novel and render it more immediate. For example, the great battles in Tolkien's novel have the scope and sweep appropriate to epic. Jackson does not forgo epic sweep, but because the camera can swiftly zoom outward to cover the*

*whole field of battle and then inward to catch a particular expression on
the face of a single warrior, what in the novel seems overly complicated
and even confusing is made clear. Even a reader familiar with epic cannot "enter" its action, but an audience seeing the effect of the bloodshed
and horror of battle in a character's face experiences the terror the character "feels." Jackson's narrative strategy also incorporates subsidiary
plot lines and characters into the main line of action, giving more room
to some (Arwen, for instance) and downgrading others (Denethor) in
order to make Tolkien's important underlying themes explicit. For example, take Jackson's handling of Gollum in the scenes that depict the
journey of Frodo and Sam to Mordor with Gollum as their guide. Jackson adds actions that do not appear in the novel — Gollum deliberately
driving a wedge between Frodo and Sam or Frodo's rejection and dis-
missal of Sam on the Stairs of Cirith Ungol — to bring to the surface in
action truths that are central to the novel but are never directly expressed. In consequence, a theme that flickers fitfully in the novel — that
Gollum, like all of us sinners, is capable of salvation — is enacted and
thereby reinforced. Moreover, although the novel makes clear the terrible
love-hatred for Frodo that afflicts Gollum, the movie takes us into Gollum's mind, and we hear the hateful-pitiable creature arguing with
himself. We experience the terrible war that good and evil wage for possession of him. The implicit is made explicit. Shippey expertly examines
the changes that Jackson makes to "translate" the text into drama, to
shape* The Lord of the Rings *to fit the understanding and apprehension
of a twenty-first-century audience without compromising its deep philosophical core. Shippey's "Another Road to Middle-earth" takes us on a
most exciting and enlightening journey.*

In 1958 Tolkien found himself confronted by the synopsis of a proposed animated version of *The Lord of the Rings.* As one can see from
his published *Letters,* he was originally not unsympathetic to the idea
in principle, but when he saw the script itself — it survives, with
Tolkien's amusing marginal notes, in the collection of Tolkien papers

at Marquette University — his attitude changed.[1] Not only was the script careless to the point of willful stupidity, its author showed no apparent interest in the themes of the book or the many divergent cultures of Middle-earth, the latter all flattened out to a kind of suburban if science-fictional sameness. Protesting with some degree of "resentment," Tolkien wrote: "The canons of narrative art in any medium cannot be wholly different; and the failure of poor films is often precisely in exaggeration, and in the intrusion of unwarranted matter owing to not perceiving where the core of the original lies" (*Letters*, p. 270).

"*Wholly* different"? One may agree that some aspects of narrative art will remain the same in either medium, book or film. At the same time, one has to concede that the most scrupulous shift from one medium to the other is bound to generate narrative change. So how far should a film adaptation be judged against the criteria appropriate to its written original? The answer to that question perhaps lies in the second issue which Tolkien raises: where is the core of that original, and will a moviemaker perceive it?

Speaking about a "core" meanwhile implies that there is a "periphery," and Tolkien seems tacitly to have accepted that in the distinction he drew, as early as 1957, between "abridgement" and "compression" (*Letters*, p. 261). In purely commonsense terms, the former is inevitable. Even in their extended versions, Peter Jackson's three *Lord of the Rings* movies will run to not much over twelve hours' duration. Meanwhile, marathon public readings of *The Lord of the Rings* have shown that each volume takes some forty to fifty hours to complete, while even fast silent reading of the texts would take, at the very least, considerably longer than watching the movies. Nor is it always the case that pictures convey information faster than words. There was never any question, then, but that something would have to go, and in fact Jackson has selected skilfully if ruthlessly sections which could be deleted in total, not without loss, but without having major effects on the rest of the narration: in particular, the "Tom Bombadil" chapters (effectively chapters 5 through 8 of the first book of *The Fellowship of the Ring*) and the "Parting" and "Scouring" chapters (again, effectively chapters 5 through 8 of the second book of *The Return of the King*). As the sixty-two chapters of Tolkien's *The Lord of the Rings* were converted into the approximately 170 scenes of Jackson's,[2] about a dozen vanished entirely, while several others became vestigial. As has just been said, there can be no rational objection to this in principle, while Tolkien himself observed that abridgement was far preferable to compression — meaning by the latter, trying to get everything in but at the price of hurrying everything up, "with resultant over-crowding and confusion, blurring of climaxes, and general degradation." What Tolkien feared in particular was the subordination of what he called the "Prime Action," the story of the Ring-bearers Frodo and Sam, to the "Subsidiary Action" of the great battles at Isengard, at Helm's Deep, at Cormallen, at the Black Gate.[3] It is very much part of the core meaning of *The Lord of the Rings* that the highly visual and traditional heroic displays from Aragorn and Théoden and the other high-status characters would be futile, as they themselves recognise, without Frodo and Sam, whose heroism is in an entirely different and much less visible style.

Tolkien's fears in this respect at least proved groundless. One of the strong points of the Jackson movies is that the director remains ready at all times to return the audience's attention to the Ring itself, which we see in close-up again and again, and to its effects and its temptations, on several occasions spelled out slowly, even patiently, without the predictable rush to get back to "the action." Yet in some respects *The Lord of the Rings* remains an "action movie," even a "special effects movie." There is one reason for this which seems inevitable from the very nature of the differing media. To put it bluntly, an author — especially an amateur author like Tolkien, who never gave up his "day job" — invests nothing in the creation of his work except his own spare time, and loses nothing except his own time in the event of failure. A moviemaker, however, operating with a budget measurable in millions of dollars per day, very obviously has to consider recovering the return on his expenses, and is accordingly susceptible to "audience pressure": he has to guess what his audience will like and won't like and adjust his production accordingly. Experimentation is much cheaper in a written medium, conformism much more of a threat in movies.

One has to say that there is, probably inevitably, a certain degree of bowing to popular taste in Jackson. Tolkien's perceived lack of strong female characters leads to the insertion of Arwen as Frodo's rescuer in the first movie, but the heroic role she is given rings a little hollow. Turning at the edge of the ford of the Loudwater, she defies the Ringwraiths: "If you want him, come and claim him!" (*JFR* 21, "The Flight to the Ford"). Of course they do want him and have every intention of claiming him. Arwen's defiance makes no difference and is rhetorically cheaper than Frodo's weary, solitary, and unsuccessful gesture in the original (p. 209). But it perhaps offers a moment for female viewers to place themselves in the story. In the same way, quite often, Pippin and Merry seem to be used by Jackson to appeal to the young teenage market, with their pranks and general scatter-brainedness viewed tolerantly and even approvingly: letting off the firework at Bilbo's Party, overeating on *lembas,* dancing on tables, lighting the beacon for Gandalf at Minas Tirith, all sequences added deliberately to the original. The tension between Legolas and Gimli is meanwhile made more evidently comic and tilted even more evidently towards Legolas's "heartthrob" role, so clearly aimed at the young female audience. Sequences designed for the teenage market include Legolas skateboarding down a flight of steps on a shield in the battle of Helm's Deep (*JTT* 51, "The Breach of the Deeping Wall") and the "dwarf-tossing" joke, used twice, first in the scene with the Balrog as Gimli faces a chasm he can barely leap across — "Nobody tosses a dwarf!" — and then again at Helm's Deep, where we have a sally scene written in seemingly so that Gimli can accept indignity in the cause of duty — "Toss me! . . . Don't tell the elf!" (*JFR* 36, "The Bridge of Khazad-dûm," and *JTT* 53, "The Retreat to the Hornburg," respectively). Both skateboarding and dwarf tossing are well out of place in Middle-earth. But these moments pass quickly, like some of Tolkien's own early jocularities and anachronisms — the goblin king Golfimbul in *The Hobbit* (p. 27), or the dragon passing "like an express train" in chapter 1 of *The Lord of the Rings* (p. 21).

The "core of the original" remains the Ring and what we are told about it by Tolkien: its effect is always corrupting; no-one, no matter how strong or virtuous, can be trusted with it; it cannot simply be buried or hidden but must be destroyed in the place of its forging. Unless one accepts these propositions as given, the action of *The Lord of the Rings* cannot make sense, whatever the narrative medium. Tolkien, however, set his adaptors a serious problem in the way that he communicates them. Much of what has just been stated is told by Gandalf to Frodo in the chapter "The Shadow of the Past," which takes place, one should note, almost seventeen years after the first chapter, "A Long-Expected Party." Near the end of this, Gandalf says indeed, "There is only one way [to destroy the Ring]," and further, to Frodo, "you have been chosen." Having got so far, though, Gandalf seems to put the matter off, saying, "you ought to go soon," but rapidly qualifying it with "I said *soon*, not *instantly*," staying on in the Shire himself for "over two months," departing at the end of June, and leaving Frodo to make his own departure nearly three further months later, on September 23 (pp. 59, 60, 64, 66). It is another month later, October 24, before Frodo and Gandalf meet again in Rivendell. During that intervening period, of course, Frodo has made his way from the Shire to Rivendell with several adventures and without the escort of Gandalf. But it is not till the Council of Elrond, twelve chapters and many thousands of words later than "The Shadow of the Past," that Gandalf's identification of Bilbo's ring with the One Ring is confirmed, and its whole history detailed: from Sauron to Isildur to Sméagol/Gollum to Bilbo, with the further evidence of Gollum's own tale (reported by Aragorn and Gandalf) and Isildur's scroll (sought out and read by Gandalf in Minas Tirith). I have remarked elsewhere[4] how, in the chapter "The Council of Elrond," discussion has to be repeatedly brought back to the vital questions — Is it the Ring? What shall we do with it? Who will do it? — usually by relatively minor characters such as Gildor or Erestor. Both in that chapter and in the first fourteen chapters of *The Fellowship of the Ring* as a whole, the account of the Ring itself is, to say the least, slow, tortuous, and much interrupted.

In the narrative medium of prose this has many advantages — though one may think, with hindsight, that some of the complications may have arisen in fact from the extraordinarily slow and much-interrupted gestation of Tolkien's story, as revealed in volume 6 of *The History of Middle-earth*.[5] But whatever the cause or the effect, it must have been clear from very early on that the narrative medium of film could not cope with such a roundabout and leisurely unrolling. Jackson's solution was clear, direct, immediately arresting: to begin with the history of the Ring as uncovered by Gandalf, told from start to finish with a cool and quiet voice-over set against scenes of extreme drama and violence on-screen (*JFR* 1, "Prologue: One Ring to Rule Them All"). Viewers of *The Lord of the Rings,* unlike readers, accordingly know for sure what is going on from the very start: they have quite literally been "put in the picture." Much of the approach to the Council of Elrond has furthermore been cut out — not just the Bombadil scenes but also the long delays between Bilbo's Party and Gandalf's return, Gandalf's second departure and Frodo's. The whole episode of Gandalf's imprisonment by Saruman and rescue by Gwaihir is furthermore presented as it is happening, interwoven with Frodo's flights from the Shire, from Bree, and from Weathertop, and not in the lengthy "flashback" narration to the Council, as written by Tolkien. This simplification and straightening of the plot removes much of the importance of the Council of Elrond itself, and Jackson handles this very differently from Tolkien — yet still in a way which respects its narrative core. In Tolkien, the tensions between the various parties, Aragorn and Boromir, elves and dwarves, are evident but remain reasonably suppressed, with Glóin for instance accepting Gandalf's rebuke for sniping at Legolas, and Gimli rather remarkably the only member of the Council who does not speak at all. In Jackson all this becomes much more hot tempered, and Gimli actually tries to destroy the Ring with his axe. Furthermore, in Tolkien the Council ends in exhaustion and prolonged silence: "All the Council sat with downcast eyes, as if in deep thought" (p. 263). In Jackson it ends with all parties shouting and haranguing one another. Yet in both the vital words are the same, and it could be said that Jackson even stresses them above and beyond his original. The vital words are, from Frodo, "I will take the Ring, though I do not know the way" (p. 264), but in Jackson these have to penetrate noise and confusion rather than being dropped into a silence. Frodo indeed, in the movie, says "I will take the Ring" three times (*JFR* 27, "The Council of Elrond").[6] The first time he is ignored amid the hubbub. As he walks forward to say it the second time, Gandalf turns to listen. And as the others notice Gandalf listening and fall silent, he says it a third time, this time completing it almost as in Tolkien: "I will take the Ring to Mordor. Though I do not know the way." The scene in the movie makes a point vital to the entire story. It is the small and physically insignificant characters, the hobbits, who dominate the plot, but this is completely unexpected by everyone except Gandalf, the only one among the Wise (as Tolkien makes clear in other scenes) who ever pays any attention to hobbits. Jackson's straightening and lightening of the plot, indeed, find their justification in just this moment.

One could indicate a second deft transposition. In Tolkien, in "The Shadow of the Past," there is an especially resonant exchange between Frodo and Gandalf. Slowly realising what Gandalf is telling him, Frodo says reluctantly, "I wish it need not have happened in my time," and Gandalf answers: "So do I, . . . and so do all who live to see such times. But that is not for them to decide. All we have to decide is what to do with the time that is given us" (p. 50). For English people of Tolkien's generation, the words "in my time" carry a powerful echo. In 1938, returning from the Munich conference where he gave way to Hitler, Neville Chamberlain notoriously and quite wrongly announced that he brought back "peace in our time," and the words (themselves taken from the Anglican liturgy) have become irrevocably tainted with appeasement, avoidance of duty, and failure. When Gandalf says "all who live to see such times," then, he could be taken as meaning, in unconscious prophecy, Tolkien's contemporaries and countrymen; and when he says "them," the pronoun includes Frodo and the Shire-hobbits with everyone in Middle-earth and indeed everyone at any time faced with the need for painful decision. Gandalf then softens the implied criticism slightly by changing his pronoun, including himself, and narrowing the focus: "All *we* have to decide is what to do with the time that is given *us*" (my emphasis). The echo of Chamberlain, however, might well slip past a twenty-first-century audience almost a lifetime removed from 1938 and Munich. But Jackson gives the words a renewed emphasis by moving them to a different place and moment. In the first of his movies, the words are still said by Gandalf to Frodo, but they are said in another notably quiet scene, in the dark, as the two characters talk in the Mines of Moria (*JFR* 34, "A Journey in the Dark"). Their force is furthermore established by repetition. Almost at the very end of the movie, as Frodo prepares to leave the Fellowship and set out as he intends for Mordor on his own (*JFR* 46, "The Road Goes Ever On"), he seems to hear Gandalf's words repeated, with the face of Gandalf (whom he and the viewers think at that moment to be dead) filling the screen. Only the words have once more had their pronouns changed. This time what Frodo hears is, "All *you* have to decide is what to do with the time that is given *you*." The statement has accordingly become entirely personal, directed precisely at Frodo's own single moment of decision.

This kind of switching between universal truth and individual application is, indeed, absolutely Tolkienian, exemplified several times in the hobbit poetry which Jackson has for the most part had to cut out. Once again, though, it shows a careful and sensitive response to what is exactly "the core of the original." One further example may reinforce the point. In one of the most active and violent sequences of all three movies, the armies of Mordor are battering their way into Minas Tirith, with trolls beating down a gate. On the other side of the gate, a little removed from the front line, Pippin is sitting, clearly extremely frightened, when Gandalf comes over to him and talks to him about death. Death is not the end, he says, smiling benevolently. When it comes we will find ourselves walking into a "far green country." The words are quite unexpected, and though they are Tolkien's, they come from a quite different and normally unnoticed part of his narrative — though in that narrative they are repeated twice. At the start of the chapter "Fog on the Barrow-downs" (totally omitted by Jackson), Frodo on his last night in the house of Tom Bombadil has a dream, or perhaps a vision, of "a far green country [which] opened before him under a swift sunrise" (p. 132). Many pages later, after he has left Middle-earth for ever, Frodo "beheld white shores and beyond them a far green country under a swift sunrise" (p. 1007). The next words Tolkien wrote, though, are: "But to Sam . . ." Frodo has gone on to the Undying Lands. Sam turns back to death — and of course to life, to his wife and children, and to the mortality that goes with them. But one could believe, if one wished, that Frodo's fate and vision need not be confined to him alone, might be a possibility for all mortals, and so Jackson suggests. Discussions of death, however optimistic, are not a normal part of Hollywood rhetoric, any more than the contemplation of defeat, but it could well be said that death, and the themes of the Escape from Death, and the Escape from Deathlessness, are vital parts of Tolkien's entire mythology. Once again Jackson has done exactly what Tolkien feared movie-adaptors would *not* do: subordinated noise to silence, heroes to hobbits, Subsidiary Action to Prime Action.

The whole handling of Sméagol/Gollum in the film sequence shows a similar awareness. Jackson has made the journey into Mordor much more of a "triangle" than Tolkien did, with scenes inserted to show Gollum deliberately driving a wedge between Sam and Frodo, and Frodo indeed distrusting and dismissing Sam on the Stairs of Cirith Ungol as he does not in the original. Yet Jackson in these sequences is stressing a point of great importance to Tolkien, namely, that Gollum is after all capable of salvation — for the obverse of the fact that the Ring can corrupt anyone is that no one and nothing (not even Sauron) is evil in the beginning. Jackson furthermore brings out something perhaps latent in Tolkien, namely, that there is an element of rivalry, or even jealousy, in the relationship between Gollum and Sam. It is a critical moment in the original, near the end of the chapter "The Stairs of Cirith Ungol," when Gollum finds Sam and Frodo sleeping, and creeps up, looking, for the moment, like "an old weary hobbit . . . a starved and pitiable thing," to touch Frodo's knee, only for Sam to wake and "roughly" abuse him (p. 699). Jackson catches the essence of this feeling by the repeated scenes of Gollum/Sméagol arguing with himself. In one original scene, in *JTT* 29, "Gollum and Sméagol," Sméagol (the better half, so to speak) banishes Gollum, his worse half, with the words, three times repeated, "leave now, and never come back." The exorcism is successful but not lasting. Gollum returns, in Jackson's version, when Sméagol feels himself betrayed by Frodo to Faramir at the Forbidden Pool (*JTT* 42, "The Forbidden Pool"). Though these shifts are made more emphatic by Jackson, they are entirely in line with Tolkien's intention. And there is one scene where pictures show that they can indeed do more than words, as Gollum, clutching his "precious," falls into the fires of Mount Doom. Tolkien's last word on Gollum is "Out of the depths came his last wail *Precious*, and he was gone" (p. 925). Jackson's camera follows him down and catches the expression on his face: shocked? regretful? contented? All are perfectly possible, and appropriate.

Gollum is not the only character to have his importance in a sense enhanced by Jackson. Others include Saruman, Pippin, Arwen,

and even arguably Aragorn. Possibly the stress on individual character goes along with the inevitable downplaying of a major feature
of Tolkien's original, its immense scope and complication, the sense
it conveys of a whole world of competing and often independent
powers with their own histories and geographies. When Pippin and
Merry are captured, the orcs fall into three different groups, each
with a different purpose. There are the Northerners, or "mountain-
maggots" as Uglúk calls them, out for vengeance and knowing nothing of the Ring. There are the Isengarders, led by Uglúk, who means
to take the hobbits back to Saruman. There are the orcs of Sauron, led
by Grishnákh, who wants to take them back across the River to
Barad-dûr, or Lugburz in his speech. Jackson does not mark these
distinctions, and in general presents Saruman rather as an agent of
Sauron than as a rival or treacherous and temporary ally.

   In a similar way the rather complex tactics surrounding the battle of Helm's Deep in Tolkien have been made less tactical, more personal. Tolkien has salvation come for Théoden and Aragorn from
several directions: from the Huorns of Fangorn, whom Gandalf has
summoned by negotiation with Treebeard, and from Erkenbrand of
Westfold, who had according to the report of Ceorl fallen back towards Helm's Deep but never arrived. "He was a mighty man," says
Théoden (p. 519), but Tolkien has no more to say about him. This introduction of all but anonymous characters will not do in a movie,
and accordingly much of Erkenbrand's role is given to Éomer, sent by
Jackson into exile precisely so that he can return and save the day. Another decisive intervention is awarded to Pippin. In Tolkien, Treebeard is well aware of the tree felling that has been going on round
Orthanc, and says of Saruman before the Entmoot has even started,
"Curse him, root and branch! Many of those trees were my friends,
creatures I had known from nut and acorn" (pp. 462–63). The Entmoot accordingly decides to take action — though, in a strikingly
uncinematic way, we never "see" the destruction of Isengard at all, for
Tolkien stops on the verge of Nan Curunir, the Valley of Saruman, di-

verts for more than four chapters to another strand of plot, and only describes the Entish attack in flashback, through a long account delivered by Pippin and Merry. A moviemaker could clearly never allow anything as nonvisual as this, but Jackson also shies away from allowing the vital decision to attack Saruman to be made "offstage," in the Entmoot. Pippin accordingly is made to divert Treebeard — who has decided *not* to attack — through the wasteland round Orthanc, and Treebeard is made to realise *only then* what has been going on, and to say the words cited above (*JTT* 54, "Master Peregrin's Plan," and 56, "The Last March of the Ents"). Pippin's role is enhanced, at the expense one might say of Entish independence, and another tactical issue becomes a personal one.

Could some such consideration underlie what are perhaps the three major additions or changes (rather than abridgements) made by Jackson, which I would label as "the Aragorn Intermezzo," "the Faramir Digression," and "the Denethor Downgrade"? The first of these takes place as Théoden's people — here definitely retreating in order to avoid confrontation, not making a strategic withdrawal as in Tolkien — are straggling back to Helm's Deep. They are attacked by warg-riders; Aragorn is involved in the defence, is dragged over a cliff, and lies as if dead by a river. He is brought back to life, seemingly, by a vision of Arwen, and by his horse, Brego, another character deliberately introduced (*JTT* 34, "The Wolves of Isengard," and 37, "The Grace of the Valar"). Why, one wonders, in a movie always short of time, add an apparently unnecessary complication? I would suggest that the root cause lies partly in the insistent urge of the moviemaker towards personalisation, and partly in the expectations of an audience significantly different, in the 2000s, from the one Tolkien imagined in the 1940s. To Tolkien's generation, thoroughly accustomed to war and to both victory and defeat, there was no need to explain that the forces of evil might prove stronger. In his account, accordingly, Théoden retreats before Saruman's forces not from any inner failing but because he knows they are for the moment too much for him.

They are "overmastered," says Ceorl, and Gandalf agrees, ordering the Riders back and shouting, "do not tarry in the plain" (pp. 515–16). Jackson instead has Théoden refusing to fight out of a kind of disillusionment. "The old alliances are dead," he says. "We are alone" (*JTT* 43, "Aragorn's Return"). No help will come from Gondor (Tolkien's Théoden had not expected any), no help from the elves (in Tolkien, the Riders do not even know quite what elves are). There is indeed a slightly Churchillian suggestion in all this, with Théoden saying in the same scene, "If there is to be an end, I would have them make such an end as is worthy of remembrance," much like Churchill's famous "finest hour" speech of 1940. But the sense of having been abandoned is set up, of course, only to be reversed, as a surprisingly well-drilled elvish army turns up to honor the Old Alliance and man the walls of the Hornburg. Jackson's version insists that the source of weakness is disunity, and Aragorn is once more given an expanded role as the focus of union. Back at the Council of Elrond, Elrond had indeed said, "You will unite, or you will fall" (*JFR* 27, "The Council of Elrond"). Aragorn's connection with the Elves through Arwen is stressed repeatedly. Symmetrical turning points, close together in the *Two Towers* movie, are Arwen turning back from flight over sea for love of Aragorn, and Aragorn brought back to life by love of Arwen (*JTT* 36, "The Grace of the Valar," and 38, "Arwen's Fate"). This, perhaps, is the justification for "the Aragorn Intermezzo": it is there to show that "there is always hope" (Aragorn to the boy Haleth son of Háma, *JTT* 48, "The Host of the Eldar"), that Théoden is wrong to think he has been abandoned.[7] The movie has been affected, one might say, by sixty years of NATO and of American hegemony.

"The Faramir Digression" is an even more marked plot shift. As everyone who has read Tolkien will remember, Faramir has every opportunity to strip Frodo of the Ring, about which he knows a great deal even before Sam's blundering admission, but rejects the temptation. Jackson has him succumb to it, with the declaration "the Ring will go to Gondor," and march Frodo, Sam, and Gollum off to Gondor as prisoners. In Jackson's version, Faramir intends to hand the Ring over to his father as "a mighty gift" (*JTT* 57, "The Nazgûl Attack") — and the phrase is Tolkien's, but Tolkien assigned it not to Faramir but to Denethor, rebuking Faramir for letting the hobbits go (p. 795). The "Digression," as I have called it, makes no difference in the end, as Faramir is persuaded, seemingly by Sam, into letting the Ring and the hobbits go back toward Mordor (and indeed anything else would have altered the plot terminally). So why introduce this second apparently unnecessary complication? One reason may well be to form a connection with what I term "the Denethor Downgrade" in the third movie, in which Denethor is turned into a thoroughly unpleasant character. It is true that even in Tolkien Denethor is cold, proud, ambitious, and misguided. It is his decision to defend the wall of Rammas Echor, which Gandalf thinks to be wasted labor, and this decision all but costs Faramir his life (p. 798). It was his decision also to send Boromir to Rivendell rather than his brother, although the prophetic dream was clearly meant for the latter (pp. 239, 795). It was this decision which meant that Faramir was the one to encounter the hobbits in Ithilien, as Faramir angrily reminds his father (p. 795), but Denethor refuses to take responsibility. Nevertheless, and in spite of his other disastrous errors, it is possible to feel a certain sympathy for Tolkien's Denethor: he makes his mistakes for Gondor. One cannot say the same of Jackson's Denethor. One of the more blatant uses of cinematic suggestion is the scene in the third movie in which Denethor, having sent his son out to fight, sits in his hall and gobbles a meal, tearing meat apart with his hands and munching till juice runs down his chin. He is made to look greedy, self-indulgent, the epitome of the "château general" who sends men to their deaths while living himself in style and comfort. And in a repeat of the "disunion" motif, he refuses to light the beacons to summon Rohan, till Pippin does so at Gandalf's direction.

What the "Digression" and the "Downgrade" do between them is generate a theme particularly popular in recent (American) film, that of the son trying desperately to gain the love of his father, and of the father rejecting (till too late) the love of his son. They also perhaps "democratise" the plot, as Denethor is made to stand for old-world arrogance and hierarchy, while Faramir is converted from his obedience to his father by — and this is an echo of Pippin's manipulation of Treebeard — the intervention of Sam. After dragging Frodo back from the winged Nazgûl, Sam is given a long speech (transposed from its original place on the Stairs of Cirith Ungol) on "the great stories" and the heroes of old. "They kept going because they were holding on to something," he tells Frodo, because "there's some good in this world, and it's worth fighting for" (*JTT* 60, "The Tales That Really Mattered"). His words are given total authority by being presented as a voice-over to images of victory at Helm's Deep and at Isengard, of which Sam at that moment knows nothing. He has become a prophet, a spokesman for the movie's philosophic core, and Faramir, having overheard Sam talking to Frodo, is made to recognise this by giving way and changing his mind about the Ring. There is a further parallel set up by Jackson, not absent but much less marked in Tolkien, and that is that both Sam and Faramir have to go on doing their duty despite rejection by their leaders, Denethor and Frodo. But once again the conflicting motives and independent policies of Tolkien's Middle-earth have been narrowed down to perhaps more readily understandable issues of love given and love refused, faintheartedness and mistaken loyalty.

One may say that there are no neutrals in Jackson's vision, or that those who wish to remain neutral, like Théoden and the elves turning their backs on Middle-earth, are made to see the error of their ways. Jackson is also quicker than Tolkien to identify evil without qualification and as a purely outside force (a failing of which Tolkien has often, but wrongly, been accused). In the opening voice-over we are told that after the battle of Dagorlad, Isildur had "this one chance to destroy evil for ever" (*JFR* 1, "Prologue: One Ring to Rule Them All"). For ever? When Tolkien uses the phrase, it is marked immediately as mistaken. Elrond says he remembers the day "when Thangorodrim was broken, and the Elves deemed that evil was ended for ever, *and it was not so*" (p. 237, my emphasis), but there is no such qualification from Jackson. Jackson also has Elrond say to Gandalf that because of Isildur's error "evil was allowed to endure" (*JFR* 24, "The Fate of the Ring"), but Tolkien's Wise Ones, I am sure, would be conscious that evil is always latent and will exist whether humans and elves allow it to or not. There is the kernel here of a serious challenge to Tolkien's view of the world, with its insistence on the fallen nature even of the best, and its conviction that while victories are always worthwhile, they are also always temporary. And this could, at last, be not a problem created by any failure to perceive "the core of the original," but a genuine difference between two different media and their respective "canons of narrative art."

An important if commonly unnoticed leitmotiv in Tolkien is that of vision. It comes up, for instance, in the chapter "The Mirror of Galadriel," with its strong echo/contradiction of the witches' mirror in act 4, scene 1 of *Macbeth*.[8] There one may remember that Galadriel cautions Sam and Frodo before they look in her mirror, telling them, "it shows things that were, and things that are, and things that yet may be. But which it is that he sees, even the wisest cannot always tell" (p. 352). When Sam sees what appears to be the destruction of the Shire and wants to go home to settle matters, she tells him further: "the Mirror shows many things, and not all have come to pass. Some never come to be, unless those that behold the visions turn aside from their path to prevent them. The Mirror is dangerous as a guide of deeds" (p. 354). In this case the warning seems unnecessary, as Sam has seen what is indeed happening, or about to happen. But Galadriel's warning is highly appropriate to later events, and especially to the repeated uses of the *palantíri,* or Seeing Stones. We first come across these when Pippin picks up the *palantír* thrown from Orthanc by Gríma and later sneaks a look at it when Gandalf is asleep. In the Stone, he sees Sauron, and Sauron sees him. But though

Sauron sees Pippin, he draws from this a wrong conclusion, namely, that Pippin is the Ring-bearer and has been captured by Saruman, who now has the Ring (pp. 578–79). The next day Aragorn, who has been given the Stone by Gandalf, deliberately shows himself in it to Sauron, and once again Sauron draws the wrong conclusion: namely, that Aragorn has overpowered Saruman and that he is now the owner of the Ring. It is fear of this new power arising which makes Sauron launch his premature attack, and Gandalf indeed realises that this was all along Aragorn's intention (p. 797). Gandalf further surmises that it was the *palantír* which was Saruman's downfall. As he looked in it, he saw only what Sauron allowed him to see, and so lost heart and decided that resistance would be futile (p. 584). Both Sauron and Saruman have allowed what they see in the Stones to guide their decisions, but they have seen only fractions of the truth.

The most disastrous use of a *palantír* is however made by Denethor. The sequence of events is here made especially clear by Tolkien, though it is hardly ever noticed. Aragorn shows himself to Sauron in the Orthanc Stone on March 6. On the seventh and eighth Frodo and Sam are with Faramir in Ithilien. On the ninth Gandalf and Pippin reach Minas Tirith. On the tenth Faramir returns to Minas Tirith and reports to his father that he has met, and released, two hobbits, whom both he and his father know were carrying the Ring. The next day Denethor sends Faramir to defend Osgiliath, clearly a tactical error. On the thirteenth Faramir is brought back badly wounded, and Denethor retires to his secret chamber, from which people see "a pale light that gleamed and flickered . . . and then flashed and went out." When he comes down, "the face of the Lord was grey, more deathlike than his son's" (p. 803). Clearly Denethor has been using his *palantír*, but what has he seen in it? Much later on, close to suicide, he will tell Gandalf that he has seen the Black Fleet approaching (as it is), though he does not know (though at that moment the reader does) that the Fleet now bears Aragorn and rescue, not a new army of enemies (p. 835). However, this does not seem quite enough to trigger Denethor's total despair. Surely we are meant to realise that what he has seen in the *palantír* is Frodo, whom he knows to be the Ring-bearer, in the hands of Sauron. Both Frodo's capture and Faramir's wounding take place on March 13; and one may recall that Sauron plays a similar trick by showing Gandalf and the leaders of the West Frodo's *mithril*-coat and Sam's sword in the parley outside the Black Gate. The matter is put beyond doubt, however, by what Denethor says to Pippin as he prepares for suicide. "Comfort me not with wizards! . . . The fool's hope has failed. The Enemy has found it, and now his power waxes" (p. 805). "The fool's hope" is Gandalf's plan to destroy the Ring, and "it" must be the Ring. Once again, then, Denethor has seen something true in a *palantír* and has drawn from it a wrong conclusion.

What all these scenes do collectively is to indicate the dangers of speculating. And as so often with Tolkien, that word bears both its modern meaning (speculating is guessing what will happen, trying to anticipate the future) and a more literal, etymological one (speculating is looking in a *speculum* or mirror). Warning against the dangers of speculation, and the way in which too much looking into the future can erode the will to action in the present, is surely very much part of Tolkien's analysis of his own time and his own society. The obverse of it lies in repeated scenes when we are made to realise that the fate of one character or group of characters depends on assistance coming from a direction of which they are quite unaware. Sam and Frodo cross Gorgoroth unseen because Sauron is distracted, quite deliberately, by Aragorn. Théoden King is saved at Helm's Deep by the Huorns brought by Gandalf but also by Merry and Pippin alerting Treebeard. Saruman is destroyed in a way by his own actions. For all Aragorn's doubts about his own decisions, Gandalf reminds him, "between them our enemies have contrived only to bring Merry and Pippin with marvellous speed, and in the nick of time, to Fangorn, where otherwise they would never have come at all" (p. 486). The *palantíri* mislead careless users by filling them with unjustified fear, but the whole structure of *The Lord of the Rings* indicates that decision and perseverance may be rewarded beyond hope. This, I would suggest, is Tolkien's philosophic core. He believes in the workings of Providence — the Providence which "sent" Gandalf back, and which "meant" Frodo to have the Ring (pp. 491, 55). But that Providence does not overrule free will, because it works only through the actions and decisions of the characters. In Tolkien there is no chance, no co-incidence. Characters' perception of events as chance or coincidence is a result only of their inability to see how actions connect as Shippey says.

To follow this, however, one needs a very sure grasp both of the chronology of events and of the way in which events in one plot strand (like the capture of Frodo) affect those in another (like the sui-cide of Denethor). The medium of film does not lend itself to this kind of intellectual connection. Jackson does not use the *palantiri* much. Pippin indeed picks one up in the flotsam of Isengard — though there is no explanation as to how it got there — and sneaks a look at it. But the important thing in Jackson's third movie is not Sauron seeing him, and drawing the wrong conclusion, but him see-ing Sauron, and being able to guess some part of his plan — to as-sault Minas Tirith. Aragorn and Denethor are not seen using a Stone (unless some passages are to be restored in the eventual extended ver-sion), and there is no hint that Saruman has been corrupted by it. The theme of mistaken "speculation" has been all but entirely re-moved. Meanwhile the theme of misdiagnosed coincidence is indeed present, but relatively vestigially. In the shortened presentation of Sam and Frodo's approach to Mount Doom, the two look out across the plain of Gorgoroth and see the campfires of the orcs going out as Sauron's armies move away to the Black Gate. Sam thinks and says that this is a stroke of luck, but he is wrong, because Aragorn and Gandalf have led their remaining forces to the Black Gate precisely in order to draw Sauron's attention. But other "coincidences" have been removed. In Tolkien, it was a fortunate coincidence that the sword with which Merry stabs the chief Nazgûl had been made long ago for use against "the dread realm of Angmar and its sorceror king" (p. 826), who is now the Nazgûl; but the film, having eliminated the barrow-wight sequence, makes nothing of this. Similarly, there is no doubt in Tolkien that Denethor's attempted murder of Faramir is what dooms Théoden, for as Pippin draws Gandalf away, Gandalf says, "if I do [save Faramir], then others will die" (p. 832). But this demonstration that there is always a price to pay for weakness is also no longer visible. In general, Tolkien's painstaking double analysis both of the dangers of speculation and of the nature of chance, which between them express a highly traditional but at the same time markedly original view of the workings of Providence, is on the whole not reflected in Jackson's sequence of movies. In that sense, much of the philosophical "core of the original" has indeed been lost in the movie version.

However, and here I query Tolkien's statement cited at the start of this essay, this may be because the "canons of narrative art," while certainly not "wholly different" in a different medium, are identifiably different. For one thing, the film medium has more trouble dealing with distorted time sequences than does prose fiction — and Tolkien was an especially idiosyncratic changer of time sequences. Filmmakers can easily cut from one scene to another, and Jackson often does so with strikingly contrastive effects. The implication, though, is always that the different scenes (more of them, shorter, much more broken up) are happening at more or less the same time. Simply by having chapter and book divisions, with all the familiar devices of chapter titles and fresh page starts, a novelist like Tolkien can in effect "say" to his reader, "I am now taking you back to where I left off with this group of characters." One result is that the reader is much more aware of what he or she knows, from another plot strand, that the characters in the plot strand being narrated do not know, with obvious resultant effects of irony or reassurance. This is a major difference between the two versions we now have of *The Lord of the Rings*.

Does it matter? Jackson may not have been able to cope with all the ramifications of Tolkien on Providence, but then few if any readers do. It is very difficult to say whether some part of Tolkien's intention gets through even to careless or less-comprehending readers: he would have hoped so, but there is no guarantee that he was correct. And meanwhile Jackson has certainly succeeded in conveying much of the more obvious parts of Tolkien's narrative core, many of them quite strikingly alien to Hollywood normality — the difference between Prime and Subsidiary Action, the differing styles of heroism, the need for pity as well as courage, the vulnerability of the good, the true cost of evil. It was brave of him to stay with the sad, muted, ambiguous ending of the original, with all that it leaves unsaid. Perhaps the only person who could answer the question posed at the start of this chapter would be a person with an experience quite opposite to my own: someone who had seen the movies, preferably several times over, and *only then* had read Tolkien's original. It would be interesting to gather from such a person a list of "things I hadn't realised before," as also "things Tolkien left out." Perhaps the most heartening thing one can say is that there will certainly now be many millions of people in exactly that position, new readers facing a new experience, and finding once again Tolkien's road to Middle-earth.

Acknowledgments
and Permissions

WE WISH TO THANK OUR AGENT, John Mason, for his persistence and persuasiveness; Clay Harper, Houghton Mifflin's coordinator of all things Tolkien, for his support; Phil Isaacs; and, for various technical and other help along the way, Jeff Burdick, Ellen Isaacs, Jessi Krek, and Adam Zimbardo.

For their help in the process of securing permissions, we are grateful to Ryan Bowman of McIntosh and Otis, Stacey Salling of the University of Texas Press, Grace Wherry of Curtis Brown, Pat Spacks, Mary Jaine Winokur of Heldref Publications, Debbie Campbell of the University of Notre Dame Press, Ed Meskys, Felice Rolfe, Ann Behar of Scovil Chichak Galen, Mary-Lou Pena of Fordham University Press, Ronald Hussey of Houghton Mifflin, Lee Miller and Charles Henderson of *CrossCurrents*, and Mack McCormick of the University Press of Kentucky.

We gratefully acknowledge the following permissions: for "The Dethronement of Power," which appeared originally in *Time and Tide*, October 25, 1955, was reprinted in *Tolkien and the Critics* with the permission of that paper's editors; for "The Lord of the Hobbits," copyright © 1961 by Edmund Fuller, reprinted with the permission of McIntosh and Otis, Inc.; for "The Quest Hero," originally published by *Texas Quarterly*, copyright © 1961 by W. H. Auden, reprinted by permission of Curtis Brown, Ltd.; for "Power and Meaning in *The Lord of the Rings*," originally published in *Critique* 3 (1959): 30–42, under the title "Ethical Patterns in *The Lord of the Rings*," reprinted with permission of the author and of the Helen Dwight Reid Educational Foundation, published by Heldref Publications, 1319 18th Street NW, Washington DC 20036–1602, www.heldref .org, copyright © 1959; for "Moral Vision in *The Lord of the Rings*," from *Tolkien and the Critics: Essays on*

Notes

All citations to *The Lord of the Rings* (except those in the Shippey essay) are to the revised three-volume 1967 edition.

POWER AND MEANING IN *THE LORD OF THE RINGS*

1. Edmund Wilson, "Oo, Those Awful Orcs!" *The Nation* 182 (April 14, 1956): 312–14. One notable reply to Wilson is Douglass Parker's "Hwæt We Holbytla . . . ," *Hudson Review* 9 (Winter 1956–1957): 598–609, which brilliantly refutes Wilson's attack and makes a strong defense of the trilogy. Mr. Parker is largely, though not exclusively, concerned with the success of *The Lord of the Rings* as fantasy. He reads the trilogy as most essentially concerned not with the struggle of Good against Evil but with an account of "the end of an age," an account that defines the human condition perceived in basically pagan terms. Although I agree with Mr. Parker on many counts, I must quarrel with his easy rejection of free will as a theme of Tolkien's. "Free-will," he writes, "has not, as some critics think, been restored [as a result of the Ring's destruction]; it never existed in the first place, nor did determinism reside in the Ring" (604). Surely the situation, for Tolkien as for the *Beowulf* poet, is more complicated: the universe paradoxically combines qualified determinism with qualified free will.

2. November 25, 1955.

MORAL VISION IN *THE LORD OF THE RINGS*

1. William Nelson, *The Poetry of Edmund Spenser* (New York, 1963), p. 116.

2. Edmund Wilson, "Oo, Those Awful Orcs!" *The Nation* 182 (April 14, 1956): 312, suggests that their name is "a telescoping of rabbit and Hobbs."

MEN, HALFLINGS, AND HERO WORSHIP

1. Edmund Wilson, "Oo, Those Awful Orcs!" *The Nation* 182 (April 14, 1956): 312–14.

TOLKIEN AND THE FAIRY STORY

1. Tolkien, "On Fairy-Stories," in *Tree and Leaf* (Boston: Houghton Mifflin, 1965). All of Tolkien's subsequent remarks on the fairy story are quoted from this essay.
2. Preface to *George Macdonald: An Anthology,* ed. C. S. Lewis (New York: Macmillan, 1947), pp. 16–17.
   [Ed.'s note, unnumbered in text p. 110: The passage Reilly quotes from Shelley is in *Prometheus Unbound,* act 1.]
3. C. S. Lewis, "The Dethronement of Power," above, p. 11.
4. Coleridge, *Biographia Literaria,* chap. 13.
5. Northrop Frye, *Anatomy of Criticism* (Princeton, N.J.: Princeton University Press, 1957), p. 94.

FOLKTALE, FAIRY TALE, AND THE CREATION OF A STORY

1. W. H. Auden, for example, as critic of Tolkien, usually chose to stress the quest, the heroic journey, the numinous object, and the victory of good over evil, as in his "At the End of the Quest, Victory," *New York Times Book Review,* January 22, 1956, p. 5, and in "The Quest Hero," above, p. 31, but he built his own criticism on Tolkien's essay in *Secondary Worlds,* T. S. Eliot Memorial Lectures (London, 1968).
2. Tolkien, "Mythopoeia," Introductory note to *Tree and Leaf,* in *The Tolkien Reader,* ed. Pauline Baynes (New York: Barnes and Noble, 1976), p. 2.
3. Tolkien, "*Beowulf:* The Monsters and the Critics," pp. 63–64.

4. While these matters occur in various scholarly and creative pieces, the most interesting probing occurs in his "English and Welsh," being pp. 1–41 of *Angles and Britons* (Cardiff, 1963), a collection of O'Donnell Lectures by various hands.

5. "Philology: General Works," *The Year's Work in English Studies* (hereafter *YWES*) 5 (1924): 65.

6. *YWES* 6 (1925): 32.

7. Lewis, "The Gods Return to Earth," *Time and Tide*, August 14, 1954, pp. 1082–83; and "The Dethronement of Power," above, p. 11.

8. Chesterton, *Orthodoxy* (London: Christian Classics Ethereal Library, 1908), pp. 66–102.

9. Macdonald, *A Dish of Orts* (London: Edwin Dalton, 1908), pp. 1–45.

10. The "cook" as artist, or even as an image of God as Creator, is the point of Tolkien's "Smith of Wooton Major" (1967).

11. Owen Barfield, another of Tolkien's circle of friends, the Inklings, is an anthroposophist who holds that the solid objects of the material world are but the antecedent condition for perceiving the "unrepresented" noumenal world, so that man, in failing to acknowledge this reality, has forgotten that all his knowing is ultimately a participation in the creative Word of God.

12. See Christopher Dawson, *Progress and Religion* (Oxford: Oxford University Press, 1929), pp. 86ff.

13. Tolkien, "Chaucer as a Philologist," from the annual *Transactions of the Philological Society*, 1934, pp. 1–70.

14. Willoughby, from the annual *Transactions of the Philological Society*, 1935, p. 75.

15. Lewis, "The Dethronement of Power," above, p. 11.

16. Many critics have found elements of Kafka in various parts of Tolkien's writing.

17. The subtitle of *The Hobbit* is *There and Back Again*, a phrase from Hegel which recurs in Tolkien's work and indicates the final value of distant *aventures* in the Blakean fight which enable the hero to fight at home.

18. As Auden, Tolkien's disciple, put it in *Secondary Worlds*, "Present in every human being are two desires, a desire to know the truth about the primary world, the given world outside ourselves, . . . and the desire to make new secondary worlds of our own, or, if we cannot make them ourselves to share in the secondary worlds of those who can" (p. 49).

19. This is similar to the end of *The Last Battle* (1956), the Narnia story by Lewis.

20. It is stressed in the trilogy that death is the *gift* of the One to men.

21. C. S. Lewis, Introduction in *George Macdonald: An Anthology* (London: Geoffrey Bles, 1955), p. 19.

22. Lewis, "The Dethronement of Power," above, p. 11

23. Lewis, in *Time and Tide*, August 14, 1954, p. 1083.

24. When Frodo can but recall parts of his elegy on Gandalf, these are described as "only snatches . . . faded as a handful of withered leaves" (I, 374).

25. Presumably this quality of higher growth is similar to the function of the Sea and the Far West in *The Lord of the Rings*.

26. Many of these images recall those of the prison in *Pilgrim's Regress* (1933) by Lewis, a work that was subtitled *An Allegorical Apology for Christianity, Reason, and Romanticism.*

FRODO AND ARAGORN: THE CONCEPT OF THE HERO

1. Richard C. West, "The Interlace Structure of *The Lord of the Rings*," in *A Tolkien Compass*, ed. Jared Lobdell (LaSalle, Ill.: OpenCourt, 1975), p. 80.

2. Tolkien, "On Fairy-Stories," in *Tree and Leaf* (Boston: Houghton Mifflin, 1965), pp. 19ff.

3. Ready, *The Tolkien Relation: A Personal Inquiry* (Chicago: Regnery Press, 1968), p. 101.

4. Tolkien, "On Fairy-Stories," p. 14.

5. *Beowulf*, lines 2184–88, my translation.

6. Carpenter, *Tolkien* (Boston: Houghton Mifflin, 1977), p. 188.

7. Ibid., p. 186.

8. Tolkien, *Tree and Leaf* (Boston: Houghton Mifflin, 1965), p. vii.

9. Paul Kocher, *Master of Middle-Earth: The Fiction of J.R.R. Tolkien* (Boston: Houghton Mifflin, 1972), p. 131; Daniel Hughes, "Pieties and Giant Forms in *The Lord of the Rings*," in *Shadows of Imagination: The Fantasies of C. S. Lewis, J.R.R. Tolkien, and Charles Williams*, ed. Mark Hillegas (Carbondale: University of Illinois Press, 1976), p. 91; see p. 82.

10. Carpenter, *Tolkien*, p. 176.

11. Jessie L. Weston, *From Ritual to Romance* (Garden City, N.Y.: Harcourt Brace, 1957), p. 191.

12. Tolkien, "*Beowulf:* The Monsters and the Critics," p. 67.

13. Ibid., p. 69.

14. Douglass Parker, "Hwæt We Holbytla . . . ," *Hudson Review* 9 (Winter 1956–1957): 605; Rose A. Zimbardo, "Moral Vision in *The Lord of the Rings,*" above, p. 68; George H. Thomson, "*The Lord of the Rings:* The Novel as Traditional Romance," *Wisconsin Studies in Contemporary Literature* 8, no. 1 (Winter 1967): 51–53.

15. Tolkien, "*Beowulf,*" p. 81.

MIDDLE-EARTH: AN IMAGINARY WORLD?

1. Tolkien, "On Fairy-Stories, p. 47.

2. Ibid., p. 9.

3. III, 405. Cf. similar statements at I, 17; III, 313, 385, and especially 411.

4. Tolkien, "On Fairy-Stories," pp. 24–25.

5. Ransacking the Pleistocene for niches into which to fit the ages of Middle-earth is a pleasant pastime, which one hopes the players of the game are not taking seriously. See Margaret Howes, "The Elder Ages and the Later Glaciations of the Pleistocene Epoch," *Tolkien Journal* 4, no. 2 (1967), which picks a span from 95,000 to 65,000 years ago.

6. Cf. Sam's bestiary poem entitled "Oliphaunt" in *The Adventures of Tom Bombadil* (Boston: Houghton Mifflin, 1963).

7. Tolkien in "On Fairy-Stories" considers communication with the animal world a basic human need. See *Master of Middle-earth,* chap. 5. On the wanton destruction of trees, see the introductory note to *Tree and Leaf* in *The Tolkien Reader,* p. 2., and of course many passages about the Ents in the epic itself.

8. The description I give of the Valar and their country in this and subsequent paragraphs is a blending of information from *The Lord of the Rings* (chiefly appendixes A and B) with elaborations later published by Tolkien in *The Road Goes Ever On* (Boston: Houghton Mifflin, 1967), pp. 65–66.

9. *The Navagatio Sancti Brendani Abbatis* is discussed in detail in my analysis of Tolkien's "Imram." See *Master of Middle-earth,* chap. 7.

10. Tolkien, *The Road Goes Ever On,* p. 66.

11. These examples come mainly from appendixes A and B, but most of them are alluded to also in the course of the three volumes of the epic.

12. Detailed readings of each of these shorter pieces of fiction appear under appropriate headings in *Master of Middle-earth,* chap. 7.

TOLKIEN: ARCHETYPE AND WORD

1. Tolkien, "On Fairy-Stories," p. 13.
2. Ibid., pp. 14, 68.
3. Lewis, "Psycho-Analysis and Literary Criticism," in *Selected Literary Essays,* ed. Walter Hooper (Cambridge: Cambridge University Press, 1969), pp. 296, 297.
4. Barfield, *Saving the Appearances: A Study in Idolatry* (London, 1957), pp. 133–34.
5. Barfield, *Romanticism Comes of Age* (Middletown, Conn., 1944), pp. 193, 202.
6. Lewis, letter to Charles Moorman, 15 May 1959, in *Letters of C. S. Lewis,* ed. W. H. Lewis (London, 1966), p. 287.
7. Tolkien, "*Beowulf:* The Monsters and the Critics."
8. Barfield, *Romanticism,* p. 193.
9. Jung, "The Phenomenology of the Spirit in Fairy Tales," in *The Collected Works of C. G. Jung,* ed. Sir Herbert Read, Michael Fordham, and Gerhard Adler, trans. R.F.C. Hull, vol. 9, pt. 1, pp. 231, 233, 235.
10. Ibid., pp. 226, 219; Jung, *Mysterium Conjunctionis,* in *Collected Works,* vol. 14, p. 325.
11. Jung, "On the Nature of the Psyche," in *Collected Works,* vol. 8, p. 203.
12. Jung, "The Spirit in Fairy Tales," in *Collected Works,* vol. 9, pt. 1, p. 239.
13. Ibid., p. 213.
14. See Jung, "On the Nature of Dreams," in *Collected Works,* vol. 8, p. 293; Julans Jacobi, *The Psychology of C. G. Jung* (London, 1962), p. 102; and Jung, *Psychology and Alchemy,* in *Collected Works,* vol. 12, p. 41.
15. Jung, *Aion,* in *Psyche and Symbol,* ed. Violet S. de Laszlo (New York, 1958), p. 6.
16. Jung, "Conscious, Unconscious, and Individuation," in *Collected Works,* vol. 9, pt. 1, p. 285.
17. Jung, *Memories, Dreams, and Reflections,* trans. Richard Winston and Clara Winston (New York, 1965), p. 392.
18. Jung, "The Psychology of the Child Archetype," in *Complete Works,* vol. 11, pt. 1, pp. 166–67.

19. Jung, "On the Nature of Dreams," p. 293.
20. Ibid., p. 227.
21. Jung, *Psychology and Religion: East and West*, in *Collected Works*, vol. 11, p. 341.
22. See Jung, *Man and His Symbols*, p. 191; Jacobi, *Psychology of C. G. Jung*, p. 117.
23. Jung, *Aion*, p. 9; see also Jung, *Man and His Symbols*, p. 216.
24. Jung, "Concerning Rebirth," in *Collected Works*, vol. 9, pt. 1, p. 124.
25. Jung, "On the Nature of Dreams," p. 293.
26. Jung, "Concerning Rebirth," pp. 146–47.
27. Jung, "The Spirit in Fairy Tales," pp. 215–17.
28. Tolkien, "On Fairy-Stories," p. 68.
29. Jung, "The Spirit in Fairy Tales," p. 251.
30. Tolkien, "*Beowulf*," pp. 91–99.
31. Tolkien, "The Homecoming of Beorhtnoth Beorhthelm's Son," in *The Tolkien Reader*, pp. 21, 22.

Myth, History, and Time in *The Lord of the Rings*

1. See Tolkien, "On Fairy-Stories," esp. p. 37.
2. William Ready, *The Tolkien Relation* (Chicago, 1968), pp. 6, 44, 83.
3. Lewis, "The Dethronement of Power," above, p. 11.
4. Ready, *Tolkien Relation*, p. 4 and passim.
5. See Tolkien, "On Fairy-Stories."
6. Ibid., p. 73.

The Lord of the Rings: Tolkien's Epic

1. Randel Helms, *Tolkien's World* (Boston: Houghton Mifflin, 1974), p. 21.
2. For its medieval (and classical) linguistic, literary, and mythological sources, influences, and parallels in general, see, for example, Caroline Whitman Everett, "The Imaginative Fiction of J.R.R. Tolkien" (master's thesis, Florida State University, 1957), chap. 4; Alexis Levitin, "J.R.R. Tolkien's *The Lord of the Rings*" (master's thesis, Columbia University, 1964), chap. 2; John Tinkler, "Old English in Rohan," in *Tolkien and the*

Critics, ed. Neil D. Isaacs and Rose A. Zimbardo (Notre Dame, Ind.: University of Notre Dame Press, 1968), pp. 164–69; Sandra L. Miesel, "Some Motifs and Sources for *Lord of the Rings*," *Riverside Quarterly* 3 (1968): 125; E. L. Epstein, "The Novels of J.R.R. Tolkien and the Ethnology of Medieval Christendom," *Philological Quarterly* 48 (1969): 517–25; Lin Carter, *Tolkien: A Look Behind* The Lord of the Rings (New York: Ballantine, 1969), passim; Kenneth J. Reckford, "Some Trees in Virgil and Tolkien," in *Perspectives of Roman Poetry: A Classics Symposium,* ed. G. Karl Galinsky (Austin: University of Texas Press, 1974), pp. 57–92; Charles A. Huttar, "Hell and the City: Tolkien and the Traditions of Western Literature," in *A Tolkien Compass,* ed. Jared Lobdell (La Salle, Ill.: Open Court Press, 1975), pp. 117–42; and Ruth S. Noel, *The Mythology of Middle-earth* (London: Thames and Hudson, 1977).

For the source and genre of *The Lord of the Rings* as northern saga, see especially Gloria Ann Strange Slaughter St. Clair, "*The Lord of the Rings* as Saga," *Mythlore* 6 (1979): 11–16; St. Clair's earlier "Studies in the Sources of J.R.R. Tolkien's *The Lord of the Rings*," *Dissertation Abstracts International* 30 (1970): 5001A; and more recently, St. Clair, "An Overview of the Northern Influences on Tolkien's Works" and "Volsunga Saga and Narn: Some Analogies," in *Proceedings of the J.R.R. Tolkien Centenary Conference, Keble College, Oxford, 1992,* ed. Patricia Reynolds and Glen H. Goodknight, *Mythlore* 80 and *Mallorn* 33 in one volume (Milton Keynes, England: Tolkien Society; Altadena, Calif.: Mythopoeic Press, Proceedings of the Tolkien Society, 1995), pp. 63–67 and 68–72.

On the conflict in *The Lord of the Rings* between the Germanic pessimism that *lif is læne* [life is loaned] (from Old English literature) and the medieval Christian idea that submission to God's will provides hope in a transitory world, see Ronald Christopher Sarti, "Man in a Mortal World: J.R.R. Tolkien and *The Lord of the Rings*," *Dissertation Abstracts International* 45 (1984): 1410A (Indiana University). On the similarity between Unferth (in *Beowulf*) and Wormtongue, see Clive Tolley, "Tolkien and the Unfinished," in *Scholarship and Fantasy: Proceedings of the Tolkien Phenomenon, May 1992,* Turku, Finland (special issue), ed. K. J. Battarbee, Anglicana Turkuensis, no. 12 (Turku: University of Turku, 1992), pp. 154–56; on the influence of *Beowulf* and "The Battle of Maldon" on Tolkien's epic, see George Clark, "J.R.R. Tolkien and the True Hero," in *J.R.R. Tolkien and His Literary Resonances: Views of Middle-earth,* ed. George Clark and Daniel Timmons (Westport, Conn.: Greenwood Press, 2000), pp. 39–51.

Tom Shippey analyzes the indebtedness of "Orcs," "Ents," and "Hobbits" to Old Norse and Old English etymologies in "Creation from Philology in *The Lord of the Rings,*" in *J.R.R. Tolkien, Scholar and Story-Teller: Essays in Memoriam,* ed. Mary Salu and Robert T. Farrell (Ithaca: Cornell University Press, 1979), 286–316. For analyses of the Greek, Latin, and Hebrew antecedents of Tolkienian names, see Dale W. Simpson, "Names and Moral Character in J.R.R. Tolkien's Middle-earth Books," *Publications of the Missouri Philological Association* 6 (1981): 1–5. Note that Shippey also traces the influence of Old Norse and Old English on detail used by Tolkien in the trilogy, such as the word "fallow" as an epithet for an Elven cloak, names of characters, and place names. See also Tom Shippey, *Road to Middle-earth,* rev. ed. (London: Allen and Unwin, 1992).

On Frodo compared to Gawain in *Sir Gawain and the Green Knight,* particularly in relation to the loss of innocence and understanding of self, see Christine Barkley and Muriel B. Ingham, "There but Not Back Again: The Road from Innocence to Maturity," *Riverside Quarterly* 7 (1982): 101–4; see also Roger C. Schlobin, who looks for parallels between the characters of *Sir Gawain* and *The Lord of the Rings,* in "The Monsters Are Talismans and Transgressions: Tolkien and *Sir Gawain and the Green Knight,*" in Clark and Timmons, *J.R.R. Tolkien,* pp. 71–81.

3. For religious, moral, Christian, or Roman Catholic aspects of the trilogy, see Edmund Fuller, "The Lord of the Hobbits," above, p. 16; Patricia Meyer Spacks, "Power and Meaning in *The Lord of the Rings,*" above, p. 52; Levitin, "Inherent Morality and Its Concomitants," chap. 5 of "J.R.R. Tolkien's *The Lord of the Rings*"; Sandra Miesel, "Some Religious Aspects of *Lord of the Rings,*" *Riverside Quarterly* 3 (1968): 209–13; Gunnar Urang, "Tolkien's Fantasy: The Phenomenology of Hope," in *Shadows of the Imagination: The Fantasies of C. S. Lewis, J.R.R. Tolkien, and Charles Williams,* ed. Mark R. Hillegas (Carbondale and Edwardsville: Southern Illinois University Press, 1969), pp. 97–110; Paul Kocher, "Cosmic Order," chap. 3 of *Master of Middle-earth: The Fiction of J.R.R. Tolkien* (Boston: Houghton Mifflin, 1972); and Richard Purtill, *Lord of the Elves and Eldils: Fantasy and Philosophy in C. S. Lewis and J.R.R. Tolkien* (Grand Rapids, Mich.: Zondervan, 1974).

4. Spacks, "Power and Meaning," above, p. 52.

5. For *The Lord of the Rings* as traditional epic, see Bruce A. Beatie, "Folk Tale, Fiction, and Saga in J.R.R. Tolkien's *The Lord of the Rings*," in "The Tolkien Papers," special issue, *Mankato Studies in English* 2 (1967): 1–17; as fantasy drawing upon epic, *chanson de geste,* and medieval romance, see Carter, *Tolkien,* pp. 96–133; as fantasy, see Douglass Parker, "Hwæt We Holbytla . . . ," *Hudson Review* 9 (Winter 1956–1957): 598–609; as fairy story, see R. J. Reilly, "Tolkien and the Fairy Story," above, p. 93; as a genreless work, see Charles Moorman, "The Shire, Mordor, and Minas Tirith," in Isaacs and Zimbardo, *Tolkien and the Critics,* pp. 201–2.

6. The most satisfying genre may be that of the romance, drawn from medieval or Arthurian antecedents. Characteristic of the romance are its symbolism, quest themes of search and transition, the sense of death or disaster, and the maturation of the young. But Tolkien inverts the romance structure so that Frodo relinquishes his quest at the end and the heroes peacefully overcome death. See George H. Thomson, "*The Lord of the Rings:* The Novel as Traditional Romance," *Wisconsin Studies in Contemporary Literature* 8 (1967): 43–59; Richard C. West, "The Interlace Structure of *The Lord of the Rings*," in Lobdell, *A Tolkien Compass,* pp. 77–94; Derek S. Brewer, "*The Lord of the Rings* as Romance," in Salu and Farrell, *Scholar and Story-Teller,* pp. 249–64; and David M. Miller, "Narrative Pattern in *The Fellowship of the Ring*," in Lobdell, *A Tolkien Compass,* pp. 95–106. See also, for the influence of French and German Arthurian romance (and the Perceval story) on Tolkien in *The Lord of the Rings,* J. S. Ryan, "Uncouth Innocence: Some Links Between Chretien de Troyes, Wolfram von Eschenbach and J.R.R. Tolkien," *Inklings-Jahrbuch* 2 (1984): 25–41; and *Mythlore* 11 (1984): 8–13. For a tracing of the Fellowship's journeys through various kinds of landscape in *The Lord of the Rings,* see the fifty-one maps in Barbara Strachey, *Journeys of Frodo: An Atlas of J.R.R. Tolkien's "The Lord of the Rings"* (London: HarperCollins, 1998; Boston: Houghton Mifflin, 1999).

7. For Aragorn as hero, see Kocher, *Master of Middle-earth,* chap. 6; for Frodo, see Roger Sale, *Modern Heroism: Essays on D. H. Lawrence, William Empson, and J.R.R. Tolkien* (Berkeley and Los Angeles: University of California Press, 1973); and for Aragorn as the epic hero and Frodo as the fairy-tale hero, see Levitin, "J.R.R. Tolkien's *The Lord of the Rings*," pp. 60–76. Because heroism and *ofermod* are incompatible, it is

difficult to choose "the hero" of the work; see Miesel's brief mention of this idea in "Some Religious Aspects of *Lord of the Rings*," p. 212; further, real heroism depends more on service than mastery, making Sam, who resembles Niggle in "Leaf by Niggle," the best choice for hero: see Jack C. Rang, "Two Servants," in "The Tolkien Papers," pp. 84–94. See also Flieger's concept of the split hero, in four individuals, which she identifies with the multigenre form of *The Lord of the Rings:* for Frodo as the fairy-tale hero, Aragorn as the epic hero, Gollum as the *Beowulf* monster (who combines Grendel and the dragon), and Sam Gamgee as the loyal servant Wiglaf in *Beowulf* and Bedivere in *Morte Darthur,* Verlyn Flieger, "Medieval Epic and Romance Motifs in J.R.R. Tolkien's *The Lord of the Rings*," *Dissertation Abstracts International* 38 (1978): 4157A (Catholic University of America); and the article that epitomizes her argument, "Frodo and Aragorn: The Concept of the Hero," above, p. 122.

8. For other views of structure in the trilogy, see, for example, Helms, "Tolkien's World: The Structure and Aesthetic of *The Lord of the Rings*," chap. 5 of *Tolkien's World.*

9. Quoted from a letter by J.R.R. Tolkien appended to Everett, "Imaginative Fiction," p. 87.

10. In addition to the innovative Millennium Edition (London: HarperCollins, 1999), *The Lord of the Rings* has also been published in a single-volume, "India-paper" deluxe edition, with slipcase, by Allen and Unwin (London, 1968); again, without a slipcase and on regular paper, in 1991 (HarperCollins); and in quarter-leather with a slipcase and in limited numbers (HarperCollins, 1997). That these formats change the way the reader understands *The Lord of the Rings* is important in grasping Tolkien's intentions.

11. See David Calloway, "Gollum: A Misunderstood Hero," *Mythlore* 37 (1984): 14–17, 22.

12. Boethius, *The Consolation of Philosophy,* trans. Richard Green (Indianapolis: Bobbs-Merrill, 1962), p. 97 (book 4, poem 6). On the Great Chain of Being, the "fair chain of love," and the Renaissance concept of *discordia concors* (also found in Hugh of St. Victor) and its influence on order in the trilogy, see Zimbardo, "The Medieval-Renaissance Vision of *The Lord of the Rings*," in *Tolkien: New Critical Perspectives*, ed. Isaacs and Zimbardo (Lexington: University Press of Kentucky, 1981), 63–71: there is a place for all beings and things in Middle-earth, so that

the evil arises when one being or thing seeks its own desires without regard for the whole. For the Boethian reconciliation of Providence, fate, and free will, as a source for the conflicting statements Tolkien makes in the trilogy about chance and intentionality in the universe, see Kathleen Dubs, "Providence, Fate and Chance: Boethian Philosophy in *The Lord of the Rings*," *Twentieth-Century Literature* 27 (1981): 34–42.

13. For an incisive discussion of the origins, kinds, and natures of the rings, see Melanie Rawls, "The Rings of Power," *Mythlore* 40 (1984): 29–32.

14. For a classification and discussion of good and/or evil species, see Zimbardo, "Moral Vision in *The Lord of the Rings*," above, p. 68; Thomas J. Gasque, "Tolkien: The Monsters and the Critters," in Isaacs and Zimbardo, *Tolkien and the Critics*, pp. 151–63; Robley Evans, *J.R.R. Tolkien* (New York: Warner Paperback Library, 1972), chaps. 3–5; and Kocher, *Master of Middle-earth*, chaps. 4–5.

15. The insignificance and ordinariness of Tolkien's heroic hobbits are glossed in several of his letters, particularly 180, 181, and 246; see J.R.R. Tolkien, *Letters,* selected and edited by Humphrey Carpenter, with the assistance of Christopher Tolkien (London: Allen and Unwin, 1980; Boston: Houghton Mifflin, 1981), pp. 230–32, 232–37, and 325–33.

16. For a discussion of the descent into hell in the second book and its traditional implications, see Huttar, "Hell and the City," pp. 117–42.

17. On Old Man Willow and Tolkien's empathy with trees, see Flieger, "Taking the Part of Trees: Eco-Conflict in Middle-earth," in Clark and Timmons, *J.R.R. Tolkien,* pp. 147–58.

18. On Tom Bombadil as an embodiment of the classical and medieval god of nature (or human nature), drawn in part from John Gower's *Confessio Amantis,* see Gordon Slethaug, "Tolkien, Tom Bombadil, and the Creative Imagination," *English Studies in Canada* 4 (1978): 341–50. On Tolkien's theology of nature and grace, see also Colin Duriez, "Subcreation and Tolkien's Theology of Story," in Battarbee, *Scholarship and Fantasy,* pp. 133–49.

19. On the names of the Dwarves, see Patrick Callahan, "Tolkien's Dwarfs and the Eddas," *Tolkien Journal* 15 (1972): 20; and for their connection with Norse mythology, see Brunsdale, "Norse Mythological Elements in *The Hobbit,*" *Mythlore* 3 (1983): 49–50; and Lynn Brice, "The Influence of Scandinavian Mythology in the Works of J.R.R. Tolkien," *Edda* 7 (1983): 113–19.

20. See also, for Tolkien's paradise, U. Milo Kaufmann, "Aspects of the Paradisiacal in Tolkien's Work," in Lobdell, *A Tolkien Compass*, pp. 143–52; and for Valinor as based on the earthly paradise, Gwyneth E. Hood, "The Earthly Paradise in Tolkien's *The Lord of the Rings*," in Reynolds and Goodknight, *Proceedings*, pp. 139–56.

21. On the Roman Catholic and religious features of *The Lord of the Rings*, see Miesel, pp. 209–13; Catherine Madsen, "Light from an Invisible Lamp: Natural Religion in *The Lord of the Rings*," *Mythlore* 53 (spring 1988): 43–47; and Carl F. Hostetter, "Over Middle-earth Sent unto Men: On the Philological Origins of the Earendel Myth," *Mythlore* 65 (spring 1991): 5–8.

22. On the Anglo-Saxon and Germanic heroism of Frodo, see George Clark, "J.R.R. Tolkien and the Hero," in Clark and Timmons, *J.R.R. Tolkien*, pp. 39–51.

23. The emphasis on sight and seeing is often linked in the trilogy with the *palantíri*, one of which Saruman has and that Sauron uses to control him, so that Frodo's "sight" here atop the hill opens up new vistas and visions beyond his capability: see J.R.R. Tolkien, *Unfinished Tales of Númenor and Middle-earth*, ed. Christopher Tolkien (London: Allen and Unwin, 1979; Boston: Houghton Mifflin, 1980), pp. 421–33.

24. For the two towers of this volume as central symbols, see also Tolkien's own unused designs for the cover, in Wayne G. Hammond and Christina Scull, *J.R.R. Tolkien: Artist and Illustrator* (New York: Houghton Mifflin, 1995), pp. 179–83. The two towers were used recently on the cover of a HarperCollins reissue, for the second of the three volumes (London, 2000).

25. *Ancren Wisse* treats the deadly sins as animals. . . . Tolkien himself links propensities to different sins among different species — sloth and stupidity, with the hobbits; pride, with the Elves; envy and greed, with the Dwarves; a type of pride ("folly and wickedness"), with men; and a more dangerous form of pride ("treachery and power-lust"), with wizards, in letter 203 (*Letters*, p. 262). On deadly sin in *The Lord of the Rings*, as well as *The Hobbit* and *The Silmarillion*, see Charles W. Nelson's recent discussion, "The Sins of Middle-earth: Tolkien's Use of Medieval Allegory," in Clark and Timmons, *J.R.R. Tolkien*, pp. 83–94. See also, for a comparison of the battle between Sam and Frodo and Shelob and the battle between the Vices and Virtues in Prudentius's *Psychomachia*, J. S. Ryan, "Death by Self-Impalement: The Prudentius Example," *Minas Tirith Evening Star* 15 (1986): 6–9.

26. Genesis 11:1–4, *The Jerusalem Bible*, ed. Alexander Jones (Garden City, N.Y.: Doubleday, 1966). Tolkien participated as a principal collaborator (one of twenty-seven) in the translation and literary revision of this Bible.

27. For parallels between *The Lord of the Rings* and *The Silmarillion* and Milton's *Paradise Lost*, see Debbie Sly, "Weaving Nets of Gloom: 'Darkness Profound' in Tolkien and Milton," in Clark and Timmons, *J.R.R. Tolkien*, pp. 109–19.

28. On the Ents, Treebeard, and Old Man Willow, and Tolkien's indebtedness to the Green Knight, see Flieger, "The Green Man, the Green Knight, and Treebeard: Scholarship and Invention in Tolkien's Fiction," in Battarbee, *Scholarship and Fantasy*, pp. 85–98.

29. For information about the wizards, see Tolkien, *Unfinished Tales*, pp. 405–20.

30. For the theological concept of the Word of God (=Jesus Christ, his Son, or the incarnation of God's love), as the basis for Tolkien's literary aesthetic, see S.T.R.O. d'Ardenne, "The Man and the Scholar," in Salu and Farrell, *Scholar and Story-Teller*, p. 35. Just as the combination of adjective and noun in the Anglo-Saxon kenning gave the Anglo-Saxon *scop* with his *wordhord* control over the thing described, so kennings allow Tolkien to create his own world, through the compounds and epithets for the One Ring, the Ring of Power, the Ring of Doom, Gollum's Precious, etc. Tolkien's constructed languages also give insight into the peoples who use them: Dwarvish is Old Norse; Quenya and Sindarin, High Elvish and Common Elvish, as languages of song, mirror Faërie's desire for good; Black Speech is suited to a race whose dentals consist of fangs and is therefore not a good language for song. See Anthony J. Ugolnik, "*Wordhord Onleac*: The Medieval Sources of J.R.R. Tolkien's Linguistic Aesthetic," *Mosaic* 10 (winter 1977): 15–31. In this case, "Sauron," as a name that describes his being, derives from the Greek for "lizard." See Gwyneth E. Hood, "Sauron as Gorgon and Basilisk," *Seven* 8 (1987): 59–71.

31. For Rohan as Old English, see Tinkler, "Old English in Rohan."

32. My translation of lines 92–93. See the original in George Philip Krapp and Elliott Van Kirk Dobbie, eds., *The Exeter Book, The Anglo-Saxon Poetic Records*, vol. 3 (Morningside Heights, N.Y.: Columbia University Press, 1936).

33. For Aragorn as a healing king, and the medieval and Renaissance ante-

cedents of the concept, see Gisbert Krantz, "Der Heilende Aragorn,"
Inkling-Jahrbuch 2 (1984): 11–24.

34. For a related discussion of the implications of return and renewal in
the last book, see Evans, *J.R.R. Tolkien,* pp. 190–93.

35. See also Jack C. Rang, "Two Servants," in "The Tolkien Papers," pp. 84–
94.

ANOTHER ROAD TO MIDDLE-EARTH: JACKSON'S MOVIE TRILOGY

1. *The Letters of J.R.R. Tolkien,* ed. Humphrey Carpenter with the assistance of Christopher Tolkien (London: George Allen & Unwin, 1981).
Letters 201 and 202 (pp. 260–61) show an initially favorable reaction, in
September 1957, but letter 207 (pp. 266–67), in April 1958, shows Tolkien "very unhappy." Letter 210, undated (pp. 270–77), gives extensive
criticism of the synopsis.

2. Page references to *The Lord of the Rings* are to the one-volume edition published by Houghton Mifflin, Boston, 2001, reprinting that of
HarperCollins, London, 1994. Page references to *The Hobbit* are to the
2001 reprint by Houghton Mifflin, with corrected text and "Note on
the Text" by Douglas A. Anderson. References to the first two Jackson
movies are by scenes as numbered in the extended DVD versions put
out by New Line Cinemas in 2002 (*The Fellowship of the Ring,* here
JFR) and 2003 (*The Two Towers,* here *JTT*). There are 46 scenes in the
former and 66 in the latter. There is no recorded version of the third
movie, *The Return of the King,* as yet available, and references here are
to the theater version released in December 2003.

3. See *Letters,* p. 275.

4. See Shippey, *J.R.R. Tolkien: Author of the Century* (Boston: Houghton
Mifflin, 2000), pp. 77–81.

5. See J.R.R. Tolkien, *The Return of the Shadow,* ed. Christopher Tolkien
(London: Unwin Hyman, 1988; Boston: Houghton Mifflin, 1989).

6. Possibly even four. Only three are subtitled, but Frodo appears to say "I
will take the Ring" completely inaudibly, as if to himself, before trying
to say it out loud.

7. Arwen says to Elrond, her father, "There is still hope," in *JTT* 38,
"Arwen's Fate," and this conversation is what brings the Elvish army to

the rescue at Helm's Deep. There is a kind of symmetry, then, in three or four scenes: Arwen persuading her father in *JTT* 38, Aragorn encouraging Théoden in *JTT* 43 and Haleth in *JTT* 48, and Sam remotivating Frodo and at the same time convincing Faramir in *JTT* 60, "The Tales That Really Mattered."

8. There is an old theatrical tradition that the "glass" which Macbeth sees at line 118ff. was, in the original production, a mirror angled towards King James I in the audience so that the latter could see himself as one of Banquo's descendants.

Index

epic, 37, 54, 56, 91, 122, 124–34, 138–39, 173
of fairy tales, 37, 122, 124–25
Frodo as, 45–51, 53–54, 57, 60–61, 83–92, 122, 124–25, 134–45, 170, 179, 188, 198, 236, 268n. 6
Germanic, 195, 198, 212, 220–22
hobbits as, 12–13, 21–23, 69, 70–71, 122, 124–25, 134–45, 170, 173–74, 179–81, 196, 206–7, 229–31, 236, 240
Jungian archetype of, 169–70
love between, 76–92
and magic, 126–27, 169–70, 173
meaning of, 100
as monsters, 199–213, 231
of quest stories, 37–40, 83–92, 122, 124–25, 170
Sam as, 83–92, 179–81, 198, 229, 236
Tolkien's interest in, 118
as villains, 38
worship of, 76, 77–78, 82–84
See also Epic genre; Quest stories; Return (of the hero); Swords; specific heroes
Hierarchies. See Chains of being; Feudal relations
History (in Lord of the Rings)
in appendices, 59, 128, 132, 146, 148, 152, 154–59, 185–86
of Middle-earth, 16, 41, 94, 146, 148–52, 159–60, 165, 178, 182, 183–94, 239, 244
of the Ring, 19–21, 206, 238–39
See also Fantasy; Realism
Hitler, Adolf, 101, 241
See also Nazism
Hobbit, The (Tolkien), 136, 199, 223
Bilbo's acquiring of the Ring in, 21–22
Gollum in, 141

happy ending of, 196
influences on, 200
vs. Lord of the Rings, 29, 53, 57, 161, 185, 196
style of, 129, 231
subtitle of, 261n. 17
Hobbit(s)
aging of, 78–82, 176
in chain of being, 70–72, 204
encounters of, with legendary being, 189
in Fourth Age, 155
Frodo's inability to live among, after his return, 51, 73, 91–92, 144
Gollum as fallen, 72, 141, 171, 201, 202
as heroes, 12–13, 21–23, 69, 70–71, 122, 124–25, 134–45, 170, 173–74, 179–81, 196, 206–7, 229–31, 236, 240
as historians, 187–88, 192
return of, to Shire, 82, 90–92, 115, 136
as species in Lord of the Rings, 17, 53–54, 149, 158–59
See also Shire; names of specific hobbits
Holy Grail quest, 37, 134, 144
"Homecoming of Beorhtnoth Beorhthelm's Son, The" (Tolkien), 162, 179, 231
Homer, 23, 56, 125
Hughes, Daniel, 130
Hydrogen bomb, 13–14, 26–27
Hygelac (Beowulf character), 137

Iliad (Homer), 23, 125
Imaginary worlds. See Fantasy
Imagination
"esemplastic," 93, 97, 112
as like a tree, 108–9, 119–21
in Lord of the Rings, 95–99, 192
"secondary," 97–99, 103–4, 116
Tolkien on, 111–16, 155–56